# Ambassadors in Pinstripes

# Ambassadors in Pinstripes

## *The Spalding World Baseball Tour and the Birth of the American Empire*

Thomas W. Zeiler

ROWMAN & LITTLEFIELD PUBLISHERS, INC.
*Lanham • Boulder • New York • Toronto • Plymouth, UK*

ROWMAN & LITTLEFIELD PUBLISHERS, INC.

Published in the United States of America
by Rowman & Littlefield Publishers, Inc.
A wholly owned subsidiary of The Rowman & Littlefield Publishing Group, Inc.
4501 Forbes Boulevard, Suite 200, Lanham, Maryland 20706
www.rowmanlittlefield.com

Estover Road
Plymouth PL6 7PY
United Kingdom

British Library Cataloguing in Publication Information Available

**Library of Congress Cataloging-in-Publication Data**

Zeiler, Thomas W.
  Ambassadors in pinstripes : the Spalding world tour and the birth of the
American empire / Thomas W. Zeiler.
    p.  cm.
  Includes bibliographical references and index.
  ISBN-13: 978-0-7425-5168-8 (cloth : alk. paper)
  ISBN-10: 0-7425-5168-7 (cloth : alk. paper)
  ISBN-13: 978-0-7425-5169-5 (pbk. : alk. paper)
  ISBN-10: 0-7425-5169-5 (pbk. : alk. paper)
    1. Spalding, A. G. (Albert Goodwill)  2. Baseball—United States—
History—19th century.  3. United States—Foreign economic relations.
4. Civilization, Modern—American influences.  5. Globalization—History—
19th century.  6. Globalization—History—20th century.  I. Title.
GV863.A1Z44  2006
796.357092—dc22
[B]                                                              2006012901

Printed in the United States of America

♾ ™ The paper used in this publication meets the minimum requirements of
American National Standard for Information Sciences—Permanence of Paper for
Printed Library Materials, ANSI/NISO Z39.48-1992.

# Contents

# Acknowledgments

I am indebted to many individuals and institutions, but I must single out some who provided essential guidance that went beyond the call of duty. Thanks to colleagues Marc Gallicchio, Christopher Endy, Dean MacCannell, Gerald Early, David Wrobel, and Jules Tygiel, who corrected and improved the manuscript, a few of them more than once.

I was fortunate to make friends with Bill Sear and his wife, Leslie, in Atlanta. Bill is the world's foremost collector of international baseball tour memorabilia, a font of knowledge about the game, a diehard Braves follower, and the most supportive booster of this project. He introduced me to Stephen Wong, the author of the beautiful *Smithsonian Baseball*, and Doug Allen of Mastronet, Inc., both of whom generously provided me with images for this book. Without Bill's help, I doubt this book would be presentable.

Thanks also to baseball, sports, and history scholars Patrick Carroll, John Enyeart, Terry Frei, John Freyer, Ed Hartig, Ted Hathaway, Peter Levine, J. A. Mangan, Howard Rosenberg, Dan Ross, Mike Ross, Tom Thomas, and Stew Thornley. The Center for Canadian and Pacific Studies (CPAS) at the University of Tokyo, Komaba, provided me with a forum to try out ideas; Masako Notoji, Yujin Yaguchi, and the staff and audience there were kind to hear me out. As well, I learned immeasurably from the "Empire" workshops at Kyoto University, under the direction of Naoto Kagotani. Thanks also to the Japan–United States Educational Commission of the Fulbright Program for a wonderful year of thinking and rewriting in Tokyo in 2004/2005.

Several archivists, librarians, and skilled professionals throughout the United States and abroad pointed me in the right directions. I could not have benefited from the holdings of the National Baseball Hall of Fame without the assistance of Claudette Burke and Gabriel Schechter, as well as the hospitality of Linda and John Smirk, owners of Cooperstown Bed and Breakfast. At my own University of Colorado at Boulder, bibliographer

Thea Lindquist; Dave Underwood, the manager of media design in ITS, who worked his magic with the images; Associate Dean Graham Oddie; and the Council on Research and Creative Works of the Graduate School, which provided funding for the project, deserve special gratitude. As well, the following archivists provided sources, and I appreciate them all: Becky Amato, Sean Ashby, Peter Attwell, John Cable, Betsy Caldwell, Joan Clark, Jonathan Cockroft, Jenny Cooksey, Barbara Dey, Pete Elwell, Andrea Faling, James L. Gates, Nancy Geiger, Matthew Graham, Chris Grasso, Milton Gustafson, Elizabeth Harvey, Allen Hoof, Mitzi Kanbara, Mary Ellen Kollar, Paul Livingston, Doug Misner, Chris Nicholl, Darrol Pierson, Catherine Renschler, L. A. Spring, Rosie Springer, and Sylvia Weedman.

Friends and family proved crucial to this project, as usual. Stephen and Anne Marie Cole opened their home as a base for research in London. Catherine and Jim Helwig did the same in Washington, D.C. As always, my father, Michael Zeiler, read over my work while agonizing over the Braves' misfortunes in the playoffs. Jim Small of Major League Baseball Japan and Joel Ehrendreich and Mark Jackson of the U.S. Embassy in Tokyo kept me focused on the delights of baseball during the year in Japan. My children, Jackson and Ella, thought this project was cool and accepted my souvenirs from the Hall of Fame. My wife, Rocio, has never been a baseball enthusiast, but as she knows, I have always been her greatest fan for everything she has done for me.

Parts of "A Night at Delmonico's: American Identity and the Spalding World Baseball Tour," *International Journal of the History of Sport* 23, no. 1 (February 2006): 28–45, were reprinted in chapter 5.

# Introduction

## Baseball, Globalization, and Empire

In Jules Verne's classic fantasy novel of 1873, Phileas Fogg circled the Earth, from London and back again. At the time, modern ships and trains had shrunk time and distance so much that he was able to beat his deadline of eighty days. Fifteen years after this fictional feat, two actual teams of baseball players took off in the opposite direction. In October 1888, they headed west from Chicago to San Francisco. They traversed the Pacific and Indian oceans to the Suez Canal, crossed Europe and the Atlantic, and returned to the Windy City six months later. They have received less attention than Verne's protagonist, but they shared in the world's wonders, encountered a fascinating array of people, and benefited from technology in travel and communications. These tourists even bested Phileas Fogg, for they played baseball, too. They differed, most significantly, in that their trip reflected American identity, power, and dreams.

The baseball tour revealed roots of the future American empire. In 1888–1889, this imperial domain remained in an embryonic stage of ideas and desires, but the dynamic, integrative processes of globalization promised to convert it to reality. For that reason, the baseball adventurers relate to the ascendancy of the United States during the late nineteenth century. This book explains their expression of empire through globalization's instruments of free enterprise, webs of modern communications and transport, cultural ordering of races and societies, and nationalistic values that galvanized elites to think of their country as exceptional. To be sure, the baseball tourists cannot be linearly connected to the eventual American empire; in fact, they might be viewed as quite odd representatives of budding imperial notions. But even the baseball establishment, it turned out, was not completely removed from the nationalistic and globalizing impulses that pointed to expansion and Great Power status.

As famous cultural figures who participated in a movement across international frontiers, the "baseball tourists"—that is, the touring Spalding group—represented many of the ideals later realized after 1898, when the United States acquired its empire.[1] Like politicians, the business community, missionaries, and others, they discerned America's ascendancy as a potential imperial power. To achieve this goal, the tourists engaged in globalization, a process that had existed at least since the eighteenth century of creating unified markets and cultural harmony in the world through technological advances and economic growth, openness, and integration. World War I interrupted this convergence, which, since roughly the 1850s, had been characterized by a free flow of labor, capital, goods, and culture under Anglo-American stimulation and oversight, especially in the Atlantic basin and British Empire.[2] Within this interconnected world economy, the baseball tourists followed the example of other enterprising cultural and commercial "transnationals" (or private, nonstate actors who interacted with other people across national borders) such as William "Buffalo Bill" Cody.[3] They carried into foreign lands the values, ideas, and influence trumpeting American ways and beliefs—with mixed success, to be sure, but with purpose all the same. When added to the cacophony of other imperial-minded voices, the entourage became part of a larger project of reshaping the world in the coming century under American leadership.

Their American mission abroad occurred through tourism, which, like today, reaped sizable monetary rewards for adept and visionary planners. For centuries, missionaries and scientists had launched expeditions, knights had set out on heroic travels, conquistadors had embarked for riches and pilgrims for the Church, philosophers pondered the goodness of mortals, and millions traveled just out of plain old curiosity and amusement. Oftentimes, tourists combined an entrepreneurial spirit with principles as well as imperial intentions. This was so for the baseball tourists, or at least for their inspired organizer, driven promoter, and confirmed expansionist—the business magnate who ruled the sport, Albert Goodwill Spalding.[4]

Baseball's most influential figure, Spalding was an entrepreneur who launched the idea of the baseball tour both as a way to advertise his sporting goods empire and market the popular national pastime as a global game. The two-word "base ball," as most referred to it at the time, had become an American institution that some even equated with a civil religion. It flourished within the U.S. market system, as well as in its culture, and Spalding had taken advantage of that national status as a skilled, energetic captain of industry (or robber baron, depending on the opinion of him). Thus, in his eyes, the world tour, while losing money, would in the long run bring him a windfall of fame and fortune by spreading

American beliefs of free enterprise, progress, racial hierarchy, cultural virtue, and exceptional national greatness. A baseball tour, he and the sport's power structure understood then (as it still does today), could form the basis of informal imperial relationships through the process of globalization.

In sum, Albert Spalding linked baseball to a U.S. presence overseas, viewing the world as a market ripe for the infusion of American ideas, products, and energy. Through globalization during the Gilded Age, he and other Americans penetrated the globe. Tourists of all types (actors, reformers, academics, and aristocrats) imparted mass American culture and goods abroad, while also bringing an awareness of the world to the cloistered people at home. World fairs, fantasy travel novels, and even daring races helped Americans grasp the opportunities to be had abroad. For instance, in mid-November 1889, just months after the Spalding entourage returned to Chicago, *New York World* publisher Joseph Pulitzer sent his audacious female reporter, Elizabeth Cochrane—known as Nellie Bly—around the globe to beat Phileas Fogg's record. The stunt won great acclaim, as the spunky Bly returned to New York on January 25, 1890, in just over seventy-two days, handily besting Verne's hero by a week.[5]

Thrilling though it was, the Bly exploit also revealed the compression of time and space—the essence of globalization. Tourism joined trade, investment, fairs, and entertainment forms like minstrel shows as an element in global exchange. The powerful force of movement and mobility created communities among and between societies that presaged formal empire.[6] Spalding, no less, became part of this process, and in so doing, revealed an America that was coming of age and longed for imperial status, a rank that came to fruition a decade later.

In short, the baseball tour exposed the foundations of America's rising international power in the 1880s. Eager imperialists could not count on military muscle, which grew agonizingly slowly at the time; "Big Navy" advocates decried the nation's puny force and warned of threats from such laughably intimidating states as Chile, Turkey, and Haiti. Formal diplomacy also seemed hardly a strength. Although the United States eyed European activity in the Western Hemisphere, criticized British imperialism, grasped for Hawaii, and even briefly confronted Germany in far-off Samoa, these concerns reflected the old fears of national security and self-defense rather than expansionist impulses. Congress occasionally debated (and usually rejected) treaties to acquire new territories. Thus, the old diplomacy of nonentanglement and inwardness prevailed into the 1890s. This was simply not an era of government activism in foreign policy; domestic affairs took precedence, and America stood by quietly as Europeans scrambled for empires.[7]

No matter, for the world economy, shaped by the constant pressure of

Anglo-American globalization and the "soft power" of U.S. business and other transnational contacts, held the promise of imperial rewards. Despite the official torpor, U.S. citizens were busy overseas "spreading the American dream" of abundance and mobility through technology and mass consumption.[8] Thus, through the process of globalization, entrepreneurs joined a parade of cultural agents who built a national identity, through private means, by forging a self-image of a future imperialist power.

These empire-seekers did so, in large part, through globalization, which itself hinged on modernization through industrialization. Spalding benefited from major technological innovations of the last half of the nineteenth century. He lived in the Second Industrial Revolution; the decade of the 1880s was among the years, claims historian David Landes, which "saw the lusty childhood, if not the birth of life-changing technology."[9] Advanced nations such as Germany, France, Great Britain, and the United States modernized rapidly under innovations. Even underdeveloped agricultural countries throughout Europe witnessed rapid, small-scale growth of their industrial sectors. A great age of steel and chemicals flourished in midcentury, creating in the latter decades new centers of energy and power based on railroads, steamships, engines, and electricity. Although the human toll was sizable, the combination of science, invention, and profit—joined with investment, rising incomes, and general global peace—rolled technology's changes through economies worldwide. Workers contested management and government over the pace and cost of laboring under rapidly evolving conditions of mechanization. The baseball tourists were not immune to such strife, as imminent player conflict with Spalding over contracts later demonstrated. Yet in this milieu of booming, integrated manufacturing, the pull of globalization elevated the United States as a world-class power. These processes established the country's wealth and tied it to various parts of the world, mainly the European empires and parts of Latin America and Asia. Colonial subjects saw their living conditions altered, often to their detriment, but globalization persisted in a never-ending cycle of innovation, profit, sacrifice, and change.

America's rise remained a constant from the late nineteenth century onward, and baseball, as a cultural icon, played a role. Of course, most of these tourist-players should not be judged other than as uninformed foreigners who journeyed for pleasure to a number of places. They were mere athletes, after all, and in general, possessed at most a high school education even though they were skilled professionals in their sport. Significantly, baseball promised economic gains for team owners and, in Albert Spalding's case, for his business of sporting goods. As well as profit-seeking, the tour projected the rules, organization, and styles of this peculiar sport and thus served, in its way, to market Americanism. What did "American" mean? Defining national identity was, implicitly, what the baseball tour set out to divulge. The tourists sounded the message that the world faced a new era of American ambition and, they hoped, global influence.

By examining aspects of globalization that promoted American imperialism, the ensuing chapters reveal the importance of the Spalding tour in the formative history of the American empire. The first chapter launches the endeavor in Chicago within the context of market capitalism and business ethics. Then, as the tourists made their way from Chicago to Hawaii, chapter 2 discusses the new American West of transportation and communications that integrated the region with the rest of the world. Chapters 3 and 4 move the tour into the cultural realm of identity by exploring, respectively, the racial hierarchy of empire and European resistance to American ways. The final chapter addresses the return of the tour to U.S. soil, when nationalistic outbursts expressed notions of American exceptionalism that built confidence in the coming course of empire.

This last topic pinpoints the essence of why Spalding's trip was important: how could Americans prove they were exceptional, when, relative to others who had far-flung empires and glorious pasts, they were mere infants in the game of greatness?[10] One answer might be found by examining the baseball trip. In what Henry Chadwick—by 1888, baseball's most venerable journalist—called "the greatest event in the history of athletic sports," the Spalding world tour amounted to an unofficial missionary movement on behalf of a rising United States. Even more than an attempt by Albert Spalding to "extend an American presence in the world," as his biographer claims,[11] the baseball tour was an attempt by agents of business and culture to further imaginings of a not-so-distant empire.

## NOTES

1. It is important to note that this book is not concerned with the nature or consequences of empire, nor even a definition of the term. It does not consider concepts of imperial subordination or inequality, nor formal and informal empire. The terms *empire* and *imperialism* are used merely as markers of what was to come, of the ambitions of leaders. This book focuses on the ideas and expressions behind the formation of empire. That is, the world tour, by attempting to inject the American cultural icon of baseball abroad, gave a sense of the exceptionalism of the United States and the hope of elites of the future greatness, and, thus, imperial power, of the country. Furthermore, the term *baseball tourist* is used here in reference to the Spalding entourage and should not be confused with traveling baseball fans.

2. For early globalization, in which the British dominated the Atlantic economy through free trade, open capital markets, the gold standard, and dominance of shipping, sea lanes, and communications, see O'Rourke and Williamson, *Globalization and History*; Eckes and Zeiler, *Globalization and the American Century*, 9–37; and Davis and Gallman, *Evolving Financial Markets*. For a long view of globalization's vast scope, including its non-Western origins, see Hopkins, *Globalization in World History*.

3. For transnationalism, see Field, "Transnationalism and the New Tribe," and Thelen, "Nation and Beyond."

4. Feifer, *Tourism in History*, 2, 164. See also MacCannell, *The Tourist*.

5. See Marks, *Around the World in 72 Days*. Pulitzer sponsored a contest—which more than 1,000,000 people entered—to determine when Nellie Bly would return to New York. Beating her rival Elizabeth Bisland, who was sponsored by the rival Pulitzer newspaper, Bly arrived to a huge crowd on January 25, 1890, breaking the fictional record set in *Around the World in Eighty Days* with a time of 72 days, 6 hours, 11 minutes, and 14 seconds. Promoting the feat, backers created trading cards and a board game called "Around the World with Nellie Bly." Songwriter Joe Hart wrote "Globe Trotting Nellie Bly" to commemorate the adventure.

6. Leed, *Mind of the Traveler*, 16–21. For the nineteenth-century beginnings of American cultural exportation conducted by the process of globalization, see Rydell and Kroes, *Buffalo Bill in Bologna*. See also Dulles, *Americans Abroad*, 86–96, and Stowe, *Going Abroad*. For an example of entertainment exports, see Blair, "First Steps toward Globalization."

7. Robert L. Beisner, in his *From the Old Diplomacy to the New*, 32–71, chose the year 1889 (when the baseball tour ended) as the last moment of the "old paradigm" of unsystematic, reactive diplomacy. See also Heiss, "Evolution of the Imperial Idea," 524–25, and Jedediah Purdy, "Universal Nation," 104–6.

8. See Rosenberg, *Spreading the American Dream*. Rosenberg explores an era following the period of this book, but the argument that a private system of investors, entrepreneurs, philanthropists, and media leaders fostered U.S. foreign relations holds for the post–Civil War years of 1865–1890.

9. Landes, *Unbound Prometheus*, 235; see also pp. 276–92.

10. See Ninkovich, *United States and Imperialism*. See also Kaplan, *Anarchy of Empire*, and Streeby, *American Sensations*.

11. Levine, *A. G. Spalding*, 99.

# 1

# Marketing

## Albert Spalding's Chicago

ILLINOIS
Chicago, Saturday, October 20, 1888—*Chicago* 11, *All-America* 6

Mighty Casey was a snarling, intimidating batter, but ultimately, a tragic failure. On June 3, 1888, readers awoke to the slugger's exploits in their morning edition of the *San Francisco Daily Examiner*, a newspaper run by William Randolph Hearst, who had received it from his father. Readers that morning found a poem by reporter Ernest Lawrence Thayer, a Harvard College friend of Hearst who had been brought out to California by Hearst along with two other writers from the satirical *Harvard Lampoon*. Thayer published under the byline "Phin," and on this Sunday, he entitled his article, "A Ballad of the Republic, Sung in the Year 1888." The poem told the tale of the potent Casey (named after a high school acquaintance of Thayer's) who played for the "Mudville Nine." With his team down to its final out in the ninth inning of a pressure-packed game, trailing the opponent by two runs but with two men on base, the great "sturdy batsman" came to the plate to take his swings. A frenetic hometown crowd screamed in agony for him to deliver them victory by smacking the ball and bringing in the winning runs. But there would be no joy in Mudville that day. The great hitter took two called strikes, and then, with "teeth clenched in hate," he whipped a violent swing through the air. Mighty Casey had struck out.

Little did author Thayer realize that in May 1889, a month after Albert Spalding's world tour ended, New York actor DeWolf Hopper would recite his poem at the Wallack Theater between acts of the play *Prince Methusalem*. The ballad had been reprinted in the *New York Sun* under the byline "Anon," and a sharp-eyed New York author named Archibald Gunter had saved it for future reference. In August, Gunter gave the newspaper

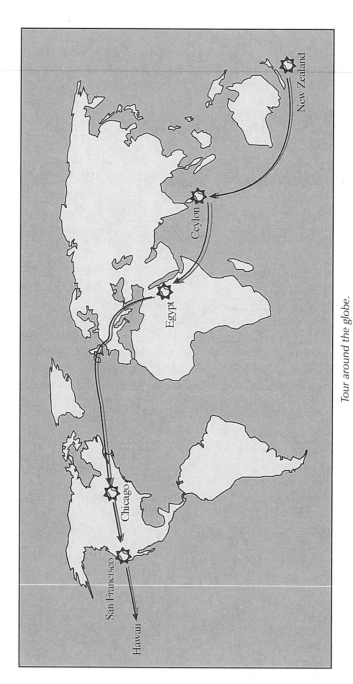

*Tour around the globe.*

(David Underwood, Graphic Design, CU-Boulder)

clipping to Hopper, and the actor first performed the poem at the Wallack Theater after a series of games between the New York Giants and the Chicago White Stockings, and before an audience that included Civil War general William Sherman and other luminaries. Nine months later, once again, the White Stockings and Giants, among others, enjoyed the show.

The long-legged, loose-jointed Hopper, beloved for comic opera as an eccentric comedian with a deep voice and clear diction, gained more fame for performing the ballad than for anything else he ever did. At least ten thousand more times before his death, eager fans heard recitals of "Casey at the Bat" vividly executed with wit, drama, and superb timing in exactly five minutes and forty seconds. The poem defined Hopper's career, and it went down in history as the most recognizable baseball performance piece, alongside the 1908 song "Take Me Out to the Ball Game." In fact, Hopper—six times married, a socialite of the sporting world, and an avid baseball fan—would greet Spalding's tourists upon their return to New York City at a gala in their honor by adding on some stanzas to the poem that addressed their globe-trotting glories.[1]

At home in Chicago, Albert Goodwill Spalding read the ballad with glee because it added to the lore and legend of the national pastime over which he was king. Keeping baseball in the news could only boost his fortunes—which he had made from pitching, leadership in the fledgling National League, ownership of the Chicago White Stockings, and promotion of his sporting goods company. For Thayer, Hopper, and Spalding in 1888–1889, baseball was a venue for profit and promotion, and the entire nation—indeed, the whole world—became their stage.

Baseball was an easy and popular sell, at least at home; by the 1880s, all classes, genders, ages, and colors had—oftentimes fanatically (the word *fan* derived from the sport's "fanatic" spectators)—seized upon baseball as their national pastime. Once rules were imposed and athletic skills and tactics perfected through midcentury, it had evolved from a child's game into an adult sport. For the United States, self-conscious about national meaning—the Statue of Liberty had just been erected in 1886 to welcome the masses of non-Americans—baseball became a source of identity. Abroad, especially in the British Empire, sporting men seemed primed to receive the game, steeped as they were in the values of strenuous outdoor pursuits. A savvy and determined entrepreneur with an eye for the big, seemingly limitless, world picture, might use the business and technological tools of Anglo-American globalization at his disposal to reap great profits.[2]

The so-called national pastime had no more zealous a promoter than Albert Spalding. One of his ambitious marketing projects—if not his most ambitious—was his international tour, which expanded well beyond its initial conception of terminating in Australia. Spalding's trip eventually girdled the entire world. In doing so, he launched another group of Americans into the world arena, helping to project U.S. business and culture abroad. He had never before undertaken an endeavor on such a grand scale, but he jumped at the chance in 1888, and unlike Casey, he did not disappoint. In part, Spalding's audacity emerged from his experiences and optimism cultivated in his business stomping grounds, the energetic city of Chicago, where the world tour began.

## SECOND CITY

Bustling Chicago was one of the fastest growing and most vibrant metropolitan areas in the world, and it held the seeds of Spalding's marketing frenzy and genius. Disparaged as the idiot child of cities, Chicago suffered from urban disorganization stemming from rampant commercialism based on an ethic of wide-open competition, factories and slaughterhouses, and political patronage. Yet, guided by ruthless and go-getting business and political leaders, and fueled by raw materials and the muscles of masses of workers—many of them immigrants—Chicago had remade itself after the Great Fire of 1871 and burst its seams as a commercial center. Within a decade, it rivaled New York as America's economic hub, led by risk-taking entrepreneurs who jumped on such innovations as steel-skeleton construction, food processing, and mass electrification and directed them into money-making enterprises. Chicago transformed itself into the nation's second city, as well as a modern nexus of national and international global economies—a tumult of technology, construction, politics, greed, and ambition that fueled globalization and, through this process, imperial dreams.

A dynamo of a city that linked the nation's transportation systems, Chicago was a "perpetually unfinished" metropolis situated at the heart of market capitalism and linked to the world by the modern accoutrements of transport and communications that typified the late-nineteenth-century period of globalization. It served as the point for raw materials to be bought, processed, and distributed into manufactured goods. Chicago was "nature's metropolis"—so powerful an economic provider of goods and services that, for instance, in 1889, the city's beef and pork packers, benefiting from refrigeration, stunningly outsold New York City meat suppliers in Gotham's own backyard of Long Island.[3] The volume of business was critical to the city; bank deposits, Board of Trade clearings, merchandise consumed, manufactures, publishing, grain storage capacity—all reached enormous proportions by the late 1880s. Claimed Mark Twain's *Gilded Age* collaborator, Charles Dudley Warner, Chicago had grown beyond everyone's expectations. By the eve of the Spalding world tour, trade had rocketed to more than $1.1 billion. The city's population would soon top one million, and Dudley doubted that there was "anywhere congregated a more active and aggressive million, with so great a proportion of young, ambitious blood."[4] Chicago was a remarkable place of energy, daring, manipulation, and organization. Businessmen there possessed, above all, a vision for profit.

It is instructive to delve into the city's economy, and its national and global links, to understand the roots of Spalding's own vision for profit. Merchants of all sorts negotiated their trades in Chicago. By the 1880s, entrepreneurs found their opportunities by meeting the demands of developing urban markets rather than by building new industries as in the pre–Civil War period. Self-made entrepreneurs maneuvering in a maelstrom of exchanges of money and goods, they built empires of private enterprise and developed industries in a beehive of business activity. Cyrus McCormick had built his famous reaper plants in Chicago and thereby changed rural America; he also built up a huge international trade that ran through the city and outward across the country and the seas beyond. Lumber mills proliferated, surpassed in number and size only by the millions of animals delivered for butchering to the multibillion-dollar operation of the Union Stockyard. Meat barons like the Armours and Swifts developed assembly lines and demanded not only good rail transportation to get their bacon to market but also luxury travel for themselves. George Pullman met their demands by establishing the Pullman "Palace" sleeping car, similar to the elegant trains that the baseball tourists would board for the initial cross-country leg of their journey.

Other empire-builders peopled Chicago. Marshall Field owned the largest wholesale and retail dry goods concern in the world, employing three thousand workers in his shops. Aaron Montgomery Ward created his retail empire by launching a general mail-order business in 1872, a company that, along with competitor Sears, Roebuck (founded in 1884), had a goal of selling through mail-order catalogs anything a farmer or urban dweller might need.[5] Coincidentally, though Aaron Ward was no baseball mogul, his younger cousin John Montgomery Ward, a star pitcher and batter for the New York Giants, captained one of the teams on Spalding's world tour.

Success in one of the commanding heights of capitalism, however, bred problems, too, among them labor troubles. Some of U.S. history's most violent strikes occurred in Chicago before and after the Spalding tour— the Haymarket Riot of 1886 and the Pullman Strike of 1894 were engineered by increasingly activist labor unions. In October 1888, the month that Spalding's entourage took to the rails, a strike by three thousand streetcar drivers and conductors erupted, compelling more than half of Chicago's residents to walk and nearly one thousand policemen to clear the obstructionist unions from the tracks with clubs. Supported by large mobs, the strikers retaliated with stones; sticks of dynamite were found on one rail line. Another struggle over labor rights and pay centered on construction of the city's Auditorium Building.[6]

It was in this environment that John Montgomery Ward guided baseball's earliest union, the Brotherhood, which he had formed in 1885. Like workers in other industries, baseball players contested their work and living conditions, especially the tight grip of industrial capitalists on their paychecks and freedom in the workplace.

Yet modern industrial capitalism possessed an allure for the masses, too, and magnates such as Pullman, Field, and Spalding capitalized on the desires of workers for their piece of the pie. Chicago's hundreds of thousands of laborers lent the city its commercial creativity in a diverse and young workforce willing to partake of the American dream of prosperity, even if hopes did not often meet expectations. The stream of immigrants pouring into the city further revealed Chicago's connection to global networks. The swelling thousands of managers and clerical staffers—white-collar, middle-class workers who worked in accounting, advertising, and other business organizations that represented the rising U.S. corporate sector—shopped at new retail outlets like Marshall Field's, mail-ordered through Montgomery Ward, and spread the city outward in a frenzy of home ownership eased by bankers who revolutionized mortgage practices.[7]

Chicago embraced the Gilded Age in all its glitter, illusions, wealth, struggle, and dynamism, but this city on the make also exemplified the vibrant hum of globalizing America. The United States stood poised on the leading edge of the modern push for worldwide cultural and economic integration. Travelers from abroad noted Chicago's rough edges, its newness and blatant fixation on profit. Loud promoters and prominent billboard advertising mingled with extensive parks and boulevards as well as libraries and other cultural institutions that made Chicago a city of contrasts. It was, said one tourist, "teeming with life and commercial activity," a modern urban center of enterprise that was "unsurpassed by any city in the world." Chicago prompted visitors to "hold their breath in astonishment" over the gigantic scale of its physical accomplishments.[8]

Visitors recognized Chicago as an economic linchpin in world trade, finance, and business development but also as an emerging cultural center. Considering that the population of London was about five times that of Chicago in 1888, it was "perfectly amazing," proclaimed a French traveler, that an average of 620 readers sat in the rooms of the British Museum on a daily basis that year, while the Chicago Public Library welcomed an impressive 1,569 per day.[9] Indeed, Charles Dudley Warner argued against the common assumptions of outsiders—and Chicagoans themselves—

that they lacked culture, reform, and social graces. Like everything in Chicago, however, the clubs, schools, settlement houses for immigrants, and libraries (and their funding and holdings) came on a grand scale that often surpassed the scope of similar institutions overseas.[10]

Foreigners observed both the upsides and downsides of the modern industrial society of the Gilded Age, yet their commentary usually centered on Chicago's technological wonders, which were drivers of globalization. Entering the "seething" maelstrom in 1888, British traveler John Aubertin arrived at the Chamber of Commerce building that was "clamorous with business" and the twang of ubiquitous, constantly moving elevators, "the almost only recognized American staircase." He encountered other innovations: construction of a seemingly endless tramway system; grain elevators and depots; a sophisticated, titanic waterworks system called "one of the wonders of the world"; and a hub for twenty-six converging railways. And, of course, there was the assembly line of wheels, lines, pulleys, and conveyors, along with tanks, barrels, freezing rooms, and other repositories, in the "interminable system of rapid mechanical manual labour" in the city's slaughterhouses. Chicago was "the future," Aubertin concluded, lying at the convergence of rail, road, and inland sea that absorbed and then thrust out into the world the goods "to supply the varied wants of an increasing civilization."[11]

In this city that had, just a half-century before, been a solitary outpost for wolf hunts and small schooners bringing in provisions, now, wrote Capt. Willard Glazier, "the bears of the Stock Exchange alone rage and howl" while "there swarms a fleet of vessels of all descriptions, bringing goods from, and sending them to, every quarter of the world." To many observers, he added, "Chicago is a great and a magnificent city, embodying more perfectly than any other in the world the possibilities of accomplishment of the Anglo-Saxon race, given its best conditions of freedom, independence, and intelligence."[12] City leaders, as well as influential men in the professions—including baseball's Spalding—agreed with this view, which they injected into their daily dealings.

Such race-laden sentiment of Anglo-Saxonism seems anachronistic today, but it expressed a positivist faith in modernity integral to nineteenth-century globalization and, indeed, globalization in the late twentieth century. The latter juxtaposed such jarring notions of clashes of civilizations with ideas of homogeneity, as well as revealing the tensions of opportunity tempered by inequality; profit burdened by risk; wealth burdened by poverty, dirt, and unsanitary conditions; and cultural and economic world integration confronted by nationalism. Aptly, then, an English clergyman commented a century before that "Chicago is a very large, and a very lively, but it is not a nice child, and nobody wants to fondle it."[13]

Still, Chicagoans got high marks for their energy, ambition, and individualism, and that applied to baseball magnates as well as bankers and butchers. Baseball, too, held promises both real and false for its participants. In fact, the sport articulated the city's character very well, emerging as a professionalized enterprise that reflected not just Chicago's dynamism. In the 1880s, Chicago went "baseball crazy" as its White Stockings won five National League pennants in a seven-year span.[14] Thus, success in the baseball business, as in other enterprises, rang supreme in the city.

## THE MAKING OF A MAGNATE

Into Chicago's baseball ferment landed Boston Red Stockings star pitcher Albert Goodwill Spalding, recruited by White Stockings owner William Hulbert in 1876. The first president of the new National League, Hulbert spoke to the city's centrality by supposedly telling Spalding, "I'd rather be a lamppost in Chicago than a millionaire in any other city."[15] With business flourishing all over the city, cultural institutions followed in the 1880s, and just around the corner, the famous World's Fair of 1893 would make Chicago a global focus. Baseball, and particularly Spalding, played a large role in the culture and economy of Chicago, as well as the country as a whole. Like McCormick in agricultural machinery and Gustavus Swift in meatpacking, Albert Spalding became the baron of baseball, a captain in a newly professionalized industry in which he had a controlling interest in both playing the sport and supplying it with its equipment. Both proved to be lucrative endeavors that gave him unparalleled influence.

He was a product of the Gilded Age. Born in 1850, Spalding lived his first twelve years in the farming town of Byron, Illinois, before his father passed away after building a modest fortune through wise real estate investments and selling horses. His mother, determined to foster industriousness among her children, sent him to Rockford, more than seventy-five miles west of Chicago, to reside with an aunt for a year before she and his two siblings joined him and the aunt there. It was here, in a railroad hub set among highly productive farmland, that the lonely Spalding could not help but focus on his ambitions. Homesick for smaller and simpler Byron, Albert sought relief by watching baseball being played on the Rockford common. Overcoming his shyness, he then participated in the games himself, and took to it quickly. He initially distinguished himself by catching a lofty fly ball in center field and throwing it home, without a bounce, to the catcher. So marked the beginning of this naturally gifted fifteen-year-old's baseball career, for in 1865 Rockford's new prestigious club, the Forest Citys, recruited him to pitch.

Spalding learned how to play the sport—and also got an idea of the marketing behind it. The team, sponsored by businessmen who hired players in the off-season and by town boosters wishing to promote Rockford's status, attracted amateur players looking for an outlet to play competitive baseball in the region. Spalding exceeded them all, soon reaching national acclaim. In 1867, his Rockford team played in a typical summer tournament; this one included the Washington (D.C.) Nationals, a touring squad of nine government employees and college students said to be the best team in the country. The Nationals had just blasted a Columbus, Ohio, club by a score of 90–10, and then followed by wiping out the Indianapolis nine, 106–21. Few elite teams showed mercy in those early days of baseball.

At the tournament in late July at Chicago's Dexter Park, the Washington side embarrassed the Forest Citys' archrival, the Chicago Excelsiors, 49–4, and the Rockford nine then stepped up to the slaughter. In what he later called his proudest accomplishment in baseball, Spalding, just seventeen years old, pitched the Forest Citys to a stunning 29–23 victory. Touted as an up-and-coming pitcher by the sport's best-known journalist, Henry Chadwick, Spalding was feted for a week by the proud civic boosters of Rockford. The big (over six-foot) kid seemed headed toward a stellar career, earning his chance for the big time by joining the Excelsiors. The opportunity proved short-lived, but Spalding got a taste for the city that he never lost.

Migration from rural America to the city during the Gilded Age was typical for young people like Spalding. Bolstered by success manuals and the famous examples of the numerous wealthy who had made fortunes by hard work and enterprise, motivated youth left the fields and small towns for the promise of the city. Self-help, determination, and good character were the maxims of the Second Industrial Revolution, and with cleverness and luck, achieving the American dream fell within reason. Spalding lived by these moral guideposts, and with his keen observation, he also knew the value of business acumen as well as integrity. Skillful maneuvering and focused insights could lead to cornering markets, building monopolies, and promoting profits. Baseball offered lessons as well as warnings about the ills of bad behavior such as drunkenness and gambling, dishonesty, and dissipation. By moving to Chicago, Spalding experienced the interplay of instinct and calculation, of character and emotions, and of energy and efficiency that served him when he built his baseball empire less than a decade after his arrival in the city in 1867.

Spalding became a proponent of Andrew Carnegie's gospel of wealth, and specifically the notion that, like animals in the jungle, individuals battled for survival—in business as in life. While others noticed the need for reform, social justice, and labor rights, there is no evidence that Spalding absorbed such thought as he set out on his career. In fact, like most rising corporate leaders of his time, he sought to tame the market jungle and corral labor by collusion, cooperation, and combination in following the ethic of the Gilded Age so instrumental to the aggressive marketing required in the Anglo-American era of globalization.[16] Baseball gave him that opportunity.

The Excelsiors offered Spalding a chance to play in the limelight of America's second city. Under the rules of the sport's top-flight organization of the late 1860s, the amateur National Association of Baseball Players, Spalding could not earn a salary, but he nevertheless managed to find paid employment. Typically, players were employed by local boosters. In Spalding's case, a wholesale grocer gave him a job as a clerk, with a flexible schedule that did not interfere with his pitching. However, he played in only one game before the grocer went bottom up and Spalding was forced to leave Chicago and return to Rockford to make a living. It is difficult to discern the magnitude of his disappointment, but in any case, over the next few years, attracted to the "business end of the game," in his words, Spalding worked and played baseball in a town that seemed challenging enough to reward him.

It was clear that Rockford, a place that promised ample wealth and thus kept alive the pecuniary dreams of Gilded Age America, continued to shape his thinking. As Spalding's biographer has noted, he "grew up in a town preoccupied with self-promotion and in a society that offered constant hints on how to achieve material success." The key to success lay in "money-getting," and Spalding responded to this message by including in his scrapbooks of the late 1860s several clippings on banking and currency. Even more indicative of his future, he cut out and saved articles about the prospect of earning a salary as a baseball player. In this way, he joined business and baseball.[17]

Professionalization in America at this time had resulted in the growth of the industrial and service sectors, as well as the creation of a thriving middle class that marched in tune with elites and entrepreneurs. Chicago, of course, witnessed such professionalism, and sports was not immune to it. Baseball soon shrugged off its amateur, gentleman's club organization and evolved into a professional sport because it had little competition from other pastimes, like football and hockey, which did not fully professionalize until the 1920s. In 1869, like many baseball fanatics, Spalding monitored the rise of the Cincinnati Red Stockings, baseball's first all-salaried team. President Aaron Champion and his manager, Harry Wright, applied business skills, civic boosterism, and a background in English cricket to sign the top players, advertise the team's greatness, and give Cincinnati a field to brag about as their team barnstormed the Midwest and East, defeating all comers. Professionals seemed to perform better than amateurs, and fans appeared to be willing to pay to see them play.

Taking note of the Red Stockings' success, in 1870 the Forest Cities—led by their ace Albert Spalding, winner of forty-five out of fifty-eight games over the previous three years—headed east to play seventeen contests. They won thirteen and tied another; one of the victories was Spalding's victory over Wright's vaunted wage-earners, the Cincinnati club, 12–5. A year later, Wright bought Spalding from Rockford, contracted the pitcher for $1,500 a year, moved his Red Stockings to Boston, and devised the first professional baseball league, called the National Association.[18] Spalding, a pitcher but also a keen student of the game's business and management, was present at the creation of a fully professional major league organization. Cincinnati boosters, by the way, would later form another team, calling it the Redlegs, then Reds for short.

After playing in Boston for six years, Spalding finally returned to Chicago, but before he did, he turned out to be an apt pupil of the talented Harry Wright. This cricketer and key figure in the development of baseball had turned out to be a superb teacher of organizational skills, money management, and baseball itself, although ultimately, he failed to transfer his ideas and personal skills to the professional league, which staggered for five years until it folded. Wright tutored his star, Spalding. At six feet, one inch, and 170 pounds, "Big Al" Spalding now joined his physical prowess with a keen intellect. He adapted to changes that favored skilled players over the gentlemanly amateurs of yesteryear. Earning the club's top salary of $2,000, by 1874 he also gained a reputation for proper conduct off the field—an oddity for a sport plagued by gamblers, drinkers, and spitting. Most significantly, Spalding observed as Wright calculated and expanded Boston's budgets and organized the team's schedule, advertising, and negotiations with players. In a critical learning experience for Spalding, Wright then fulfilled a dream by taking the best team in America to his native England to demonstrate his adopted sport. Big Al came along not only as a Red Stockings pitcher but also as Wright's chief assistant.

The tour lost money (and Wright, in the typical behavior of a magnate, recouped the losses by cutting the players' pay), but Spalding gained immeasurably. The nearly two-month trip of 1874 pitted Boston against the rival Philadelphia Athletics in fourteen exhibition games, as well as seven cricket matches against British clubs in which the Americans won six and drew the seventh due to rain. Having faith in his pitcher's business qualifications, Wright sent Spalding to England to make travel arrangements and plan the matches. The British were politely unimpressed by baseball, validated in their view that the Americans were "a nation so busy, so bent upon getting on" that they did everything possible to complete their games in three hours, rather than the day or two it took to play the much more sophisticated sport of cricket.[19] For his part, Spalding was immeasurably impressed by the professional demeanor of the U.S. sides—so much so that he would insist upon similar upright behavior during his own, grander world tour fifteen years later. He also became more famous as a thinking-man's player, an organizational mastermind, and a dignified representative of the game. Spalding joined the crusade, alongside advocates of decency such as Boston's Wright, Cincinnati's Champion, and newsman Chadwick, against baseball's unsavory reputation.

As Wright's "business agent," moreover, Spalding could also not help but grasp the entrepreneurial nature inherent in baseball. The foreign promotional sports tour gave him one example. A more immediate financially rewarding one that exhibited the profits to be won in baseball arose as the motivated Spalding noted the success of a New York sporting equipment store owned by Harry Wright and his brother George that sold to an eager consuming public. Baseball promised monetary gains and, therefore, social status—the two Grails of the Gilded Age.

In 1875, Spalding applied his education at the hands of the Wrights when he was lured back home by William Hulbert, who promised a more disciplined league and a promotion for Big Al to captain and manager of the newly refurbished Chicago White Stockings.[20] The next year, Hulbert and some other owners gave birth to the National League, and they drafted Spalding to write its constitution. That was an honor, but the profit came when Spalding's sporting goods company, based in Chicopee, Massachusetts, won exclusive rights to manufacture National League baseballs. After also cornering the market on the new American League's baseballs in 1901, the Spalding monopoly provisioned Major League balls for the next one hundred years, until the Rawlings company received the contract in 1976.[21]

Headquartered in Chicago, Hulbert's National League attracted key players, but the pivot to its success turned out to be Albert Spalding. To be sure, his playing days were nearing their end. Earning a huge salary of $2,000, plus one-quarter of all White Stockings gate receipts, in 1876—the year Chicago won the first National League championship behind his forty-seven wins—Spalding moved to first base the next year. In 1878, Spalding gave up his captaincy of the White Stockings, playing in just one game and retiring at age twenty-seven for the monetarily greener pasture of team secretary.[22]

## BUSINESS MOGUL

Financial independence built from his sporting goods firm helped Spalding advocate for the team and the game. Through the early 1870s, he had built his company, and by 1877, a year after capitalizing it in Chicago (its store just down the street from White Stockings headquarters) with his brother, J. Walter, Albert had made so much money that he could easily give up active work on the diamond the following year. Yet Spalding did not neglect Chicago. Upon Hulbert's death in 1882, Big Al assumed the presidency of a White Stockings ball club that dominated baseball during the decade. And for the magnate Spalding, the 1880s turned out to be a time of merging baseball and business that gave him decisive influence over the game and, to an extent, in the city as well.

Just thirty-two, he was now an owner who was arguably the most significant baseball figure in the country because he took it upon himself to represent the sport and preach about its improvement. It helped his standing that the Spalding Bros. partnership became the biggest sporting goods commercial house in the nation, selling the league-endorsed *Spalding's Official Base Ball Guide* to hotels and advertisers as baseball's bible. Edited by journalist Henry Chadwick, the *Spalding Guide* enjoyed a national circulation of fifty thousand in 1884, becoming the sport's handbook, a major advertising venue for his equipment company, and a forum for National League officials and magnates to editorialize about their wise governance. Spalding sold it at his booming sporting goods stores, which included fourteen new outlets in 1886 located in a commercial swath from Maine to Colorado. The firm sold more than baseball bats and balls, too, as it entered into contracts to make and distribute turnstiles, grandstand cushions, books, bicycles, golf and gymnasium equipment, and sportswear for athletes and hunters. Observers noted how the Spalding brothers engaged in mergers and acquisitions that smacked of the monopolistic practices in meat-packing, oil, and tobacco trusts. Spalding Bros. both manufactured baseball equipment and became its chief purveyor. The proverbial sky was the limit; Spalding proclaimed his motto "Everything is possible to him who dares."[23]

Dominating the business of balls, bats, gloves, bases, and uniforms made Albert Spalding king of the national pastime. He provided the league with balls. In addition, bats had been customized as early as 1884, as John Andrew "Bud" Hillerich, a former butter-churner who converted to wood-turning, designed the first specially tailored bat for the original "Louisville Slugger," Pete Browning. Within a few years, Hillerich had fashioned more than three hundred bat models then in use, and by the 1890s, he had registered the Louisville Slugger trademark. Spalding sold these and other bats to professionals and amateurs alike. He adhered to official measurements; bats were restricted to a maximum length of 42 inches under National League rules, and initially to a diameter of $2^1/2$ inches, though that expanded a half inch in 1894.

Spalding also got exclusive rights, albeit just for a year, for supplying all National League teams with uniforms. In 1882, just before his death,

*Albert Goodwill Spalding.*
(New York Public Library)

league president Hulbert reacted to the chaos that ensued from a one-year experiment in which each position player wore a different colored uniform. Hulbert ruled that teams could no longer wear a rainbow of shirts— nor, for that matter, would he allow them to choose the style of uniform. Thus, for example, he assigned to Chicago a white uniform and designated Boston in red. White belts, stockings, knicker pants, and ties were required of all teams. The following year, the restrictions ended, except for the stockings, but teams stuck with the same colors, high-collared shirts, and knee-length pants. Spalding Bros. provided all of these items. Of note, too, Spalding also sold caps, too, in either the White Stockings' pillbox style or the ever more popular beanie.[24]

From the late 1870s through the 1890s, Spalding bought up smaller sporting goods concerns, secured new inventions, reincorporated the company in New Jersey to take advantage of tax breaks, and established a national retail and wholesale marketing network that distributed the company's lines in nearly three dozen American cities and six foreign ones, including Cairo, Egypt. Globalization opened up valuable opportunities for Spalding. His was a "monstrous" empire that won nearly total market control over baseball and some other sports as well. Indeed, as his biographer has noted, with the company's publications alone, Spalding's promotion of his goods through advertising, in the firm's catalogue, and by sponsorship of sports manuals "had nearly become a business in itself."[25] Spalding therefore enjoyed a vital connection to Chicago, a city populated by young men like himself in prominent management and ownership positions who had ambitions to reach city, regional, national, and global business horizons.

Spalding's sense of enterprise included gaining and holding power over the gate receipts, and this meant luring large numbers of fans to games. The 1870s "enclosure movement" had enabled owners to charge admission and place fans in boxes, seats, or bleachers—and prevent them from crowding onto the field. Consolidating their rising profits, owners then poured money into renovating or building baseball playing grounds. These wooden structures, such as New York's original Polo Grounds, constructed in 1880, and Lakefront Park in Chicago, remodeled in 1883 to seat ten thousand (the largest seating capacity in the country at the time), held the possibilities of ever larger gate receipts. Whether in building new playing grounds for his team, as he did in 1885 with the West Side Grounds, also known as the Congress Street Park, or outfitting these venues with modern facilities, Spalding remained a bold experimenter with an eye on elevating the game. In the Lakefront facility, for instance, Spalding installed a private curtained box for himself and built eighteen others. He tried electric lights at the Congress Street Grounds in 1886, and even put in a toboggan slide and an ice-skating rink next to it as means of attracting middle-class customers.[26]

Creative marketing boosted his profits, but the conservative effort at combination and control boosted Spalding to the top of his profession. As a magnate at home and a leader in the National League, he conspired with other owners in 1887 to merge with the rival American Association. The so-called beer and whiskey league allowed alcohol on its baseball premises, while the National League did not, and thus it proved to be an able competitor for patrons. Spalding also hoped to bankrupt weak teams and forge a monopolistic hold over professional baseball. This effort failed, but only for the moment; the National League would hold a monopoly over the sport in the 1890s. In addition, along with other owners, Spalding constantly tinkered with governance, trying to create a tiered arrangement of leagues and teams to generate more stable revenues. Some of his experiments failed and others had only temporary success, but still others endured. The key to understanding them all lay in

Spalding's tireless promotion of his interests in tandem with sports that gave him a perch at the top of the baseball business.

This position, and his views and monopoly practices, made him a target for a labor activists. Spalding understood player grievances, having been a pitcher himself, but he stood with his fellow magnates by the late 1880s on the divisive issue of contracts and salaries. He devised a system in which minor league teams paid to the White Stockings and other major league teams $1,500–2,000 per player per season for the rights to "reserve," or protect from being bought by the rich clubs, their best players. This form of bribery prevented a mass exodus from their teams; the National League and American Association would no longer rob players from each other or sign non–big league personnel. This minor league "reserve clause" was a version of the infamous and better known major league reserve clause, instituted in 1879, which became a source of contention for a century. It allowed magnates to hold onto a dozen or so players by tying them to one-year, renewable contracts. The reserve clause subjected players to the whims of the owners, who routinely limited salary raises or cut wages altogether. Not surprisingly, such suppression of rights developed into the rallying point for players until the reserve clause was modified by free agency in the mid-1970s.

In 1885, the reserve clause had induced players to establish the National Brotherhood of Professional Baseball Players, an organization that Spalding superficially endorsed in order to quell labor rebellion, but whose members—led by the Giants' John Montgomery Ward—fully recognized him as a key enemy in the fight for players' rights. Spalding was undeterred. He continued to engage in boss politics over the players, blocking their moves against the reserve clause, maneuvering different coalitions of owners and players against the Brotherhood, and cunningly claiming he was a friend of labor in baseball while always backing all but the very worst of magnate behavior. Spalding knew who controlled the purse strings of the sport, and he determined, quite successfully, to protect his interests from the players, who he deemed dumb, misled, or selfish.[27]

## THE BASEBALL TOURISTS

Spalding got away with such brashness because he was a success off the field, but also because he owned one of the best teams in baseball. In the 1880s, the White Stockings were the National League's first dynasty, built around the greatest hitter of the day—the first major leaguer to collect 3,000 hits. The highly respected leader of the Chicagos, first baseman Adrian Constantine "Cap" Anson joined Spalding and the White Stockings in 1876 and remained with the team for the next twenty-one years.

From 1887 onward, the young writer Finley Peter Dunne filed colorful stories about the team and made Anson—known variously as "Baby" or "Pop," but most often as "Cap"—an American hero and household name.

Anson's batting was legendary. He hit .300 or better for twenty years, including .399 in 1881, and he once swatted five home runs in five consecutive times at bat. A large, gruff, sometimes impulsive, but generally good-natured man, this aggressive captain/manager was a natural leader and thus shepherded players on the world tour. He had tourism experience, having joined the 1874 trip to England. Most significantly, Anson was the unmatched field general of the sport. Teammates trusted him for his honesty, his forthright manner, and his utter loyalty to his players, team, and the sport. In 1879, Anson took on the role of manager, directing Chicago to five National League pennants in the 1880s. In 1888, he signed a ten-year contract proffered by Spalding that gave him control over field operations and a substantial share of stock in the White Stockings. An innovator, Anson is credited with inventing managerial signals to players on the field as well as developing spring training, base stealing, coaching boxes, and pitcher rotations.

Despite his Hall of Fame hitting and considerable stature, Anson went down in history as a bigot when he became a vocal proponent of drawing the color barrier against black players. He might have been trying to disguise his background, for he was the first white child among Native Americans in Marshalltown, Iowa, in 1852. The circumstances in Iowa at that time, where slavery was still legal and Native Americans were considered barbarians when compared to the dominant white culture, also explains his racist views.

Racism aside (and Anson was not the sole segregationist in baseball), Anson was, simply, the linchpin of his team. Spalding believed him "one of the greatest players that ever lived" and essential to maintaining proper behavior, including dress codes, in the public arena of the world tour.[28] Anson guided the White Stockings on the world tour, and later wrote one of the two major accounts of the trip in his autobiography, one of baseball's first self-narratives. He was also a good choice to assist Spalding in maintaining discipline among the rowdy players of the late nineteenth century. As manager, Anson did not permit his players to consume alcoholic beverages, smoke cigarettes or cigars, or use drugs. He rewarded players with kindness when they worked for him. Players respected him, and some adored him; tourist and young pitcher John Tener remarked that this "fine fellow" had a personal "magnetism" that drew people to him, especially those with discipline and a work ethic.[29]

Spalding had other players to bolster his powerhouse team and his standing as baseball's premier businessman, but among them, Mike "King" Kelly turned out to be immune to Big Al's boosterism. This colorful,

*Adrian "Cap" Anson.*

hard-drinking base-stealer played most positions, but with Chicago, he stood behind the plate at catcher and roamed in right field. Like Anson, Kelly batted with his back to the catcher, making it impossible for opponents to guess where he would hit because they could see neither his feet nor his bat pointing in the desired hitting direction. And he hit often, leading the league in average in 1886. Yet his fame arose in large part from his base-stealing abilities. As the crowds yelled "Slide, Kelly, slide" when he took off from first base for second, Kelly dove into the bag with a roundhouse kick. This famous hook style became known as the "Chicago slide"; two decades later, Ty Cobb would nickname it his own "fallaway" maneuver. An impeccably dressed, handsome, and tall figure with a handlebar mustache, Kelly was adored by spectators—especially females—for his play and his outlandish behavior.

Kelly rarely disappointed the fans, while he greatly annoyed the authorities. He made up for his average speed with a quickness of mind that often stupefied umpires. Though morally lazy, he assiduously studied the game and its rules in a way that allowed him to invent ingenious trick plays. In once instance, he jumped off the bench and caught a foul ball that had careened out of reach of his teammate, Silver Flint, taking advantage of the substitution rule and shouting, "Kelly in for Flint!" More often, he adopted such tactical moves as dropping his catcher's mask on home plate to distract a runner.

Appreciative of his plays that helped the White Stockings, Anson nonetheless became enervated with Kelly, who mocked the manager's discipline by acting the playboy and hitting the whisky bottle. The league's most popular star of the mid-1880s, Kelly would cross the teetotaler Anson, who had originally signed him, and would eventually convince Spalding that his investment in his star was not worth the headache. Spalding sold the King before the 1887 season to the Boston Nationals for the unheard-of fortune of $10,000, more than ten times the average workingman's annual salary. Still, because of his fame and abilities, Spalding asked Kelly to join the world tour two years later. In many respects, Kelly and Spalding were peas in a pod. Both were entrepreneurs—one a clever operator on the field of play, the other a schemer off of it.[30]

Kelly's departure from Chicago did not ruin the team, for the White Stockings were blessed with many other sensations, as well as future world tourists, and they benefited, as well, from Spalding's largesse during this early golden era of baseball. Players like second baseman Fred "Fritz" Pfeffer, a member of Chicago's famous "stone wall infield," expertly fielded without a glove, notched more than forty stolen bases a year, and, as a German speaker, drew large numbers of that ethnic group to the ballpark. Completing the stone wall infield were Anson at first base; Tom Burns, a quick shortstop; and large, strong-throwing Ed Williamson at third base. The latter two switched positions after 1885, but their air-tight fielding endured. Other youthful players completed a superb team. Mark Baldwin earned a reputation as a stellar pitcher, while young George Van Haltren, whom Anson brought into the National League in 1887 from Oakland, was both a solid hitter and pitcher. Young Jimmy Ryan debuted with the White Stockings in 1886 as an outfielder with a strong arm, an early relief pitcher, a superb lead-off hitter who batted for power, and one of a handful of position players in history to bat left-handed but throw with his right. Ryan kept a diary of the world tour—an appropriate pastime for one of professional baseball's first collegians.[31] This collection of players won championships, lifting Spalding to a position of influence in American society.

## PLANNING THE VENTURE

Spalding looked beyond Chicago, however, in his vision for the sport, for in his eyes, baseball linked directly to American identity, and he had a plan to exhibit its worth to audiences at home and abroad. In the first history of the game, Spalding's own *Base Ball: American's National Game,* published in 1911 just four years before his death, Spalding charged the magnates "to preserve Base Ball as a game worthy of the great American Nation."[32] Indeed, the nearly unanimous acclaim for the book the world over placed baseball as "an American enterprise" of the first rank.[33] Read-ers agreed that Spalding had linked business and sports in a celebration of American character and customs, and they remembered that his most compelling deed in this regard had been the globe-trotting trip of 1888–1889.

Spalding's inscription at the Hall of Fame describes him as an organiza-tional genius, but it also notes his sponsorship of the first round-the-world baseball tour in history. At its heart lay the future of baseball expansion, and of the future U.S. empire, with the Chicago ethic of vibrant and daring commercialism—a cardinal element of globaliza-tion—at the fore. Extending the empire of baseball from Chicago outward was paramount to Spalding, and he conceived of the marketing ploy of a global trip to capture the public's imagination and further entrench his standing as the sport's spokesman. He also hoped to mute baseball's most serious labor insurgency against his power by hustling out of the country John Ward, the organizer of the anti–reserve clause Brotherhood player's association. The payoff was potentially immense, in terms of prestige and profit, and Spalding did not disguise his intentions. Thrilled to be asked both to pitch on the Australian trip and keep the accounts, pitcher John Tener noted that the White Stockings president "has made and is still

SPORTING **EXTRA** CIGARETTES.

THE CHICAGO B. B. TOURISTS.

*Some of the touring Chicago White Stockings. Left to right:* Bob Pettit, Mark Sullivan, Mark Baldwin, Tom Burns, Cap Anson, Fred Pfeffer, John Tener, Jimmy Ryan, and the mascot, Clarence Duval.

(Doug Allen, Mastronet, Inc.)

making money 'hand over fist' out of base-ball [and] is also a very much respected business man."[34] As Spalding told a reporter in the fall of 1888, he was headed abroad, destined for the British colony of Australia, noted for its love of field sports, "for the purpose of extending my sporting-goods business to that quarter of the globe and to create a market for goods there."[35]

Promotion required money, a feasible itinerary, planning, and, above all, a knack for advertising. Unlike his situation during the 1874 tour, this time, Spalding enjoyed wealth, experience, and unrivaled stature. Thus, he deposited $30,000 in a Chicago bank as a safeguard against the kind of financial loss incurred on the English trip. As an effective promoter, moreover, Spalding determined to make a splash by having the baseball tourists travel in style. To attract attention, they crossed land and sea in special, luxury train coaches and ocean steamers, sleeping in the best hotels and dining in the finest restaurants. Spalding did not expect to make money on the tour; rather, the venture was an investment. He aimed to draw attention to the game of baseball and make business contacts for his own long-run financial gain. No expense would be spared in making this sensational promotional opportunity a success.

To oversee the U.S. portion of the journey, Spalding tapped Jim Hart, manager of the Milwaukee club of the Western League and a long-time friend. In 1888, Hart's charge focused on generating paying crowds at home large enough to cover Spalding's expenses should the Hawaii-to-Australia leg lose money. Hart did his job, and U.S. fans gave the baseball tourists a loud, and lucrative, reception before they left the country and when they returned.[36]

Spalding left arrangements for foreign travel to the seasoned Leigh Lynch, a manager of dramatic enterprises and former administrator of the Union Square Theater. Lynch had conducted numerous visits to Australia, where he had obtained many important acquaintances. Spalding worried that other magnates might compete with him by trying out their own trips or continue their jealous harping about the supposed bad quality of his player-tourists. Not taking any chances, before publicly announcing the global endeavor, Spalding sent Lynch to Australia, in February 1888, in order to organize a viable itinerary. On the way, Lynch stopped in Hawaii and New Zealand and set up the accommodations, schedules, and the exhibition matches. He then reserved Australia's best cricket grounds for games before returning to the United States in April, after which promotional activity for the tour went into overdrive. Some delicate negotiations were in order. For instance, the Oceanic Steamship Company announced in August its intention of withdrawing its fleet from the San Francisco-to-Sydney run sometime in autumn. However, the company agreed, after substantial prodding by Lynch, to keep one vessel in Sydney to transport the players back to America.[37]

Leaving no stone unturned, Spalding looked to every venue possible for advertisement once he had made his world tour intentions known. By mid-August 1888, he had signed on players from his White Stockings team. Then in a marketing coup, he obtained an audience in October for the Chicago club with President Grover Cleveland at the White House, through the services of Illinois congressman Frank Lawler. This was a busy time for the president, who was engaged in his reelection campaign, which he ultimately lost to Republican Benjamin Harrison. Yet he took time to visit the Chicago side, perhaps in recognition that the grand trip represented a milestone in the projection of American culture and business around the globe.

After awaiting the departure of the new Chief Justice Fuller, the White Stockings filed into the Blue Room of the White House to meet the president. Cleveland happily received them, for he claimed to know them well, especially the famous Cap Anson. After shaking hands with each, a nervous Anson asked for Cleveland's endorsement of the trip by his signature on a letter that proclaimed the White Stockings and their all-star opponents, the "All-America" team, to be the best players in the United States. A politician to the last, Cleveland cheerily replied that he would ponder the request. As the players left, Anson said, "Mr. President, it may interest you to know that a majority of my men are Democrats," and although they would not be present on election day to vote, they would be "pulling for" him. Cleveland smiled, reportedly replying, "Then they cannot be beaten."[38] Although he ultimately refused to give his formal endorsement to the trip, he did call the immaculately dressed players "the best representatives of the national game to the Australian people."[39] Spalding contentedly received an ink drawing of the meeting with Cleveland, wringing all possible advantage out of the event by distributing five thousand copies during the tour.

Notably, such print advertising preceded the tourists and aroused considerable interest in the Spalding enterprise. By the late 1880s, the metropolitan press experienced tremendous subscription growth, as such features as sports pages proved popular with a growing readership. Thus, Spalding wisely included three correspondents on the tour. One worked for the *New York Sun*, another hailed from the Chicago *Inter Ocean*, and the third, Spalding's friend Harry Palmer, wrote for the *New York Herald* but also reported for the *Chicago Tribune*, *Boston Herald*, and baseball's journal of record (and Spalding–White Stockings mouthpiece) *Sporting Life*. In 1889, Palmer published the most authoritative account of the world tour in his long book, *Athletic Sports in America, England, and Australia*, which Anson cribbed for his memoirs.[40]

Regardless of his prudent plans and extensive boosterism, to Spalding's dismay, the conceptualization of the tour did not receive a uniform endorsement. There were naysayers, especially from the *Sporting News*, a rival of Spalding's ally *Sporting Life*. A correspondent for the opposition paper labeled the tour a fraud, for many of the announced players on the All-America team balked at the invitation to travel abroad. This was true. Spalding had listed hurlers Charles Comiskey of St. Louis, Pete Conway of Detroit, King Kelly, and Brooklyn's Bob Caruthers as team members, but none joined up in the end. Even Anson, *Sporting News* claimed, seemed to have soured on the tour because it might exhaust his White Stockings before the arduous 1889 season. Worse, an opposition newspaper noted that across the Pacific Ocean, Australians seemingly puzzled about this "strange undertaking" to play a child's game in the Antipodes. Even Spalding, the consummate entrepreneur, could not honestly anticipate "making money out of the venture, for such is out of the question."[41] In the face of this criticism, Spalding promised to release any player in demand from his team when the tour returned to the States in April 1889 and continued the drumbeat of promotion for the trip.[42]

Still, in general, most newspapers provided positive coverage of the endeavor, attracted by its global ambitions and the novelty of playing in "Kangaroo Country." The tour seemed refreshingly unique, with America's sports heroes and a national icon in Spalding traveling to exotic lands. It simply piqued the imagination. Opined the *New York Times*, should the attempt to bring baseball to the Antipodes through sports globalization prove successful, "the 'world's championship' may one day cease to be equivalent to the championship of the United States."[43]

Spalding had worked hard, to be sure, to receive such media support. Taking issue with the critics who were merely trying to embarrass the Chicago owner, the august Henry Chadwick, the editor of the *Sporting Life* and Spalding's close ally, wrote a few days before the tour's departure: "A. G. Spalding has done more for the game of base ball in this country than an army of [owners] could ever accomplish. He has been a tower of strength in the work of raising it to a position that enables the professional clubs to pay the salaries they now obtain." A partisan of the magnates and the White Stockings, Chadwick begged off Spalding's invitation to go on the tour due to his advanced age. Yet he minced no words in saluting his visionary friend. Spalding, he declared, "has been the king-pin in organization and wise legislation, and now when he puts his money and his ability and his efforts into an enterprise that will do more to popularize the game and widen the breadth of its influence than anything that has yet been undertaken in its interest," a bunch of "small-calibred" individuals were trying to cause him financial loss and humiliation.[44] Concluded Chadwick in September, there was no reason for criticism. The players had signed fair contracts which paid all expenses, plus a bonus, from October 15, 1888, to April 15, 1889. During that half-year period, their sole obligation was to play baseball, cricket, football, and other sports, as well as travel and dine lavishly. Meanwhile, Spalding proceeded "with the same enterprising and liberal spirit with which he conducts all his business affairs, and my word for it, it will yield him the same creditable success all his other business undertakings have."[45]

Further endorsements from the baseball establishment overwhelmed the critics. For instance, the venerable George Wright—the old British infielder who had quit cricket, joined the all-professional Cincinnati Reds in 1869 under the management of his brother, and became the game's best hitter over the next few years—joined the entourage. He was the senior member of the sporting goods firm Wright and Ditson, and Spalding asked him along as a sports promoter and a cricketer who could teach the teams the British game. Wright was a paramount sportsman and marketer himself; he introduced golf to Boston in 1890 and Canadian ice hockey to America later on, as well as boosting U.S. interest in tennis. Wright also shared Spalding's fondness for innovation. The first batter in the history of the National League in 1876, Wright had also been an early proponent of a fielding glove, which he had donned in 1870 to protect a bruised hand.

Entertainers also flocked aboard, lending a circus atmosphere to the tour. Humorist Frank Lincoln accompanied the players to Australia, not the last of the literati to be associated with them. In Omaha, Spalding picked up Clarence Duval, Chicago's black "mascot," to entertain players and dignitaries alike. Duval's value seemingly arose partly as a throwback to slavery; he practiced a demeaning jig, called "plantation dancing," in front of clapping audiences. He also played the role of drum major, leading the tourists into playing grounds. Furthermore, in San Francisco, the tour welcomed an "aeronaut," or hot-air balloonist, Michigander "Professor" Bartholomew. The "Proff," as the players called him, leaped from a hot-air balloon, intrepidly performing gymnastic routines as he floated down under a parachute. Spalding surmised correctly that the Proff might catalyze crowds abroad to come out for baseball exhibitions should the sport not naturally roust them from their homes. The exhibitionists, along with the sporting figures, writers, and actors, proved to be amusing sidelights and cumulatively gave Spalding's world trip the status of other large-scale American tours of the time, such as Buffalo Bill's Wild West Show or Nellie Bly's race around the world.[46]

## RECRUITING FROM THE LABOR POOL

Regarding the teams, Spalding also managed to ensure a turnout because of the many star players on the field. Cap Anson and Jimmy Ryan by themselves owned most of the season's batting titles. Others held considerable appeal, such as pitcher John Tener, called up to the White Stockings in September 1888. He had received a drubbing in his first game, but then threw in another twenty-nine, ending with as many wins as losses for the season. Ten Chicagos signed up for the tour, but they needed an opponent. Spalding chose the "All-America" team, a moniker designed to highlight the tour as a great national spectacle. In part, he picked its members according to their "clean habits" as well as playing abilities. He did not need the added worry of bad behavior; on the contrary, he sought men who "would reflect credit upon the country and the game."[47] He found those with the proper deportment after a careful selection process determined which men understood that the trip would showcase the national pastime on the international stage. Spalding tried to tilt the playing field by ensuring that the All-America nine did not match the level of his Chicago club.

To his consternation, the White Stockings had not qualified to play in the National League "World Series" in 1888. This unfortunate result denied him a marketing tool, for in finishing second to the New York Giants, the White Stockings could not be labeled as "world champion" tourists. Yet he remedied that situation by boosting the tour as a championship of an all-star squad against, in his opinion, truly the best team in baseball. His critics were correct in viewing the All-America team as a weakling. No All-America player had finished among the top five hitters or pitchers in 1888, for instance. Some recruits for this set-up crew, like King Kelly, backed out after signing on. The National League's best defensive outfielder, and a leading base-stealer and power hitter, Giants "Silent Mike" Tiernan—so-called because he preferred to avoid publicity by not talking to the press—also stayed home due to a mysterious illness.[48]

Not permitting these absentees to undermine his project, Spalding welcomed some key players to All-America, the most important being Giants shortstop John Ward, who captained the team. He had just led New York to the 1888 championship as a top base-stealer. The year before, Ward had earned his college and law degrees from Columbia University, achievements which prepared him to engage the National League over the monopolistic reserve clause that indentured players to the owners. Players rallied around him in 1885 when he wrote a charter for the Brotherhood union; two years later, this labor association had chapters in every National League city. A highly paid star with enough money to buy real estate when the tour went through Denver, Ward tweaked the owners. For example, he told a reporter that he might continue around the world after visiting Australia, returning to the United States in June after the tourists came back and the regular season had begun. That got the dander up of Giants president John B. Day, who responded that Ward had better return on time, for he was certainly replaceable by several men.[49] This was mere bluster, however, for the shortstop was too valuable to fire. Ward was no stranger to Spalding-type marketing himself.

Despite his wealth, Ward accused owners and officials of corrupting the reserve clause, claiming that it clamped a lid on salaries rather than maintaining stability by preventing players from hopping around to various teams. Because no player "reserved" by his current team could seek employment on another, owners could set any salary they wanted. Of course, stars like Ward earned handsome salaries, but most of the fourteen reserved players on each team were subject to the whims of their owners. In 1887, Ward famously criticized the reserve clause in *Lippincott's* magazine, calling players "chattel in a reserve system" that had started out as an "institution for good" but which had "become an evil; instead of a measure of protection, it has been used as a handle for manipulation of a traffic in players, a sort of speculation in live stock, by which they are bought, sold, and transferred like so many sheep."[50] Control of workers typified monopoly rule in the Gilded Age; it was how industrialists ran the city of Chicago and how Spalding remained at the top of baseball's hierarchy.[51] Ward shunned it in his profession.

Ward was not a revolutionary, as he prevented his own Brotherhood from demanding long-term contracts from the owners as a tactic to nullify the year-to-year reserve system. Instead, he advocated an amended reserve clause and limiting the movement of players over the alternative: a free-for-all bidding war that played into the outright greed of the magnates. Ward could compromise and split differences, like a good lawyer, and he also got on with the owners, but his loyalty lay with the players, and he demanded recognition of the Brotherhood union from National League president Nick Young. As a result of his activism, he became the target of continually circulating rumors about his imminent trade from the Giants. Yet he steadfastly remained the nineteenth century's version of Marvin Miller, leader of the player's union from the late 1960s until the early 1980s. Ward warned that despite the sport's prosperity, disaster lay around the corner. While the public chafed at high salaries, the real problem was that "extravagant management, money thrown away on useless experiments, [and] bad faith among clubs" had conspired to undermine baseball. The answer lay in breaking the Spalding–National League monopoly by having players join the Brotherhood union and demand revisions of the rules that curbed the excesses of the reserve clause.[52]

*John Montgomery Ward.*

(Library of Congress, Prints and Photographs Division, LOT 13163-05, no. 218, Digital ID bbc 0290)

Ward, therefore, was newsworthy as an influential counterweight to Spalding, and to Chicago captain Pop Anson as well. For starters, he had recently entered into a closely watched and stormy marriage with actress Helen Dauvray, née Helen Gibson, a friend of "Casey at the Bat" performer DeWolf Hopper. Also, during the 1888 Major League championship between the Giants and St. Louis of the American Association for the Dauvray Cup—named after his new wife—Ward published an article in *The Cosmopolitan* discussing the sport's appeal but also noting the labor struggles as baseball marketed itself as a worthy pastime. Considering his advocacy of player rights, one would not expect that this thorn in Spalding's side would be invited on the tour. Yet with the Brotherhood up in arms over magnate behavior, it was likely that Spalding wished to hustle the union's ringmaster out of the country to prevent him from organizing a protest or strike.[53]

Was Spalding trying to weaken the Brotherhood rebellion by stealing away with Ward before the beginning of the 1889 season? And would the magnate and the Giant's captain square off during the tour? The answers were uncertain. For one thing, as mentioned above, Ward felt ambivalent about the reserve clause, as he had allowed its inclusion in all player contracts in 1888. Second, for the immediate needs of Spalding, Ward served as a useful intermediary in rounding up players, helping Spalding recruit players to the All-America team. Third, the shortstop seemed game for the world tour.

In any case, Ward did his part by assembling and leading the All-America side. His teammate, Ed Crane, a teetotaler pitcher with a beautiful tenor singing voice, met Spalding's requirements of clean living and expertise. Crane's powerful arm also served the promotional effort, as Spalding scheduled hurling exhibitions along the way. Another All-America teammate, "Foxy" Ned Hanlon, later went down in history as the famous manager of the scrappy Baltimore Oriole championship teams of the 1890s. He hailed from the Detroit Wolverines, a team in disarray at the time. Hanlon, only in his midtwenties, was more a leader than a star on the tour, although he did have an ability to reach base.[54] He was also a man of character of whom Spalding approved.

It was true that Ward's All-America bunch did not marshal the statistics and, in most cases, the experience of Anson's Chicago White Stockings, but they would provide good competition. From Philadelphia came popular James Fogarty, a speedy outfielder and base runner. His teammate, "Dandy" George Wood, combined power at the plate with a cannon for an arm in the outfield; twice in his career, he led all outfielders in assists and putouts. Solid-hitting Californian Fred Carroll arrived from Pittsburgh to assume the catching duties. Infielder Ed Hengle also joined

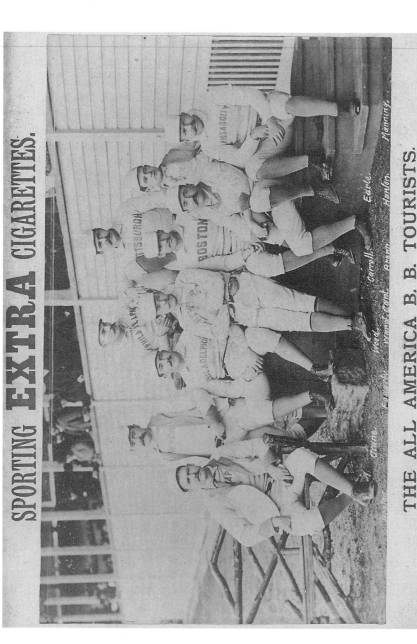

The All-America tourists. *Left to right:* John "Egyptian" Healy, Ed Crane, John Fogarty, George Wood, John Ward, Fred Carroll, Tom Brown, Billy Earle, Ned Hanlon, and Jim Manning.

(Doug Allen, Mastronet, Inc.)

Ward's squad, while from the American Association came Kansas City Blues' captain Jim Manning, a popular outfielder and pitcher. Herman Long, also of Kansas City before spending thirteen years in Boston, played a quick-footed but error-prone shortstop and exhibited ample base-running and hitting skills. Frank Silvester "Old Silver" Flint, a distinguished veteran readying for his final season for the White Stockings, agreed to assume the catcher position until King Kelly joined All-America in Denver. Overall, these and other well-behaved All-America players would competently oppose the powerful White Stockings while not eclipsing Anson's team—or at least so Spalding hoped.[55]

## DEPARTING FROM THE HUB

Plans completed, arrangements made, and the press notified, on Saturday, October 20, 1888, the tour got under way in Chicago, and fans could not but understand that Big Al was the maestro of the endeavor. Always the showman, Spalding had rushed back from the send-off by President Cleveland in time to parade through the west and south sides of Chicago in carriages drawn by fancy horses decorated with plumes and black blankets announcing the "Australian Tour." On a cold, windy afternoon, a military band led the two teams, suited in their new uniforms, to the park. The spectacle was vintage Spalding, who kicked off the play with his faded pitching prowess before a few thousand shivering but delighted spectators. In response to a request by four hundred members of the Chicago Board of Trade "to see you once more in uniform on the ball-field prior to your departure for the Antipodes," Spalding donned the light gray uniform and black stockings of his team. He opposed All-America, which wore white flannel uniforms designed by Ward's wife, with silk scarves doubling as belts in the design of American flags. Spalding threw underhanded curveballs for four innings, giving up just five hits, before giving way to John Tener. Errors hurt both teams—but All-America more in their 11–6 drubbing at the hands of White Stockings, the first of many expected losses. The crowd was enthusiastic, cheering Spalding loudly, especially when he hit a double but legged it out only to first base. Ed Williamson received a gift of shirt studs, and Jimmy Ryan an umbrella, to commemorate their play.[56]

All seemed in order, and Spalding was content. King Kelly had impressed the White Stockings president the night before by traveling from New York City and conferring about the world tour. Knowing Kelly's drawing power at the gate, Spalding met with this showboat for two hours on Saturday night. The ballplayer agreed to travel to Australia after getting his New York affairs in order, joining the tourists in Denver. In fact, Kelly seemed to make good on his intentions by playing the opening game in Chicago as catcher for All-America.

That evening, the teams and their entourage of nearly three dozen people gathered at Chicago's Union Station. Present were players' and executives' wives; a handful of Spalding friends such as former mayor of Chicago Carter Harrison and his longtime advisor Hiram Waldo; entertainers including Proff, the balloonist; businessmen such as sporting goods company magnate Irving Snyder; and baseball officials such as Harry Simpson, manager of the Newark team and Spalding's assistant on the tour. Spalding made a majestic entrance half an hour before departure. On his arm walked his elegant and stately mother, who traveled with the group partly to exercise "a restraining influence over the more impulsive members" of the tour. Banners hung from the train depot signaling "Spalding's Australian Trip," and newsmen noted the farewell as the most boisterous seen in Chicago in years.[57]

If the send-off was orchestrated, the actual departure was sure to impress as Spalding's final marketing ploy. The Chicago, Burlington & Quincy Railroad operated two specially equipped Pullman sleepers and a dining car that allowed the tourists to travel in style while avoiding the expense of hotels. The crowds that waved good-bye in Chicago, and the multitudes that greeted the baseball tourists en route across the country, witnessed not only stars but also the most regal train service available. As outfielder Jimmy Ryan noted, "People collected to see our departure and also view the newly decorated and handsome sleeping car, Galesburg, and the dining car, Cosmopolitan, which were consigned to the party until our arrival in Denver, Colorado."[58]

The tour left the station, and it was evident that Albert Spalding's promotional efforts and business acumen had elevated baseball—a sport maligned as the domain of uncouth louts, degenerate behavior, and rough athletics—to a prominent position in American enterprise and culture. The world tour surely represented his interests, and he vowed to make the most of his efforts. The profiteering of Chicago defined the era in which he thrived, and within this milieu, Spalding directed his energies to cornering the market on baseball. Yet the sport had also emerged as the national pastime, and that development fed baseball into the expanding national economy, as well as linking it and American commerce to markets throughout the world. Spalding hoped to make such connections nationally and internationally, on his own behalf and for the benefit of the sport as a whole, and capitalize on the process of globalization.

*Tour poster.*

(Harry C. Palmer, *Athletic Sports in America, England, and Australia.*
Philadelphia: Hubbard Brothers, Publishers, 1889, p. 150)

## NOTES

1. Light, *Cultural Encyclopedia of Baseball*, 138–39, 149; Ernest Lawrence Thayer, "Casey at the Bat," *San Francisco Examiner*, June 3, 1888, available at www.base ball-almanac.com/poetry/po_case.shtml; Banham, *Cambridge Guide to World Theatre*, 455–56; Hartnoll, *Oxford Companion to the Theatre*, 449–50; Sullivan, *Early Innings*, 175.

2. Lamoreaux, "Baseball in the Late Nineteenth Century."

3. Cronon, *Nature's Metropolis*, 244.

4. Warner, "Great West: III," 871; see also p. 870.

5. Cronon, *Nature's Metropolis*, 333–36; Chandler, "Entrepreneurial Opportunity."

6. See Twombley, "Cuds and Snipes."

7. Ruble, *Second Metropolis*, 5, 15, 18, 31, 40–46, 52–55, 60; "The Mob Uses Violence," *Chicago Tribune*, October 10, 1888; "Strike and Riot in Chicago," *Frank Leslie's Illustrated Newspaper*, October 20, 1888, p. 155; D'Eramo, *Pig and the Skyscraper*, 99. On the press and development of sports, see also Moore, "Ideology on the Sportspage," 230, and Furst, "Image of Professional Baseball."

8. Glazier, *Peculiarities of American Cities*, 168, 169, 171.

9. O'Rell, *A Frenchman in America*, 209.

10. Warner, "Great West: IV."

11. Aubertin, *A Fight with Distances*, 56–61, quotes on 56, 58, 59.

12. Glazier, *Peculiarities of American Cities*, 175.

13. Hole, *Little Tour in America*, 249.

14. Miller, *City of the Century*, 527–29. On the developing baseball craze in Chicago, which erupted with the end of amateurism once business and middle-class city boosters demanded a professional team, see Freedman, "Baseball Fad in Chicago."

15. Light, *Cultural Encyclopedia of Baseball*, 148.

16. Moore, "Great Baseball Tour," 436, 444.

17. Levine, *A. G. Spalding*, 3–9; quotes on 9. See also McMahon, "Al Spalding."

18. Levine, *A. G. Spalding*, 9–14.

19. "The American Invasion" and "Our Athletic Cousins," newspaper clippings, 1874, in *Albert Spalding Scrapbook*, vol. 1, microfilm reel 9, Albert Spalding Collection, Society of American Baseball Researchers Lending Library, Cleveland, Ohio (hereafter cited as Spalding Scrapbooks). See also Stout, "1874 Baseball Tour."

20. Levine, *A. G. Spalding*, 17–20.

21. "They Won't Have This Spalding to Knock Around Anymore," *Boston Globe*, October 28, 1976. Spalding bought out Alfred James (A. J.) Reach's ball-manufacturing firm at the turn of the twentieth century, and thus made American League, as well as National League, baseballs. Perhaps to avoid outcries against his monopoly, he left the Reach name on the balls.

22. The White Stockings evolved into the Chicago Cubs at the turn of the twentieth century, while former pitcher Charles Comiskey formed a new White Stockings team—soon nicknamed the White Sox to save space in newspaper headlines—in the rival American League in 1901.

23. Bartlett, *Baseball and Mr. Spalding*, 146; see also 143–44.

24. Light, *Cultural Encyclopedia of Baseball*, 78–79, 135, 606, 765–66.

25. Levine, *A. G. Spalding*, 76–95; quote on 86. See also Koppett, *Concise History*, 25–36; Warner, "Great West: III," 877; and "From Base Ball Player to Senator," newspaper clipping, Albert Spalding Biographical File, National Baseball Hall of Fame, Cooperstown, New York (hereafter cited as NBHOF). For marketing, see *Spalding's Official Base Ball Guide*, available at http://memory.loc.gov/ammem/spaldinghtml/spaldinghome.html; first published in 1877, the guide advertised equipment, scorebooks, and stores where Spalding Bros. goods were sold, as well as railroad company travel and Harry Palmer's account of the world tour, for $3.50 in cloth. See also Fielding and Miller, "ABC Trust," for another episode in Spalding's monopolistic ways—this one in regard to an attempt to corner the bicycle market and then dominate the auto industry.

26. Light, *Cultural Encyclopedia of Baseball*, 49–50.

27. Levine, *A. G. Spalding*, 46–47, 56–58, 78.

28. "Sam Crane Writes Series of Stories on Fifty Greatest Ball Players in History," December 20, 1911, newspaper clipping, Adrian Anson Biographical File, NBHOF. Also in the Anson File, see "Hero of National Game," April 20, 1922; Billy Murphy, "'Taking Care' of Anson When He's Dead and Gone is Poor Stuff"; Grantland Rice, "Baseball Loses One of Its Own"; and Mrs. Arthur C. Dodd (Anson's daughter), "Adrian Constantine Anson: Grand Old Man of Baseball, August 11, 1954. See also Anson, *A Ball Player's Career*, 132, and Rosenberg, *Cap Anson*, 175–262.

29. John Tener to Maud, September 16, 1888, John K. Tener Biographical File, NBHOF (hereafter cited as Tener File). See also Porter, "Cap Anson of Marshalltown."

30. Cappio, "Slide, Kelly, Slide," 10–14; "Thought Out Plays," newspaper clipping, November 7, 1907, Michael Joseph Kelly Biographical File, NBHOF; Cox, "When the Fans Roared," 124, 126; Light, *Cultural Encyclopedia of Baseball*, 965.

31. "N. Fred Pfeffer," newspaper clipping, Philadelphia, August 22, 1896, Nathaniel Frederick Pfeffer Biographical File, NBHOF; William McMahon, "Thomas Everett Burns," fact sheets, Thomas Everett Burns Biographical File, NBHOF; Dennis Goldstein, "Edward Nagle Williamson," Edward Nagle Williamson Biographical File, NBHOF; "Dr. Baldwin, Buc Pitcher, of Early Nineties, Dies," newspaper clipping, November 10, 1929, Mark Baldwin Biographical File, NBHOF; Frances Pendleton, "George Edward Martin Van Haltren,"; "Forgotten Oaklander has Hall of Fame Statistics," *Tribune*, September 4, 1983, George Edward Martin Van Haltren File; Arthur Ahrens, "An Assist for Jimmy Ryan," 66–67, James Edward Ryan Biographical File, NBHOF; William McMahon, "James E. Ryan," fact sheet, James Edward Ryan Biographical File, NBHOF.

32. Spalding, *Baseball*, 421.

33. C. Mifflin Frothingham to Durand Churchill, October 29, 1911, Spalding Scrapbooks, vol. 6, microfilm reel 9, Spalding Collection.

34. Tener to Maud, September 16, 1888, Tener File.

35. Levine, "Business, Missionary Motives," 61. See also Spalding, *Baseball*, 251.

36. "James A. Hart Dies at His Chicago Home," *Sporting News*, 1918 clipping,

James A. Hart Biographical File, NBHOF; "The Late James A. Hart," clipping from *The Reach Official American League Base Ball Guide*, 142–43, James A. Hart Biographical File, NBHOF. In the late 1890s, Hart succeeded Spalding as president of the White Stockings and renamed them the Cubs of the National League.

37. Henry Chadwick, "The Australian Trip," *Sporting Life*, August 15, 1888, p. 3.

38. Henry Chadwick, "Baseball: The Great Trip," *Sporting Life*, October 17, 1888, p. 4; "Great Day for Chicago," *Chicago Tribune*, October 9, 1888, p. 3. See also "Anson and Grover," newspaper clipping, Spalding Scrapbooks, vol. 10.

39. Tener to Will, October 8, 1888, Tener File. See also Levine, *A. G. Spalding*, 100–101.

40. Palmer, *Athletic Sports*.

41. "The Chicago Players," *Sporting News*, October 20, 1888, p. 2. See also Schlereth, *Victorian America*, 182–84; and "Lot of Players Who Will Not Make the Australian Trip," *Sporting News*, September 29, 1888, p. 4.

42. "Spalding Is Not That Kind," newspaper clipping, Spalding Scrapbooks, vol. 10.

43. "The Ball Players," *New York Times*, October 15, 1888, p. 4.

44. Chadwick, "Baseball: The Great Trip," p. 4.

45. Henry Chadwick, "The Australian Trip," *Sporting Life*, September 12, 1888, p. 7.

46. "George Wright," newspaper clipping, May 17, 1890, George Wright Biographical File, NBHOF; Frederick Ivor-Campbell, "Wright, George," *Biographical Dictionary of American Sports: Baseball*, 626–29; Brock, "The Wright Way," 40; Spalding, *Baseball*, 251; Palmer, *Athletic Sports*, 153–54, 160–61; Anson, *A Ball Player's Career*, 142.

47. Spalding, *Baseball*, 252. See also Robert E. Jones, "Tener, John K.," *Biographical Dictionary of American Sports: Baseball*, 1527; and "How to Judge a Man's Success," newspaper clipping, Tener File; "John K. Tener," notes, February 1913, Tener File, NBHOF.

48. Randy Linthurst, "Michael Joseph Tiernan," fact sheet, Michael Tiernan Biographical File, NBHOF; Palmer, *Athletic Sports*, 155.

49. "To Go Around the World," *New York Times*, October 7, 1888, p. 2.

50. Ward, "Is the Base-Ball Player Chattel?" 313. See also Voigt, "Serfs versus Magnates," 101.

51. Di Salvatore, *A Clever Base-Ballist*, 192.

52. Ward, "Our National Game," 455. See also John Redding to Shirley Saccone, November 18, 1971, John Montgomery Ward Biographical File, NBHOF; Stevens, *Baseball's Radical*, 67–73; Lowenfish, *Imperfect Diamond*, 32; and the following newspaper clippings from the John Montgomery Ward Biographical File, NBHOF: "Details of the Affair—The Future Intentions of the Happy Couple"; "The Issue Defined," September 28, 1887; "Washington after Ward," August 17, 1887; "From New York," July 20, 1887; and "What They Want," September 14, 1887.

53. Di Salvatore, *A Clever Base-Ballist*, 244–45.

54. Frank E. Butler, "Ned Crane—the Great Long-Distance Thrower," Edward

Nicholas Crane Biographical File, NBHOF; Ned Hanlon fact sheet, Edward Hugh Hanlon Biographical File, NBHOF.

55. "Fogarty Dead," *Public Ledger-Philadelphia*, May 21, 1891, James Fogarty Biographical File, NBHOF; George A. Wood fact sheet, George A. Wood Biographical File, NBHOF; "Death of Fred Carroll," newspaper clipping, Frederick Herbert Carroll Biographical File, NBHOF; "News from England," Edward S. Hengle Biographical File, NBHOF; "Blind 4 Years, Ex-Pitcher Cured by Miracle, He Says," newspaper clipping, James Manning Biographical File, NBHOF; Herman C. Long fact file, Herman C. Long Biographical File, NBHOF; Palmer, *Athletic Sports*, 708.

56. John Tener letter, October 19, 1888, Tener File; "The Great Trip," *Sporting Life*, October 31, 1888, p. 4; "Anson's Australian Tour," *Chicago Tribune*, October 12, 1888, p. 2; "Spalding Will Pitch," *Chicago Tribune*, October 21, 1888, p. 6.

57. Palmer, *Athletic Sports*, 159. See also "Their Farewell Game," *Chicago Tribune*, October 21, 1888, p. 11; John Tener letter, October 19, 1888, Tener File; and Levine, *A. G. Spalding*, 101.

58. James Ryan, *Tour of the Spalding B.B.C. around the World* [diary], October 20, 1888, p. 9, James Edward Ryan Biographical File, NBHOF.

# 2

# Movement

## The American West

MINNESOTA

    St. Paul, Sunday, October 21, 1888—*Chicago* 9, *All-America* 3; *St. Paul* 8, *Chicago* 5

    Minneapolis, Monday, October 22—*All-America* 6, *Chicago* 3; *Chicago* 1, *St. Paul* 0

IOWA

    Cedar Rapids, Tuesday, October 23—*Chicago* 6, *All-America* 6

    Des Moines, Wednesday, October 24—*All-America* 3, *Chicago* 2

NEBRASKA

    Omaha, Thursday, October 25—*All-America* 12, *Chicago* 2

    Hastings, Friday, October 26—*Chicago* 8, *All-America* 4

COLORADO

    Denver, Saturday, October 27—*Chicago* 16, *All-America* 12

    Denver, Sunday, October 28—*All-America* 9, *Chicago* 8

    Colorado Springs, Monday, October 29—*Chicago* 13, *All-America* 9

UTAH

    Salt Lake City, Wednesday, October 31—*All-America* 9, *Chicago* 3

    Salt Lake City, Thursday, November 1—*All-America* 10, *Chicago* 3

CALIFORNIA

    San Francisco, Sunday, November 4—*All-America* 14, *Chicago* 4

    San Francisco, Tuesday, November 6—*Greenhood and Moran* 12, *All-America* 2

    San Francisco, Thursday, November 8—*Pioneer* 9, *All-America* 4

    Stockton, Thursday, November 8—*Chicago* 2, *Stockton* 2

    San Francisco, Friday, November 9—*All-America* 16, *Stockton* 1

    San Francisco, Saturday, November 10—*Chicago* 6, *Haverly* 1

    San Francisco, Sunday, November 11—*All-America* 9, *Chicago* 6

The baseball tourists headed west toward the foreign embarkation point of San Francisco, from which they would sail further west

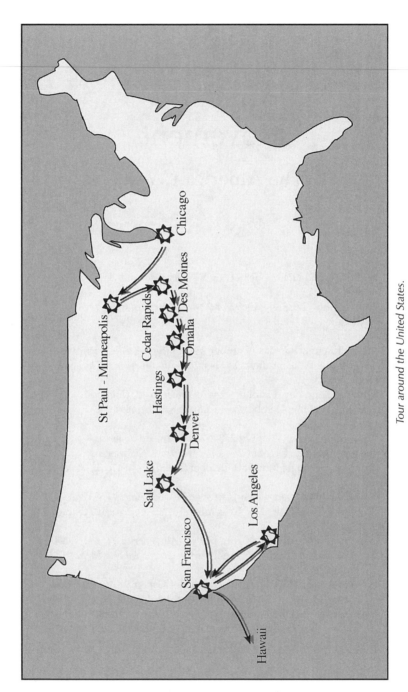

*Tour around the United States.*
(David Underwood, Graphic Design, CU-Boulder)

across the Pacific Ocean to Hawaii. As they traveled the rails across America, touring the majestic sites of the American West and playing baseball, they symbolized the drive, energy, and materialism of the masses who preceded them in the nineteenth century. Yet it is simplistic to view their trip as a journey across a mythical Wild West. In actuality, they took part in the communications and transportation networks that had revolutionized the region.

The Spalding tourists challenged historian Frederick Jackson Turner's thesis of 1893 that the frontier had shaped a distinct culture until a settled population lost the wilderness spirit. Turner anguished over the end of the frontier, from which Americans supposedly had drawn so much of their rugged individualism, and he and others looked to overseas expansion as a new, noncontiguous frontier.[1] Spalding expressed such values as a proponent of myths, personal and national greatness, and domination by the fittest. Baseball sneered at gentility and embraced turmoil, combativeness, and creativity in the style of play. In short, it echoed the stories of pioneers who peopled the American West, a reminder of the frontier. In reality, though, that characterization was sheer hokum by 1888. Scholars have questioned such romantic notions, portraying the West as an arena more typical of others in the nation's development, as well as a crossroads of globalizing, border-crossing exchange. The vast region comprised a meeting place of opportunists, and one not built solely by Spalding-type entrepreneurs. Instead, the federal government facilitated corporate exploitation of the area's vast resources. Thus, a juggernaut of capitalists, government officials, and railroad barons manipulated the region.[2]

They created a web of travel and communication networks that gave advantages to profit seekers like Spalding. The dramatic advent of the "iron horse" revolutionized travel by faster and ever more luxurious means. Through modernizing rail, ship, and information systems, the New West became fertile ground for linking Eastern U.S. power centers to the Pacific Rim and beyond to the British Empire. This process did not close the frontier; rather, it opened up immense prospects for global connections as industrial and finance capitalism disciplined the world economy and provided a springboard for empire. The Spalding tourists used these transportation and communication drivers of the globalization process to make their way westward.

## AGE OF RAILROADS

Americans had available thousands of miles of track, and after transcontinental service began in 1872, they journeyed across the country in style.

In the decade before, the first luxury saloon and sleeping cars were put into service by the Pullman Company. Peak railway construction occurred between 1875 and 1890, and railways blossomed in Latin America, India, the Congo, and into Africa and the Middle East. In the 1880s, due to the railroads, Americans in particular began thinking of tourism across the United States as a feasible option, rather than just travel to a destination or resort spots, as was the custom throughout most of the century. The sleeper carriage brought thousands of travelers into the public parks and spaces of the West, where they slept in hotels often built by the railroads and found guidance in escorted group tours of the type envisioned by British travel entrepreneur Thomas Cook. Belching through small towns and across beautiful landscapes, trains represented "man's triumph over time and space."[3] Before their six-month journey around the world was over, the Spalding baseball tourists had clicked over nearly ten thousand miles of rail across four continents.

By 1888, the 150,000 miles of railway in the United States alone were enough to girdle the globe twelve times, but it was where trains went that served the purposes of tourists. No canyon, valley, or mountain was too forbidding for the railroad, and where just a few years before, donkeys had carried supplies and men up to remote mines, now a railway did the work. Road construction had become a science and an art. Engineers cut through points of rock cut and set foundations for trestles and tunnels, oftentimes (depending on the terrain) by risky surveying on rope ladders by bold architects or by persistent construction crews who worked underwater inside huge caissons hammering away with pneumatic equipment. Steel or bridges replaced wooden trusses; magnificent suspension spans and cantilevered structures (some as enormous as the Brooklyn Bridge, built just five years before) served the railways and facilitated traffic.[4] Such technology allowed the baseball tourists to get through formerly impassable surroundings as sightseers or to cover great distances in shorter times than ever before.

Ever since the Union Pacific and Central Pacific railroads had been joined in Utah in 1869, the railroads scrambled to claim new territory and fill out the West. By the 1880s, railroad corporations perfected their empires, having built vast networks across the country and provided increasingly comfortable cars, depots, and terminals. Railroads garnered huge profits, often operating beyond the control of government regulation, which was weak to begin with. Even scheduling changed; when the myriad of local times caused confusion, the American Railway Association divided the nation into four time zones, though Congress lagged in officially adopting this standard until 1918. Without federal or state oversight, there was fierce competition for routes, with resultant monopolies, vicious price gouging, and corrupt stock buying and selling. New towns sprung up around commercial depots for ranchers and produce. People moved westward to California to take advantage. Eastern and European investors, sinking funds into completing and extending railroad lines, irrigation, hydraulic mining, and big corporate ranches, had transformed the American West into a business zone.[5]

Commerce and consolidation changed a way of life. The individualist cowboy and the rampaging Indian vanished, despite a yearning for such figures. "Buffalo Bill" Cody satisfied audiences with reenactments of the Wild West, but the domestication of the region through fences, irrigation networks, and reservations halted cattle drives as well as native and animal migratory patterns. Bandit Belle Starr was gunned down in 1889 and other outlaws sat in prisons. The disappearance of the Old West sparked interest in it, and writers and artists like Teddy Roosevelt, Owen Wister, and Frederick Remington added further to its lore. Entertainers, including Buffalo Bill, earned good incomes touring Europe in the late 1880s. The illustrators Currier and Ives further popularized the West by romantically depicting everyday life in thousands of lithographs. Yet the empire of railroads and ranchers, as well as telegraphs (400,000 miles of wire by the early 1880s) changed communications and, with it, the isolated ways of the prairie farmer, lone cowboy, and drifting miner.[6]

Trade, law, bourgeois customs, urban growth, and tourism—the trappings of commercial modernity—organized Western U.S. society, enhancing its accessibility as a resource and capital base for globalizing business. White Americans occupied the West and turned to industrialization and commercialization. The baseball tourists found modern societies when they left Chicago, but they also encountered a modernizing West, one that imitated the innovation and energy of the East. Money and markets transformed the region, and the Spalding entrepreneurs, like other businesses, were the beneficiaries. Industrial development paralleled that of the entire nation, with large corporations, city–periphery relations, and the harnessing of labor providing a dynamic process. People and towns were connected—by railroads and telegraphs from east to west, and by steamship from continent to continent. People bought in a national market, serviced in various cities linked to outlying areas by rail, thereby regularizing and expanding consumption and mass production. A region representative of U.S. national aspirations and a source of European imperial wealth, the New West was for sale, a place for making money.[7]

Spalding's troupe passed through in a way befitting the New West, and they even symbolized regional behavior. The entourage arrived and left by elegant train car, partook of top-notch tourist venues, sent messages by the modern communication of wire service, and played the cultural and social cutting-edge sport of baseball that excited Western populations. Westerners were like any other Americans, wrote another British visitor. They seemed bereft of serious attention to such subjects as party politics only after the circus left, or when "a base ball match is to be played."[8] They also represented an America of rising pride and self-promotion. Wrote traveler Matthew Arnold in 1888, by their "self-glorification and self-deception" on a scale never witnessed before, "the new West promises to beat in the game of brag even the stout champions" of the Eastern Establishment.[9] The world tourists linked East and West in this regard.

Spalding's itinerary called for the baseball tourists to take the Burlington route to trunk lines running to the Pacific coast, where the teams would join the steamship *Alameda* for the voyage to Hawaii and beyond to New Zealand and Australia. The Chicago, Burlington, and Quincy was a tremendous railroad system, with more than four thousand miles of track that stretched from Chicago north to Minnesota, criss-crossed Missouri and Iowa, and traversed Kansas and Nebraska on its way to Denver. In addition, the company boasted over six hundred engines and twenty-four thousand cars, which grabbed the attention of Western legislators bent on both extending it further and sharing the profits of its shipping and passenger rates.[10] Albert Spalding's grand adventure advanced into the New West under the power of eastern America's bastion of capitalism: the railroad corporation.

Once out of Union Station in Chicago, the entourage entered into card games, told jokes, sang songs, and listened to mandolin and guitar played by members of the party, including many of the wives who permitted the players to smoke and gamble well into the evening. Many noted the luxurious accommodations; some of the older travelers could recall the old uncomfortable stage coach bodies on trains and the era before sleeper cars. Day and night travel had eased by the addition of parlor or drawing-room cars (known as "palace cars"), then dining and hotel cars (with waiters), and, in 1887, the "vestibuled" train in which cars were connected by elegant structures to allow for movement between them.[11] The Galesburg and Cosmopolitan cars offered the comforts of modern travel, including well-ventilated windows, from which the players waved to the small assemblies of cheering crowds at way stations along the tracks to Minnesota.[12]

## GATEWAY TO THE WEST

The teams pulled into a chilly St. Paul, Minnesota, a "wide open town" of about 150,000 people, wrote Cap Anson, to be greeted by a remarkably large crowd for 7 A.M. on a Sunday morning. By "wide open," he meant Western-style libertarian regarding regulations and restrictions.[13] Playing baseball on Sundays, for instance, was prohibited at first in National League cities but was allowed in many Western towns. Cincinnati had been tossed from the National League in 1880 for violating the ban, and St. Louis quit in 1886 in protest. Still, towns in the Midwest and West, many of them hosting "beer and whiskey league" teams from the American Association, permitted baseball on the Sabbath, which prompted ministers and temperance crusaders to prowl the grandstands and shame immoral baseball fanatics. It was not until 1892, when the National League absorbed the rival American Association, that the restriction eased, although the state of Pennsylvania prohibited play in Philadelphia and Pittsburgh on the Lord's Day until 1933.[14] The looser Western mores fit the travelers just fine.

Minnesotans living in the two cities of St. Paul and Minneapolis, grandiloquently called the "twin columns of the eastern gateway to the magnificent west" that stretched to the Pacific, came out two thousand strong to see Chicago run up the score again and record its second victory over All-America in as many games, a 9–3 drubbing in six innings on Sunday. The all-star squad did score points, though—with uniforms sporting the national colors. Patriotism, and links to the established cities farther east, were not surprising to find in this area of the country that teemed with opportunity. Residents of St. Paul boasted a multiplying population occupying the west bank of the Mississippi River and extending to the eastern side as well. Above the riverside factories and wholesale houses, plateaus rose one above the other to provide ample ground for retail stores, public buildings, churches, and homes, many of which were built with local blue limestone. The setting, which included local lakes and a city park on nearby Lake Como, was picturesque. St. Paul stood at the head of navigation of the Mississippi, just downstream from the Falls and Rapids of Saint Anthony. From this juncture, the city supplied thriving towns in Minnesota and Wisconsin as a transit point from Chicago and points east for farm supplies and machinery.[15]

The residents also fell in love with baseball, and their local team, the St. Paul Saints, but it took them a while to realize they were victims of a clever ploy by Spalding. Behind the plate, Silver Flint was an imposter standing in for their beloved King Kelly, whose name had been printed on the scorecard. Spectators cheered "Rah for Kelly!" applauding the "$10,000 man," and most never caught on that Flint was in for Kelly.[16] The game was shortened to allow the White Stockings to face off with the local St. Paul side, which stunningly handled Chicago in seven innings in front of more fans than had watched the All-America nine lose. The day was cold, and fielding suffered as a result, but so elated was St. Paul manager John Barnes that he challenged Cap Anson to a rematch the next day in

Minneapolis, just nine miles away. Taking up the challenge, the tourists had their train run to the city the next morning.

Located at the Falls of St. Anthony, which generated power for the huge Pillsbury flour mills, and at Minnehaha Falls, immortalized by Longfellow, Minneapolis had an oftentimes jealous rivalry with its sister city, St. Paul. Now citizens greeted the tourists with a twenty-one-piece brass band replete with a drum major hoisting a stock with a silver ball on one end; there were a dozen landaus and horses draped in gold plumes and blankets. The teams marched to the ballpark in even colder weather than the day before, but the air was just as dry. They played in front of 1,800 spectators, many of whom had arrived by streetcars that left every half-hour from various parts of the Twin Cities.

This time, All-America got its first victory of the tour, 6–3, in a game shortened to four innings to meet the stomping demands of the audience for the Chicago–St. Paul Saints rematch. Minnesotans cheered for a win, but after four innings of shutout ball, Fred Pfeffer crossed the plate with the winning run on a ground out, after a fielder's choice got him on base, a steal sent him to second, and a wild throw placed him on third. It was an exciting visit for the tourists, who, after being feted by a farewell parade, boarded their luxury train that evening for Iowa.[17]

Ever since its admission to the union in 1845, the state of Iowa had boomed. By the 1880s, it had the nation's tenth largest population, with over two million residents. They were there because Iowa served as an overflow area for hard-working wheat and corn farmers; cattle, hog, and horse raisers; small townsmen; and Southern blacks. This was a predominantly agricultural state of many outlying communities; the capital city of Des Moines numbered no more than forty thousand people. In 1850, not an inch of train track ran through the state, but by the early 1880s, more than 6,100 miles of railroads crisscrossed its interior, placing Iowa fifth in mileage in the country. Transportation links made the state a breadbasket for the nation and the world. Iowa was a stronghold of self-sufficient, well-schooled, and solidly prosperous westerners who engaged in both moderate and populist politics and who leapt at the spectacle of the grand baseball tour.[18]

Reportedly netting about five hundred dollars from the Minnesota games, Spalding more than doubled that figure in Cedar Rapids, a town boiling over with enthusiasm for baseball and the all-star group of players. After a night of travel punctuated by the practical jokes of the impish pitcher Tom Daly, who kept his unfortunate targets awake through the night, the entourage pulled into Union Depot in Cedar Rapids at 8 A.M. on Tuesday, October 23. Accessibility was crucial. Having converged on the city from towns and farms, brought in by a half-dozen special trains that offered a special rate, the crowd roared its welcome. The arrival was special for Cap Anson, a native Iowan, whose father took an excursion from Marshalltown to see his famous son. Exciting "as much curiosity as Barnum's circus," wrote outfielder and pitcher Jimmy Ryan, the tourists dressed, ate breakfast, and climbed into their carriages under the curious gazes of the throngs.[19]

A drum major furiously waved a seven-foot-long baton with a knob "as big as an Iowa pumpkin" as he led the tourists before applauding throngs and past businesses shuttered for the occasion to the fairgrounds, where they played an exhibition before more than four thousand spectators. The early innings were blessed with cool, sunny weather but the temperature went south—to forty degrees in cloudy skies—by game's end.[20] Despite the cold, the teams performed well, as Chicago's Ryan crossed the plate with the winning run in the ninth inning. Spalding, who had been requested to umpire, presided over the White Stockings' 6–5 win. Business boosters then joined the tourists in the Cosmopolitan dining car for champagne before the train pulled out, at 6:30 P.M., for Des Moines, amidst the continued din of cheering fans.[21]

The next morning, the tourists arrived at the state capital, having played cards and smoked in the Galesburg sleeping car as the train glided past seemingly endless rolling farmland. Trains might have been luxurious, but they defied the meteorlike names, such as *Lightning* or *Cannonball*, often given to them when it came to speed. Typically, the cars on the Burlington route did not exceed speeds of forty-five miles per hour; speed records in America and Europe hit about seventy miles per hour at this time, but most expresses averaged in the high forties to low fifties. This explains why the baseball tourists traveled all night to their next destination.

In Des Moines, at the request of some city leaders, two local players joined All-America and helped the team win another close contest against the White Stockings that afternoon. More than 1,500 people watched the game—a good turnout considering the weather. Afterward, monologist Frank Lincoln joined the tour, which left the city late that night of October 24 and continued west past the stacked, ripened corn of the prairie and crossed the Missouri River into Nebraska, the "gate of the great West," Ryan recalled.

The next day, another large reception met the players. In Omaha, members of the Johnson and Slavin Minstrel Company boarded the train and led a parade that morning in the city.[22] That entertainers met the players proved appropriate, because the Spalding tourists encountered one of their own returning performers—Clarence Duval. It was a notable event so far for the tour. This dancing and baton-twirling, diminutive, young (of indeterminate age but likely in his late teens) black troubadour had met Cap Anson in Philadelphia earlier in the 1888 season, and Anson had recruited Duval as the White Stockings "mascot." Many baseball clubs had such figures in their employ, mainly as good luck charms. Oftentimes, mascots were people with disabilities, entertainers, or, years later, characters costumed in animal outfits. Along with hunchbacks, dwarfs, and the like, black youths were also common. For instance, Hall of Famer Ty Cobb would later rub the head of one "L'il Rastus" during the 1908 season before going to bat.[23]

In the case of Clarence Duval, this exhibitionist had deserted the Chicago White Stockings in New York for the stage show of a noted French actress then touring the United States. He now turned up in Omaha, apparently out of work and contrite, to rejoin Anson's side despite the scorn he endured for having left the team in the first place. Still, for Anson and the players in this age of black inferiority, the "dusky" and "sorry looking little 'nig'" Duval, as they referred to him, was an endearing kid. He also knew his place, showing that the New West absorbed other national traits—in this case, bigotry—as well as business and finance from the East (and South). After suffering Anson's wrath as a deserting "little coon," Duval joined the tourists' parade to the ball ground in Omaha, jumping from the carriage with baton in hand.[24]

*Clarence Duval parades the teams.*

(Harry C. Palmer, *Athletic Sports in America, England, and Australia.*
Philadelphia: Hubbard Brothers, Publishers, 1889, p. 169)

Duval paraded the tourists into the ballpark that afternoon, where 1,800 fans buzzed with excitement over politics as much as the baseball tour. A 12–2 shellacking of the Chicago side by All-America, which finally figured out Ryan's slow curveball, the game proved banal to aficionados of the game. Instead, people focused on the upcoming presidential election, which was less than two weeks away. The Sackville-West letter, linking the incumbent, President Grover Cleveland, to the despised British, had just been made public. The baseball tour and the election, already linked by the White Stockings' visit with Cleveland, became more intertwined with national and international affairs.

Boarding the train the evening of their Omaha exhibition, the tourists arrived early the next morning in Hastings, Nebraska, just over 100 miles to the west. The skies were blue, the sunlight warm, and the politicos were out in force. On this Friday afternoon, the Democrats tried to rally the crowd at the ballpark by marching out a boy with a pro-Cleveland banner. Pandemonium ensued when Republicans grew angry at the grandstanding. The police were called to quell the outbreak between Democrats and Republicans, who interrupted the game for a full ten minutes.[25]

This otherwise quiet prairie town had graciously received the teams that morning, as three thousand spectators came from the surrounding area to watch Chicago dismantle the All-America pitching this time around in an 8–4 triumph. As was common on the tour, spectators awarded money (in this case, forty dollars) to the best players, and then held a fireworks display. Some who traveled to Hastings for the game were more impressed by the Democratic rally than the play. Fans from nearby Juniata, for example, found "the great ball game at Hastings" to be "an average specimen of the playing of those celebrated men, they are no great shakes. Juniata players can do better than that."[26] Before the game, some players rode broncos, validating the Spalding entourage's image of the Wild West and the pioneers who peopled the Great American Desert.

The reality was more mundane, however, as commerce trumped legend. By 1888, the Platte Valley, a rather dreary endless prairie, had benefited from the presence of the Union Pacific railroad, which, initially, had been the sole trunk line to cross Nebraska. Soon most other railroad companies followed, crisscrossing the territory in a gridiron of tracks. The tourists' own Burlington Railroad had control of the lines west of Denver and thus served as a carrier for people and produce through the Rocky Mountains to the Pacific Ocean. Nebraska became a transit area between the east and west coasts. Surplus Midwestern populations, along with Easterners, pushed into the territory in the 1870s, living in sod houses to farm the productive soil. They fought locust scourges and drought, which were the subject of sensationalized newspaper coverage in Eastern cities, but they enjoyed generally decent winter weather (punctuated by the occasional blizzard, as in the legendary recent winter of 1886–1887) as they homesteaded the prairie. Still, most settlers had their eyes on lands farther west. Thus, Nebraska engaged in migratory patterns of globalization while it had its share of permanent residents, was also temporary home, wrote a chronicler of the region, to a "resistless sea of population which is steadily rolling toward the Pacific slope."[27]

A town just fifteen years old, Hastings had a population of fifteen thousand who enjoyed such conventions of the modern city as waterworks, gas and electric lights, streetcars, free mail delivery, and streets lined with handsome brick houses. In 1888, it sparkled as an agricultural community that attracted enterprising people who quickly prospered.[28] Unfortunately, symbolic of that rather rapid rise to success, the Hastings crowd came out in such droves to see the game that a hastily built section of the grandstand collapsed before the contest, dropping more than a hundred fans about twenty feet to the ground, without serious injury. Such accidents were familiar occurrences in baseball, although the more tragic usually involved fires that destroyed wooden grandstands.

Regardless of the mishap, Spalding busied himself with completing his entourage. For one, he accepted Duval back into the fold. Spalding returned from a side trip to Kansas City to watch the mascot parade onto the Hastings field to the delight of thousands, welcoming this crowd-pleasing entertainer. The players did, too, and they chipped in for Duval's train fare for the entire journey around the world. Another star never did appear. King Kelly was nowhere to be found; he was not on his way to the arranged meeting in Denver. Frantically telegraphing back east, Spalding only managed to delay Kelly's decision. In the end, as he learned in San Francisco, Spalding could not persuade the "Ten Thousand Dollar Beauty" to join the tour. This was a blow to the star appeal of the entourage, and Kelly's absence outraged Spalding. Perhaps because he resented having been moved from the White Stockings to Boston in 1887, Kelly sought revenge on Spalding by not showing up. He claimed that business interests in New York prevented him from traveling the world. Spalding, his eye on the main promotional chance, still retained a picture of Kelly on a poster advertising the world tour. His replacement, Billy Earle, hopped on a train in St. Paul to meet the entourage in Denver.[29]

Spalding still needed to finalize his rosters. He brought Jimmy Manning of Kansas City to Hastings. Furthermore, after clinching the Dauvray Cup championship, John Ward and Ed Crane left St. Louis and intercepted the tour in Oxford, Nebraska, a junction point southwest of Hastings. With these additions, and the departure of Hengle, Long, and Flint for Chicago, both teams were complete. Spalding also talked with Pat Gilmore, leader of a famous Kansas City band, who contemplated joining the tour with forty musicians to entertain the players on board the ship across the Pacific. Though Gilmore ultimately stayed home, Spalding would try other entrepreneurial tactics to propel his profit-making tour to success in the West.[30]

## COLORADO CONNECTIONS

As the full complement of baseball tourists rolled through the prairie, they finally sighted the snowcapped Rocky Mountains when they were still forty-eight miles east of Denver. This would not be the first trick played on them by the high altitude of the high plains; indeed, they would grow exhausted from running the bases and, like professional teams a century later, marvel at both the greater distance a normally hit ball would travel and the lack of break in a curveball thrown in the rarefied air.

By this time, the bustling, bursting "Queen City of the Plains" was queen of the mountains, too. A sparse mining camp in 1858, just twelve years later, Denver was a boomtown in the midst of an alkali desert at the foot of the Rockies. Lacking natural assets, this "instant city" had zealous local boosters and benefited from the luck of gold rushes in 1859, then through the 1870s and 1880s, that brought Americans and foreigners to its gates as profiteers, speculators, and miners. Denver became a magnet for capital, a globalized distribution point along the Front Range of the Rockies for investment in minerals and a colonial outpost for Eastern bankers and foreign investors. By the late 1880s, about one hundred thousand people lived there, a twenty-five-fold increase from twenty years before. Denver was "a complete and beautiful city," claimed a British clergyman, with "spacious and imposing" public buildings, including a state capitol where mining cabins had resided just a decade before. The city boasted "more picturesque and varied private residences in its suburbs than those seen elsewhere."[31] Others found stately homes, numerous churches and libraries, good schools, an opera house, and lavish displays of wealth—all the accoutrements of a "new wealthy Western city."[32]

This tree-lined city of booms and busts was a financial and transportation nucleus for prosperous miners and mining companies, as well as ranchers and farmers in the rest of the state and region. A recent downturn in the economy had abated, as investors sunk new funds into banks, real estate, manufacturing, and citywide improvements. Self-made men like lawyer Henry Wolcott, railroad executive D. H. Moffat, and H. A. W. Tabor—a grub-staking prospector turned millionaire when his Little Pittsburgh mine yielded a bonanza—peopled the city. Railroad activity was tremendous; as a link in the global transportation network, Denver ranked with Kansas City or Omaha. Into the new Union Depot, which the Denver and Rio Grande Railway and the Union Pacific dominated, came people and goods from all directions. The Burlington entered the city in 1883, giving Denver three direct routes to the Eastern Seaboard and westward to Ogden, Utah, and San Francisco, the route of the world tour. The Leadville gold mines prompted another thousand miles of track-laying through the mountains and valleys. Nobody a quarter-century before could have imagined Denver as such a center of activity.[33]

Abounding in cultural amenities, transportation networks, and business vibrancy, Denver was a natural stopping place for the Spalding tour because its inhabitants also loved leisure pursuits. Residents availed themselves of the ubiquitous trains; scenic routes to the health resorts of Idaho Springs and Estes Park, and the Georgetown railroad loop's high-wire engineering feat, gave Denverites ample opportunity to take in their state's beauty. Denverites, world tour journalist Harry Palmer confirmed, "are great patrons of amusements of all kinds, great lovers of the good things of life, and consequently enthusiastic supporters of baseball."[34]

The Spalding spectacle hit the mark upon its arrival in Denver on Saturday, October 27. Cap Anson and the rest of the players marveled at the beautiful buildings and the signs of prosperity; the city seemed to be on display. So taken by the dynamism and the possibilities of Denver, John Ward purchased three plots of land at the edge of the business district, obviously latching on to the renewed boom then under way in Colorado. Baseball spectators took note of Ward's wife, the beautiful actress Helen Dauvray, as she sat in the stands, while they recognized Ward himself at the opera. The two stayed in Denver's finest hotel, while the other tourists resided in the second best. Frank Lincoln, the humorist, arrived in town, too.

A "showy" parade from the depot to the Windsor Hotel preceded another procession to River Front Park at 1 P.M., with Denver's Alpha Band leading Clarence Duval and the players through the streets lined with onlookers. At the ball grounds awaited 7,500 people, each having paid fifty cents for admission and some another fifty cents for reserved seating. After the celebrated bareback rider Myrtle Peek galloped the field in a fit of frontier hoopla, the two teams encountered the vagaries of the West.

Miss Peek turned out to be the athletic highlight of the day as the players gave their worst exhibition thus far, a sloppy Chicago win by a score of 16–12. The disappointed locals were used to much better play and much more enthusiasm on the field—the lack of which was blamed on the thin air. Indeed, John Tener noted that "after each exertion, no matter how slight, we found it difficult to get our breath."[35] Hoping the weary players would recuperate, the crowd looked forward to the next day's rematch, including a much-anticipated appearance by King Kelly.

They were disappointed on this last score, but the tourists got a chance for redemption before a smaller crowd on a warm Indian summer Sunday. The *Denver Times* called this game "the best ever played in Denver, especially the last four innings, which could never have been excelled."[36] Kelly, it was claimed, "was not badly missed," because Billy Earle caught a superb game, while the well-known Ward played for the first time on the tour and "put new life into the All-Americas" at shortstop. The bad field produced a spectacular catch by All-America outfielder Ned Hanlon. With the score tied 8–8 in the ninth inning, Hanlon streaked after a fly ball and tripped backward on a mound of sand, only to snatch the ball with his right hand at the last moment. The crowd roared at the catch in a fit of pandemonium "never before witnessed in Denver, and it is doubtful anywhere else," declared the *Rocky Mountain News*. The game stretched into two extra innings, with All-America sending the satisfied crowds home with a 9–8 victory. There was even an explanation for the poor play of the day before; one newspaper posited that the teams were frightened because they expected Indians to jump over the fence and massacre them at any moment.[37] But, of course, that was hyperbole in this new era of Denver commerce and famous sporting events.

That evening, after crowds saw the teams off to Colorado Springs, the tourists regretfully traded their broad-gauge train cars for the narrow-gauge sleepers of the Denver and Rio Grande Railway, which would take them to the Springs and then over the mountains to Utah. These cars were not as sumptuous and spacious as the Burlington palaces. Indeed, to this point after nearly a week and a half of travel, players like Tener could write home wishing he

> could just describe the pleasures of our trip so far, but such a thing is impossible, we have every comfort that the best railroads can provide, in the cars, receive great attention from the people in the cities where we play, couple this with the fact that our party is an harmonious one throughout, and that we have been traveling in luxury since our start, and you must I know envy us.[38]

The highlight of this leg of the journey was the scenery, which neither the jeering crowds nor miserable, six-inning exhibition game of shoddy play the next day ruined. Rather, the West was the draw; the majestic sights and tourist experiences were most memorable. Spalding arranged for carriages and saddle horses to meet the party upon its arrival at daybreak in Colorado Springs and take the tourists to the summer resort of

*Hanlon's great catch.*
(Harry C. Palmer, *Athletic Sports in America, England, and Australia.*
Philadelphia: Hubbard Brothers, Publishers, 1889, p. 175)

Manitou Springs and the towering, 380-foot-high red sandstone formations of the Garden of the Gods. Setting out just as the sun topped Pike's
Peak, eighteen miles distant, the three wagons and a dozen broncos set
out for Manitou Springs, home of wealthy Westerners who built Swiss-
style homes in the valleys and mountainsides and enjoyed the mineral
waters. A quick breakfast at Cliff House, then entry into the captivating
five hundred acres of the Garden of the Gods, preceded a look at Cheyenne Mountain and Pike's Peak. The scenery was breathtaking, so much
so that this tourist side trip had become routine among travelers who had
read up on the area through the writings of Bret Harte and John Hay's
*Pike County Ballad.* The dry, sunlit climate had combined with Manitou's
soda and iron springs, pine trees, and the briskness of the outdoors to
attract tourists the world over.

After this awe-inspiring ride, however, baseball brought the players down to Earth with a thump. Spilling off their horses in Colorado Springs, the teams played on a deadline set by the Denver and Rio Grande Railway. The company warned that the train across the Rockies to Utah would wait no longer than fifteen minutes for the players, and thus the game would have to be cut short. The scheduled departure turned out to be fortuitous, because the aborted game was terrible by all accounts.

Although living in what Easterners termed a remote outpost, the residents were not hicks or dupes, especially when it came to the national pastime. Colorado Springs itself, with hardly a house in the early 1870s, had entered the process of globalization through tourism. It now flourished as a Western sanatorium for Americans and Europeans after the railroad had been brought in, and it boasted a college and opera house that hosted a number of traveling theater companies. Baseball fans were numerous, too, and they grew indignant over the exhibition game. Excited about the game, they had scheduled a reception at the Art Loan exhibition before parading the players to the Athletic Grounds. There, Springs enthusiasm for the world tour evaporated. "It was positively the worst game of ball ever seen on the [Athletic] grounds," groaned a reporter who watched the White Stockings slog through to a mistake-filled 13–9 game of six innings. Locals were indeed "roasted," he continued, because while the players tried their best, the error made by the Springs' organizers "was in paying them any money." There was even some banter about arresting Spalding "for obtaining money under false pretenses," especially when the players could not be properly identified because they had put on a mixed batch of uniforms. "There have been a good many sham shows here but none have had the colossal cheek of Spalding's combination." All the more frustrating was that the city newspaper had advertised the game to people who were "fond of base ball— the national game," to be played by "the greatest players in the world."[39]

When the teams lit out early for the train, the spectators suffered their final indignity. Manager John Hart had to chase down the entourage, galloping for the train while holding two bags of money from the gate receipts. He hopped onto the caboose as it pulled out of the station. Tener noted that the Spalding group was lucky to catch the train "before the natives got a shot at us."[40] The fans might have been on to something. It was later discovered that Spalding had paid the winning team $55 after each game as an inducement to perform and also to prevent them from organizing a split of the revenue, which would relieve them of any incentive to win. The payments ceased after the tour departed from Australia, but it was instructive that the players, including laborite John Ward, had to be bought off. And they still played badly in Colorado Springs.[41]

## ROCKY MOUNTAIN PASSAGE

The Spalding show scurried out of town, much like outlaws of the Old West, yet the tourists would also not forget their Rocky Mountain trip because more stunning vistas were in store, thanks to railroad engineering. "The grandness of this western mountain scenery is beyond me to describe," wrote John Tener to his family.[42] An observation car attached to their train displayed the high walls of the Grand Canyon of the Arkansas River before they entered Royal Gorge, over a suspension bridge that spanned the river more than one thousand feet below. After dinner in the town of Salida, they continued up the scenic Marshall Pass on their "railway ladder," the zigzagging route over the Rockies that bridged rock faces and the surging river. Bridges were hung across the river, rather than supported by pilings sunk into the river bed. The train was separated into two sections, with one engine pulling the sleepers up the mountainside, and another chugging along with the rest of the cars. Newsman Harry Palmer noted the train above them, furnace roaring out showers of sparks and smoke, while below them lay the chasm. Once at the pass, at nearly 11,000 feet, the tourists jumped from the cars into knee-deep snow. From there it was all downhill, but still stunning. Jimmy Ryan called the scenery "almost beyond description, mountain peaks a thousand feet in height hang directly overhead, while the track, like a huge serpent, winds itself in and out through deep canyons and still gloomier tunnels."[43] This technological marvel amidst such beauty defined the advances in the movement of people that was integral to globalization and that determined the economic pace and cultural integration of the New West.

The tourists crossed the Rockies into Utah. At midnight that Monday, the reconnected tourist train passed by the dramatic Black Canyon of the Gunnison and the Currecanti Needle rising from its floor. The spectacular trip in Colorado ended in Green River the next day, October 30, at breakfast. The entourage then moved westward through the less impressive, mud-colored mountains of Utah. That evening, after winding past tiny settlements that smacked of the Old West of lore—villages peopled by those on the short end of globalization, such as "Indians, Chinamen, and rough-looking frontiersmen," wrote Palmer—they arrived in the "Mormon stronghold" of Salt Lake City.[44]

Awaking on Wednesday in the elegant Walker House, their first hotel since leaving Chicago, the tourists saddled up and rode to Camp Douglas, a U.S. Army fort in the Utah Territory. Old West images persisted, as Ryan found interesting "the daily routine of a private's life upon the frontier."[45] They spent the rest of the morning seeing the famous Mormon Tabernacle and the great Salt Lake and generally meandering around "one of the handsomest and cleanest cities that the far West can boast of," wrote Pop Anson.[46]

Salt Lake City was, of course, famous for the oval Mormon Tabernacle with its immense domelike roof, and was infamous for the practice of polygamy. By the 1880s, after the Supreme Court had upheld an act of Congress that outlawed multiple marriages, hundreds of criminal court cases were prosecuted. Over one thousand men went to prison until the Mormon Church urged members to obey the law. For Utah to progress as part of a New West, adjustments were in order. Polygamy was discontinued in 1896 in order for Utah to be admitted into the Union. Yet just as this blot tarnished the reputation of Salt Lake City as backward, the "City of Saints" had also developed into a thriving business and cultural center. Its strikingly wide, straight streets crossed at right angles, its neat blocks of houses were surrounded by lovely gardens and orchards, and the air blew fresh down from the surrounding mountain heights. Horse cars transported the twenty-five thousand residents, as well as tourists. Salt Lake was not a city known for its cultural or intellectual attributes, although it did have an opera house and good schools. The city was linked to the agricultural and mining riches of Utah and national and international commerce ever since the Union Pacific Railroad had entered the territory in the 1860s.[47]

Boosters of the city were excited about the Spalding tour. Not only were baseball fans in great number, but boosters noted with satisfaction the presence of correspondents from all over the country. Fred Scarff, the manager of the ballpark, hoped these journalists would write up descriptive accounts of Salt Lake and Utah, "giving us more free advertising than we have ever had." Residents were urged to give the players a big reception; the prospects for statehood, respect, and expanded business could only be enhanced.[48]

About 2,500 fans attended the first exhibition game in well-groomed Washington Park, underneath the Wasatch Mountains, but rain stopped it in the fourth inning, with All-America ahead 9–3. As in Colorado Springs, the fans were not happy with the play, especially a number of errors that gifted All-America several unearned runs. "The playing generally lacked the vim and earnestness the public had the right to expect," a newspaper reported, and the teams should be obligated to "show the Salt Lake City public that the highly salaried ball players of the East can and will play ball."[49] Surely, the paying public in the West might quickly grow tired of the slack play; it was clear that while the paying customers took baseball seriously, the tourists were on a "picnic."

The rain continued throughout the night, turning to snow that lay on the ground, but the muddy second game on Thursday, November 1, went on, to the detriment of the players' uniforms, the slipping outfielders' dignity, and the White Stockings. The second game got better reviews, despite the criticism launched at "umpire" Ed Crane, who preferred to loll against the grandstand rather than stand behind the plate or pitcher calling outs. Ward's squad routed Chicago again, by a score of 10–3. Still, players were awed by the weather; they looked up at a hard snow in the surrounding mountains while they played down in the ballpark in beautiful sunshine.

That evening, two hundred people saw the baseball tourists off. After Clarence Duval entertained with his baton performance and "plantation walk-around," a large omnibus carriage took them to the train station. By midnight, their train reached Ogden, where they picked up their two special sleeper cars that had left them in Denver and departed for San Francisco. Salt Lake opinion makers suggested that "the San Francisco papers ought to insist on the teams playing ball, or let the public know they are off on a hoodoo and don't care whether school keeps or not."[50] Clearly, these Westerners were no country bumpkins when it came to baseball and their leisure time.

Such sentiment was a trifle for Spalding and the players. After all, they were off-season baseball tourists on the trip of their lives and headed for a luxury ship that would sail them abroad. Furthermore, while the spectators might be angry or disappointed by their play, the entourage's members were a bit depressed by the 745 miles of rail travel that lay ahead on the way to San Francisco. A full day cooped up in the train, no matter how luxurious it was, made them aware of the vastness of the American West. The three thousand miles between Chicago and the Pacific coast had become "tiresome," wrote Palmer, as the train rolled over prairie wastes of sage, droves of jackrabbits, and packs of coyotes. The Utah and Nevada deserts seemed peopled by sparse bands of forlorn Indians, who appeared at railroad station outposts. The trials of the pioneers hit home for Anson, who complained that "how they ever managed to live and to reach the promised land is indeed a mystery." No matter how impressive this enormous pastureland, the tourists welcomed the sight of the verdant Sierra Nevada and the fertile valleys of California the next morning, Saturday, November 3. A breakfast of peaches, grapes, pears, and apples in Sacramento refreshed them, and a mob at the depot that rivaled Denver's turnout helped them forget the monotonous marathon they had just endured.[51]

## ENTRY TO THE COAST

Their two weeks in the paradise of California, which ended when they boarded the steamship for Hawaii, were full of sightseeing, socializing, baseball, and business boosterism. It all started the very first day after leaving Sacramento. In the tiny railroad crossing of Suisun City, about thirty miles northeast of San Francisco, a delegation of newspapermen and baseball managers boarded the train. They were led by Jim Hart, Spalding's stateside tour manager, who, as the tour's advance agent, had organized this reception by California's baseball fraternity. At the ferry departure point of Porto Costa, Spalding received a telegram from tycoon E. J. Baldwin, who invited the tourists to mount carriages at the bottom of Market Street once their steamer had crossed the bay to San Francisco from Oakland and take rooms at his elegant Baldwin Hotel. Working their way through the hotel hustlers at the ferry dock, the tourists arrived at the hotel, only to be whisked away again by the press and the state baseball league representatives to Marchand's, one of San Francisco's finest restaurants, and then to a performance of Rice's *The Corsair* at the Baldwin Theater. A parade and pyrotechnics for Republican candidate Benjamin Harrison resounded in the streets past midnight. The players, all dressed in formal attire, finally dropped into their beds in the early morning hours.[52]

San Francisco struck the tourists as the fitting end to this continental leg of their journey, for it was the New West's crown jewel of commerce and culture. The city had been chartered after California entered the union, in 1850. The mud flats were filled in, orchards planted, and earthquakes tolerated, and the city became a commercial center on the West Coast and a port ranking with New York and New Orleans in traffic. San Francisco controlled nearly all imports and exports on the Pacific Coast, and it had more manufacturing, trade, and investment than all other Western cities combined. It was the entry point for Asian (specifically Chinese) labor for the railroads. Pleasant summer temperatures, agricultural abundance in the surrounding hills, and sheer beauty added to its appeal, and soon cable cars and horse omnibuses climbed the steep streets. Rapid development hinging on global engagement led to fragmentation in the city; San Francisco was divided by ethnic rivalries, politics, and a lack of clear civic interest. Still, businessmen in particular had risen to dominance by building opulent theaters and hotels, including both Baldwin establishments, and in so doing had given the city a greater sense of civic pride, for baseball as well as the arts.[53]

Baseball had a history in the state. For starters, California had a tradition of turning out some of professional baseball's best talent, including George Stallings, Clark Griffith, and Billy Sunday, as well as Spalding tourists Jim Fogarty, Tom Brown, and the crowd favorite, strikeout pitcher George Van Haltren. In addition, the California League, in business since 1886, had overcome the bad reputations of earlier state associations. Players found smoking cigars on the field and managers and players who threw games were expelled from the league. The California League also capitalized on baseball's popularity by holding games in the huge fourteen thousand–seat Haight Street Park, running special cable cars there for transportation. A rival Pacific Coast League also found solid support, but in this early era of state baseball, the affections of the fans remained with the California League, which banned betting to attract a better element and reserved seats for the rich and working class alike. With prosperity came greater organizational stability, and Easterners began to take notice. By the time of the tour, the league had begun hiring nonlocal professionals. Its popularity and stability attracted Albert Spalding, and as a result, he agreed to play some of the local teams in exhibition matches.[54]

The problem for Spalding was that California cranks would not stomach shoddy play, but his clubs would not oblige, at least at first. Sunday, November 4, dawned sunny and bright, and after meeting the crowds at their hotel, a military band paraded the tourists down Market to Montgomery Street, then back to Market via California and Kearny, and finally to Golden Gate Avenue to the large Haight Street Park. A huge crowd of thirteen thousand witnessed a good pregame practice, but an error-filled game followed, played by Chicago's supposed stonewall, but tired, infield. All-America ran up the score for the third consecutive game, winning 14–4, but worse was the embarrassment of a subpar performance. High altitude could not be blamed this time around. Some wondered if the game was fixed; although most spectators had faith in the honesty of Spalding and Anson, they also concluded that the teams played like rank amateurs. Fortunately, San Francisco journalists seemed better natured than those in Colorado, and thus the tourists did not suffer the hard edge of angry criticism.

That the teams committed so many fielding gaffes was disappointing, but not surprising. Errors were common in early baseball, due to uneven field conditions. Furthermore, prior to a major rule change in 1889, many plays—including walks, wild pitches, passed balls, balks, and hit batters—were scored as errors. In addition, gloves were a relatively novel device. Catchers began using gloves in the 1860s, and the puff pillow design appeared in the late 1880s. Still, most players did not adopt hand protection until early in that decade. Albert Spalding saw his first glove—flesh-colored with a large opening in the back—on a first basemen during his days in Boston in 1875. He remembered that the player garnered much ridicule, but two years later, Spalding himself donned a black glove when he moved from pitcher to first base, and then, in typical fashion, cornered the market on sales when Spalding Bros. provided the standard glove in the remainder of the nineteenth century. The first infielder's glove, worn by shortstop Arthur Irwin of Providence, had debuted in 1883, just five years before the world tour. Although several sizes of buckskin construction too big, it caught on, especially after Giants star John Ward wore one. By 1893, pitchers used them, and the following year, Louisville third baseman Jerry Denny became the last position player to field without a glove. Such was their popularity by the mid-1890s that gloves were restricted in size, for players devised some quite extended ones.[55] Thus, mitts were in an evolutionary phase during the Spalding tour. Still, glove or no glove, San Francisco fans, like other spectators along the way, had little patience for bad plays in the field.

More humiliation was in store, however. Two days after the first game, All-America squared off against the Greenwood and Morans club in front of three thousand people. The locals hammered the tourists, 12–2, with Crane pitching badly and being given little support in the field. The local Pioneers then prompted eleven All-America errors two days later, on November 8, in another self-inflicted loss. Pioneer pitcher Joe Russell made monkeys out of the Major League hitters with his low and high drop ball, while Ward left a big hole as he went off quail shooting in Watsonville. The rest of the team should have joined him, or met up with the White Stockings, who had taken a reprieve by visiting Chinatown and the Presidio, climbing Telegraph and Nabob Hills, and roaming Sutro Heights, the gardens of Golden Gate Park, and Cliff House to view the seals.[56]

Chicago was not off the hook, however, yet pride and a renewed work ethic finally returned to the world tour. That same Thursday of the Pioneer victory over All-America, Anson took his team fifty miles west to Stockton to play the town's club. At long last, the four thousand fans, who had paid double the normal admission price, saw a pretty game, which ended in a 2–2 tie after nine innings, due to darkness. John Tener pitched a two-hitter, and Chicago collected more hits, but the Stockton hurler proved just as good and his teammates outfielded Anson's squad. Better results awaited twice-routed All-America, too, as they crushed Stockton the next day in San Francisco, 16–1. Ward's fielding, Crane's pitching, and timely hitting returned, while Fogarty put on a base-stealing clinic with seven swipes (of a total of seventeen steals).

Properly chastised, both Stockton and the Pioneers refused to play the tourists again. When the White Stockings registered a 6–1 beating of the Haverly team and their star coastal pitcher, tour journalist Palmer noted that the "unfavorable impression" of the opening game in San Francisco began to fade. Thus, nearly seven thousand very enthusiastic spectators came out on Sunday, November 11, to watch the farewell game. They muttered as Hanlon and Ward arrived an hour late, sauntering onto the field without uniforms. Still, the fabled stonewall infield returned to form, although All-America batting overcame Chicago's defense, and Ward enjoyed a 9–6 triumph. Spalding agreed to a special treat for the crowd by letting native son Van Haltren pitch.[57]

Two days after the last game in San Francisco, the teams left for Los Angeles. There they were guaranteed $1,800, but local boosters had no worries. They converted the lumber of the Democratic Party's grandstand—its usefulness expired in the wake of Cleveland's loss—into additional baseball seating and vigorously advertised the matchup of the famous Giants captain John Ward against "Baby" Anson. Leaving the Nadeau Hotel, the players toured the City of Angels until taking the County Railroad train to the ball grounds. All-America blanked Chicago in the first game, 5–0, but Anson's side then ended its five-game losing streak with a 7–4 victory. The tourists played the two games in front of a total of three thousand fans paying fifty cents for general admission at Prospect Park, which they reached by the addition of extra train cars and locomotives and an increase in the number of Temple Street cable cars.

These were the tourists' final games in the West. After attending an evening theater performance in Los Angeles, they traveled all day once again, on Friday, November 16, in their return to San Francisco. There, preparations were under way for their trans-Pacific voyage scheduled for the next day.[58]

In the meantime, Spalding had been the subject of much attention by business and baseball associates. A publisher of a California newspaper invited him, as well as Anson, Williamson, Ward, and Hanlon, out to his home in Oakland before they attended festivities in their honor at the Press Club. Leading area businessmen and corporate leaders joined state legislator Charles Alexander Bird at the Merchants' Club for another banquet for Spalding, who then returned the favor on the eve of their departure for Hawaii with a dinner at the Baldwin Hotel, where he thanked the press and California League magnates. Yet Big Al's plans hit a temporary snag. Because the Eastern and English mail was delayed a day, the tourists' ship, the *Alameda*, which carried the mail, had to postpone sailing for a day.

Seventy-five guests attended the Baldwin Hotel banquet, sitting at tables decorated in baseball paraphernalia and reading a baseball-shaped circular menu card written by humorist Frank Lincoln and designed as a scorecard with hokey designations for courses, some named for baseball plays or in honor of individual tourists. Thus, one might start with "Eastern oysters on the Home Run" and move on to "Petit paté, à la Spalding." A confectionary pyramid of a ball sitting on a tripod of baseball bats, which rested on a base and under a catcher's mask of sugar crystals, highlighted the head table. Champagne flowed freely; the grand event lasted until 4 A.M. Numerous speeches followed, with a superior court judge humorously regaling the diners about early California ballplayers and an ex–New York senator doing the same for the champion Giants. Then newspapermen, Anson and Ward paid tribute to the teams and managers, George Wright lauded cricket, and even Capt. Henry Morse of the *Alameda* spoke of his vessel's role in the world tour. Spalding ended the evening by happily thanking the attendees for a splendid two weeks.[59] Anson furthered his compliments of Californians, as well as the sentiment that the baseball tourists had experienced a full range of the American West. He thought that Californians—impulsive, genial, and business-oriented—still held the "characteristics of those early pioneers who settled there" years before.[60]

By all accounts, the stay in San Francisco had been glorious. Despite some bad baseball, the players and residents got along well, although, in a short piece for the *San Francisco Examiner*, Ward complained about the long distances, cramped muscles, and overbearing crowds on the tour. The jovial and careless nature of the tourists hurt them on the field but placed them in the good graces of the residents.

Indeed, more than two thousand fans bid them farewell at the Folsom Street Wharf on November 18. The crowd delighted in a last "breakdown" dance by Duval, the bugling of "all aboard" from Lincoln, and the cheers called out to the famous ballplayers. Jim Hart, his overseeing of the tour's American leg completed, nervously counted heads and then walked down the gangplank, the last to go ashore. As the *Alameda* slipped its berth, Spalding proposed three cheers for the city, and three more for the California League, and then a traditional howl on behalf of a local squad, the "Howling Wolves," arose from the crowd on the pier. It had not been the most "artistic" display of baseball, wrote reporters, but the visit to the city had been a financial success. And San Franciscans would remember this "epoch in the history of baseball" as one in which they had a major role.[61] The continental train crossing was over; baseball globalization continued by sea, as did the push westward to Hawaii.

## TRAVELING THE HIGH SEAS

Modernized ship voyages, ports, and routes permitted such grandiose tours as the baseball trip around the world. Sail had given way to large steam-powered vessels made of steel, itself made cheaper because of innovative production techniques and business efficiencies. Passenger travel across the English Channel had begun in 1816, and within twenty-five years, one hundred thousand people a year steamed between France and England. In 1840, the Cunard line's *Britannia* journeyed across the Atlantic in two weeks, within two years of its maiden voyage that took Charles Dickens to America. The decade also witnessed steamship travel from England to the eastern Mediterranean and up the Nile from Alexandria to Cairo. Nearby, naval officers, merchants, and tourists had long marveled at the Suez Canal. Opened in 1869, the canal proved to be a critical link in the global transportation network, making travel around the Horn of Africa obsolete and shortening the distance from Asia, Africa, and the Indian Ocean into the Mediterranean and Europe.[62]

By the time ships sailed through the Suez Canal, a new type of vessel— the elegantly appointed ocean liner—had been christened to the delight of tourists as well as the busy shipping industry. Passengers dined, drank, and danced amid intricate woodwork, ornate carpeting, luxurious upholstery, and sparkling chandeliers. By the late 1850s, the first screw-propelled steamships had driven down fares, and over the next twenty years, the Collins Line's four vessels, which combined paddle wheels and sails, were most popular with Americans until iron hulls and screws supplanted them. From the 1870s on, twin-screw, ten-thousand-ton luxury behemoths cut transatlantic travel to a week. All the while, passengers could enjoy abounding epicurean delights and the modern trappings and comforts of libraries, marbled seawater baths, and electricity.[63] The baseball tourists voyaged on some of these fast iron ships, traveling more than thirty-two thousand miles across the Pacific, Indian, and Atlantic oceans, as well as part of the Mediterranean Sea and through the Suez Canal.

Advances in shipbuilding had made the steamship the greyhound of the oceans and furthered the process of globalization through the commercial and carrying trade, tourism, and immigrant transport. By 1880, steel construction had made vessels even larger and speedier than before, and thus ships took more migrants and tourists faster across the Atlantic, in particular. In regard to lucrative passenger travel, companies such as Cunard, White Star, and Inman competed for the speediest ships during the decade. Typical was the recently constructed *City of New York*, a large modern ship that drove through the water propelled by 14,000-horsepower engines, huge boilers, and manganese and bronze propeller blades. The world was growing smaller every year due to faster and cheaper ships. Although it was not until 1889, as the tourists returned to America, that trans-Atlantic ships finally did away with sails, there were calls for ever larger and better-constructed steamships to carry freight, mail, and people worldwide, across the Pacific as well as to Europe. Vessels grew so large that some ports, such as Honolulu, were bypassed because of their shallowness. Steamship traffic was profitable, and the carrying and passenger trade, much like the railroads, promised commercial riches to those few who invested capital and built up organizational control.[64] These companies provided passage across the water that linked to the rail transportation system and allowed travelers to span the globe with more ease than ever before.

Symbolic of the globalization of transportation was the large floral bouquet that the Burlington Railroad presented to the *Alameda* when the Spalding tourists boarded and which Captain Morse placed in the social hall. Such passing off of continental train travel to ocean voyage, in a continuous global circuit, was significant. By the 1840s, networks emerged linking trains and ships, so the Burlington engaged in what was now a long tradition of moving people and goods from east to west, and back again.[65] By land and sea, markets opened to travelers and products, and the New West depot of San Francisco was the hub of this trade, both eastward into the interior and westward into the far Pacific reaches of the American realm: Hawaii.[66]

Interestingly, technology was lacking when it came to communications. On the fifth day out of port, the *Alameda* encountered another ship headed in the opposite direction. Two miles of rolling waves separated the Spalding tourists from the *Australia*, which lacked news of the presidential election because no connection existed between North America and the

The Alameda *transported the tourists across the Pacific.*

(Harry C. Palmer, *Athletic Sports in America, England, and Australia.* Philadelphia: Hubbard Brothers, Publishers, 1889, p. 208)

Hawaiian Islands.[67] The two vessels conversed by light signals, and a rocket launched into the night, which burst with hundreds of stars, confirmed Republican Benjamin Harrison's victory.

Furthermore, regardless of this globalized era of travel, schedules and planning were far from certain. Thus, the *Alameda* had been forced to wait a day for the mail to arrive. When it proved impossible for the vessel to make up the time, the ship arrived in Honolulu a day late, on Sunday, November 25. Nothing impeded Spalding's own communication skills, however, in expressing his vision. He leaked to the players that he had met S. S. Parry, the English agent of the Chicago, Burlington, and Quincy Railroad, during the stay in San Francisco. The two discussed the feasibility of extending the Australia tour to Great Britain and having the tourists travel by way of India, Egypt, Italy, and France. It was agreed that Parry would return to his base in Liverpool, scout the interest in baseball exhibitions, and then cable his findings to Spalding in Australia. Parry later reported considerable enthusiasm, and thus Spalding decided to extend the tour to render it truly globe-girdling in scope.

That decision entailed some risks, however. Spalding hoped that the expenditures projected for travel could be covered. Also, he knew that lengthening the trip would cut short the Australian leg and compel quick stays in places in order to get the players back to their respective teams by April 1, the deadline for them to report for the 1889 season. For his part, he lamented missing his first league officer's meeting, then under way in New York City, where magnates contemplated conflict with the Brotherhood union. But true to his instincts, Spalding figured that exhibiting his "baseball missionaries" around the world was smart promotion. His calculations proved accurate. The prospect of going past Australia excited the fans back home, who knew of the plans before the players did because Spalding had earlier informed journalists, who wrote feature stories about the new schedule. But the players themselves were thrilled about the change in itinerary, too—all of them except Ward. He preferred to be as close as possible to his Brotherhood compatriots to monitor magnate decisions. In addition, his wife, Helen, had decided to abandon the tour and travel with her sister to Europe, where she would rejoin her husband in Malta. Ward was unhappy about her backing out, but Helen, at thirty-one, did not want to undercut the momentum of her acting career. Being stuck on a ship with baseball players was no way to achieve that goal. Ward played on, oftentimes grudgingly.

## INTO THE PACIFIC

As with the long cross-country train trip, so with the *Alameda*—similar sensibilities of pleasure, sightseeing, and discomfort persisted and were even heightened. As the globe-trotting baseball travelers made their way through the fog of San Francisco Bay and dropped the pilot who had negotiated the ship from the harbor to the open sea, they began their 2,100-mile ocean journey to Honolulu. Soon sturdy "Molly hawk" gulls replaced the stormy petrels and albatrosses that had followed the ship a hundred miles out to sea. Meeting the other twenty-five passengers, as well as the nine officers under the leadership of Capt. H. G. Morse, the entourage tried to adjust to the rolling swells of the Pacific Ocean. It took until Wednesday, November 21, three days out, for the seasickness to subside. The "sea sorrow" plagued the unfortunates, who braved the wind and pitch of the *Alameda* by either retiring to their berths, where they slept in narrow bunks three to a room, or by lounging in the sun on the deck, on the port side where the sun shone and where Anson and Spalding had their quarters. Those immune to the rolling ship took delight in the desperate runs to the side of the ship by their retching comrades, or they engaged in superstition by placing a piece of paper over their stomachs to protect their digestion. The ship's bell, which kept time on a four-hour schedule, proved to be a curiosity to these landlubbers, as were the fire drills that occurred every afternoon at 3 P.M. All the tourists paled at this sight, however, scared of the implications.

Near the end of the weeklong journey, as the ship entered tropical waters, the seas calmed. Feeling better, the tourists bet on the distance traveled in each twenty-four-hour period, selling pools of tickets each numbered with miles at breakfast every morning. In fact, in order to seek relief from the monotony, they bet on everything, including what would be served for the next meal or whether the ship would sink before reaching Hawaii. As it grew warmer, they also spent the nights on deck with the women in the party, watching the reflection of the moon and stars on the water and enjoying whatever breeze blew up. They also enjoyed Commander Morse, a bluff, warm-hearted sailor, treating him in an overly friendly way that belied the seriousness of his job as a captain. Because of the ease of travel, passengers oftentimes trivialized the importance of steamship captains and the responsibilities they faced in providing for the safety of the vessel and its occupants.[68]

The tourists arrived in Hawaii—or the Sandwich Islands, so named by Captain James Cook—a day late, on Sunday, November 25, and thus the plans for a baseball exhibition, organized by their advance agent Harry Simpson, were dashed. A crowd, accompanied by the King of Hawaii's band, had waited at the Honolulu docks in front of the Oceanic Steamship Company office until well past noon the previous day. People were excited to see the famous players, but even more anxious for news of the presidential election, of which they had yet no information. The players had wished to play, too, but they were not disappointed when they sighted Hawaii at daybreak on November 25. As the sun rose like a fireball, it painted the rugged mountain peaks gold, orange, and rose. Volcanoes rose out of the water, covered with a lush deep green hue of vegetation. Honolulu lay in an open valley, backed by green serrated hills. In port, a small fleet of ships headed out to the *Alameda* as it steamed past Diamond Head and stopped in the placid bay. A receiving committee comprised of steamship company officials and a handful of native Hawaiians, and headed by Spalding's cousin, George W. Smith, who resided in Honolulu, reached the *Alameda* by boat. Each tourist received a lei of flowers, while a pilot, who, when hearing of Harrison's victory, raised a bandana on a foremast to inform the crowd on shore, guided the ship to the dock.

There, on this beautiful morning, more than two thousand people had gathered, after having waited through the previous day for a sign of the baseball travelers and news of either Harrison or Cleveland. The king of the island's band, the "Royal Hawaiian," played the "Star Spangled Banner," "Yankee Doodle," and other American songs, while the U.S. Navy cruiser *Alert* cheered the tourists, its sailors asking for King Kelly. Groups of Americans and government officers in white uniforms and hats clamored at the dock. The lottery participants among the baseball tourists who bet on everything during the voyage had mostly erred; the ship had arrived in seven days, precisely on schedule.[69]

It was an American scene, a reception the tourists had encountered in Chicago, and across the continent to the Pacific. The tourists had reached the periphery of the American West, having traveled over five thousand miles across prairie, mountains, and sea by rail and ship. This grand journey into the Pacific bespoke of the facility of fast, expansive, and fairly comfortable travel during the first modern-day age of globalization. The tourists experienced the integrative processes wrought by technology and culture that joined the region to the rest of the nation. Transportation networks established by railroads and steamships, themselves financed by Eastern and foreign banks and built by large-scale labor (much of it foreign), connected the United States and its overseas interests into a large economy. Cultural affinities of West and East, baseball prominent among them, reflected the socialization of the New West as truly (white) American territory. Having moved through the western United States, the Spalding tour now engaged different cultures who were also integral to the globalizing process of the era.

## NOTES

1. Turner, *Frontier in American History*, viii; Wrobel, *End of American Exceptionalism*.

2. Roth, *Reading the American West*, 1–2; Limerick, *Legacy of Conquest*, 82; Guterl and Skwiot, "Atlantic and Pacific Crossings."

3. Feifer, *Tourism in History*, 167. See also Shaffer, *See America First*; Schlereth, *Victorian America*, 19.

4. Bogart, "Feats of Railway Engineering."

5. Farnham, "Weakened Spring of Government." See also White, "Information, Markets, and Corruption."

6. Warren, *Buffalo Bill's America*; Reddin, *Wild West Shows*; Slotkin, "Buffalo Bill's 'Wild West,'" 169; Thomas, "West of Currier and Ives"; Pomeroy, *In Search of the Golden West*.

7. Robbins, *Colony and Empire*, xiii, 5–7, 83–102; Igler, "Industrial Far West"; Pomeroy, *Pacific Slope*; Rothman, *Devil's Bargains*.

8. Brierly, *Ab-O'Th-Yate*, 314, 323. See also Betts, "Immense Dimensions."

9. Arnold, *Civilization in the United States*, 178, 186, 187.

10. Warner, "Great West: IV," 124.

11. Porter, "Railway Passenger Travel," 302–11.

12. Fornay, "American Locomotives and Cars," 193.

13. Anson, *A Ball-Player's Career*, 145. See also Aubertin, *A Fight with Distances*, 74.

14. Light, *Cultural Encyclopedia of Baseball*, 709.

15. Aubertin, *A Fight with Distances*, 77; "St. Paul a Winner," *Daily Pioneer Press*, October 22, 1888, p. 1; Glazier, *Peculiarities of American Cities*, 434–37; Robbins, *Colony and Empire*, 172–73.

16. "Very Cold Sport," *Minneapolis Tribune*, October 22, 1888, p. 1.

17. O'Rell, *A Frenchman in America*, 215; Palmer, *Athletic Sports*, 164–65; James Ryan, *Tour of the Spalding B.B.C. around the World* [diary] (hereafter cited as Ryan Diary), James Edward Ryan Biographical File, National Baseball Hall of Fame, Cooperstown, New York, entry for October 21, 1888, 10–11; Bartlett, *Baseball and Mr. Spalding*, 179; "The Great Trip," *Sporting Life*, October 31, 1888, p. 4; "Will Play Today," *Saint Paul and Minneapolis Pioneer Press*, October 21, 1888, p. 8.

18. "The National Game," *Cedar Rapids Evening Gazette*, October 24, 1888, p. 4; Miller, "State of Iowa."

19. Ryan Diary, October 23, 1888, p. 11.

20. "The Great Trip," *Sporting Life*, October 31, 1888, p. 4.

21. Anson, *A Ball Player's Career*, 147–48; Palmer, *Athletic Sports*, 165–67.

22. Ryan Diary, October 24, 1888, p. 12. See also Porter, "Railway Passenger Travel," 311; "Fast Train Service," *Nation*, August 16, 1888, p. 127; "Competition in Fast Train Service," *Nation*, October 11, 1888, p. 290.

23. Light, *Cultural Encyclopedia of Baseball*, 442, 444.

24. Anson, *A Ball Player's Career*, 148–49; Palmer, *Athletic Sports*, 168–70.

25. "The Great Trip," *Sporting Life*, November 7, 1888, p. 4; Palmer, *Athletic Sports*, 168; Anson, *A Ball Player's Career*, 148; "The Antipodean Pilgrims," *Omaha Daily Bee*. October 26, 1888, p. 2; "The Slanders Met," *Omaha Republican*, October 26, 1888, p. 1; "Scored a Failure," *Omaha Republican*, October 27, 1888, p. 1.

26. "Local and Otherwise," *Juniata Herald*, November 1, 1888, p. 1. See also "Base Ball," *Omaha Daily Bee*, October 27, 1888, p. 1; and Baltensperger, "Newspaper Images."

27. Spearman, "Great American Desert," 233; see also 232, 240–42.

28. Spearman, "Great American Desert," 245.

29. Ryan Diary, October 26, 1888, p. 4; Bartlett, *Baseball and Mr. Spalding*, 180; Palmer, *Athletic Sports*, 170; Appel, *Slide, Kelly, Slide*, 135. Star pitcher Charles Comiskey, captain of the St. Louis Browns, used the same excuse as Kelly when he was invited on the tour. He claimed that he needed to start his own business—and besides, his owner, Chris von der Ahe, refused to let him go.

30. Bartlett, *Baseball and Mr. Spalding*, 180; Di Salvatore, *A Clever Base-Ballist*, 229–30; Palmer, *Athletic Sports*, 172; "The Great Trip," *Sporting Life*, November 7, 1888, p. 4.

31. Hole, *Little Tour in America*, 370. See also Ingersoll, "Heart of Colorado," 423; Robbins, *Colony and Empire*, 175–76; West, *Contested Plains*.

32. Faithfull, *Three Visits to America*, 129; Roberts, "City of Denver," 948–50.

33. Roberts, "City of Denver."

34. Palmer, *Athletic Sports*, 172–73. See also Roberts, "City of Denver," 955.

35. John Tener to Maud, October 30, 1888, John K. Tener Biographical File, National Baseball Hall of Fame, Cooperstown, New York (hereafter cited as Tener File).

36. "Hanlon's Wonderful Catch," *Denver Times*, October 29, 1888, p. 6. See also "The Ball Game To-Day," *Rocky Mountain News*, October 27, 1888, p. 3; "Spalding's Aggregation," *Rocky Mountain News*, October 28, 1888, p. 3; "A Very Poor Exhibition," *Denver Republican*, October 28, 1888, p. 2; and "Base Ball," *Rocky Mountain News*, October 26, 1888, p. 3.

37. "Grand Base Ball Game," *Rocky Mountain News*, October 29, 1888, p. 3. See also "The Great National Game," *Denver Republican*, October 29, 1888, p. 12; Anson, *A Ball Player's Career*, 152; Ryan Diary, October 27, 1888, p. 13; and Palmer, *Athletic Sports*, 174–75. In the *Rocky Mountain News* article cited above, the Hanlon catch is vividly described. Once slugger Sullivan had creamed the ball: "During the silence that followed it grew beautifully less in size, as did Hanlon in his mad race into the far center field. It was a race in mid-air and on terra firma that was supremely exciting. On and on sped the winged sphere over the kid's grand stand, and on went Hanlon, his legs oscillating with the rapidity of a jig saw until the ball lowered almost to earth, when the fleet-footed flyer fairly flew up into the air, gathered in the battered bun and fell in a heap on the ground, not without holding the ball, however."

38. Tener to Maud, October 30, 1888, Tener File.

39. "Roasted," *Colorado Springs Gazette*, October 30, 1888, p. 1; "Base Ball," *Colorado Springs Gazette*, October 27, 1888, p. 1. See also Faithfull, *Three Visits to America*, 135, 138–43; Palmer, *Athletic Sports*, 176–82.

40. Tener to Maud, October 30, 1888, Tener File.

41. Di Salvatore, *A Clever Base-Ballist*, 231–32.

42. Tener to Maud, October 30, 1888, Tener File.

43. Ryan Diary, October 29, 1888, p. 15.

44. Ingersoll, "Heart of Colorado," 418; Palmer, *Athletic Sports*, 184–85, see also 182–84.

45. Ryan Diary, October 31, 1888, p. 15.

46. Anson, *A Ball-Player's Career*, 157.

47. Gordon, "Mormon Question"; Aubertin, *A Fight with Distances*, 212–13; "Grand Opera House," *Salt Lake City Daily Tribune*, October 30, 1888, p. 3; Glazier, *Peculiarities of American Cities*, 441–47.

48. "Amusements," *Salt Lake City Daily Tribune*, October 30, 1888, p. 1.

49. "The Champion Base Ballists," *Salt Lake City Daily Tribune*, November 1, 1888, p. 4.

50. "Much Better Ball Game," *Salt Lake City Daily Tribune*, November 2, 1888, p. 4. See also Palmer, *Athletic Sports*, 185–88; and "The Voyagers," John Tener's letter to the *Pittsburgh Chronicle Telegraph*, November 12, 1888, Tener File.

51. Palmer, *Athletic Sports*, 188; Anson, *A Ball Player's Career*, 158–59.

52. Palmer, *Athletic Sports*, 189–90; Ryan Diary, November 3, 1888, p. 19.

53. Glazier, *Peculiarities of American Cities*, 452–63, 471; Hirata, "Free, Indentured, Enslaved"; Robbins, *Colony and Empire*, 173–74; Frank Mazzi, "Harbingers of the City."

54. Franks, "California League"; Franks, "Of Heroes and Boors." The California League collapsed in 1893.

55. Light, *Cultural Encyclopedia of Baseball*, 298–99.

56. Palmer, *Athletic Sports*, 190–92; Ryan Diary, November 4–7, 1888, pp. 20–22. See also "Rousing Reception" and "Anson's Anger," newspaper clippings, *Albert Spalding Scrapbook*, vol. 8, Albert Spalding Collection, Society of American Baseball Researchers Lending Library, Cleveland, Ohio (hereafter cited as Spalding Scrapbooks); "The Great Trip," *Sporting Life*, November 21, 1888, p. 4; "On the Diamond," *San Francisco Chronicle*, November 5, 1888, p. 7.

57. Palmer, *Athletic Sports*, 192–93; "A Drawn Game," *San Francisco Chronicle*, November 9, 1888, p. 6; "They Win a Game," *San Francisco Chronicle*, November 10, 1888, p. 8; Di Salvatore, *A Clever Base-Ballist*, 228; "At Haight Street," *San Francisco Chronicle*, November 12, 1888, p. 5.

58. "The American Teams," *Los Angeles Times*, November 11, 1888, p. 4; "Amusements: Prospect Park," *Los Angeles Times*, November 13, 1888, p. 1; "Baseball," *Los Angeles Times*, November 15, 1888, p. 6.

59. Palmer, *Athletic Sports*, 194, 197–98; "A Baseball Banquet" and "At the Plate," newspaper clippings, Spalding Scrapbooks, vol. 8; Levine, *A. G. Spalding*, 102.

60. Anson, *A Ball Player's Career*, 170.

61. "Off for Australia," newspaper clipping, Spalding Scrapbook, vol. 8, p. 34. See also "The Great Trip," *Sporting Life*, December 5, 1888, p. 4; Di Salvatore, *A Clever Base-Ballist*, 230.

62. Buzard, *Beaten Track*, 41.

63. Dulles, *Americans Abroad*, 45–49, 105; Sloan, "Nightingale and the Steamship."

64. Rideing, "Building of an 'Ocean Greyhound'"; "Recent Steamship Development," *Nation* 48 (February 14, 1889): 134–35; Perry, *Facing West*, 138–45. For advances in ship travel, see Keeling, "Transportation Revolution."

65. "Southward Ho!!" newspaper clipping, Spalding Scrapbooks, vol. 8, p. 35.

66. On Hawaii as part of the West, see Whitehead, *Completing the Union*.

67. Pacific cable communication would not exist until the turn of the century, although the Americans and the British were readying plans and financing for it. See Dwyer, *To Wire the World*; Hills, *Struggle for Control of Global Communication*.

68. Palmer, *Athletic Sports*, 200–205; Spalding, *Baseball*, 255; Di Salvatore, *A Clever Base-Ballist*, 232; Stevens, *Baseball's Radical*, 74; "On the Ocean," *Sporting Life*, January 2, 1889, p. 4; Tener to Maud and Will, November 29, 1888, Tener File; Passenger list, S.S. *Alameda*, Oceanic Steamship Company, Spalding Scrapbooks, vol. 10; Ryan Diary, November 18–24, 1888, pp. 25–28; Anson, *A Ball Player's Career*, 173; "Story of the Trip," Spalding Scrapbooks, vol. 8; Kennedy, "Captain's Work."

69. "Arrival of the Alameda," *Pacific Commercial Advertiser*, November 26, 1888, p. 1; Palmer, *Athletic Sports*, 206; Aubertin, *A Fight with Distances*, 162; Ryan Diary, November 25, 1888, p. 28; "At Honolulu," *Sporting Life*, January 9, 1889, p. 4.

# 3

# An Empire of Race

## Southern Seas

NEW ZEALAND
  Auckland, Monday, December 10, 1888—*Chicago* 22, *All-America*
  13
AUSTRALIA
  Sydney, Friday, December 15—*All-America* 5, *Chicago* 4
  Sydney, Sunday, December 17—*All-America* 7, *Chicago* 5
  Sydney, Monday, December 18—*All-America* 6, *Chicago* 2
  Melbourne, Saturday, December 22—*Chicago* 5, *All-America* 3
  Melbourne, Monday, December 24—*All-America* 15, *Chicago* 13
  Adelaide, Wednesday, December 26—*All-America* 19, *Chicago* 14
  Adelaide, Thursday, December 27—*Chicago* 12, *All-America* 9
  Adelaide, Friday, December 28—*Chicago* 11, *All-America* 4
  Ballarat, Saturday, December 29—*All-America* 11, *Chicago* 7
  Melbourne, Tuesday, January 1, 1889—*Chicago* 14, *All-America* 7
  Melbourne, Saturday, January 5—*Chicago* 5, *All-America* 0
CEYLON
  Colombo, Saturday, January 26—*Chicago* 3, *All-America* 3
EGYPT
  Cairo, Saturday, February 9—*All-America* 10, *Chicago* 6

Dear Sir: We, the undersigned, members of the St. Louis baseball club, do not agree to play against negroes tomorrow. We will cheerfully play against white people at any time, and think, by refusing to play, we are only doing what is right, taking everything into consideration and the shape the team is in at present.

This letter of September 10, 1887, sent from eight players to St. Louis Browns' owner Chris von der Ahe, hinted that integrated professional baseball was in jeopardy. Three years earlier, the college-educated Moses Fleetwood Walker, and his brother Weldy, had debuted as the first

73

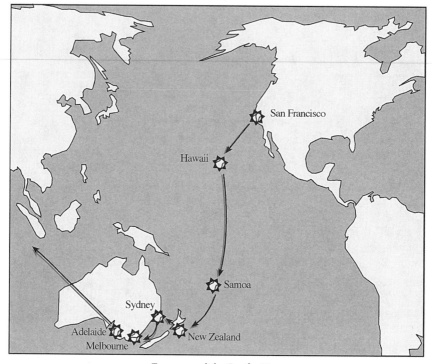

*Tour around the Pacific Rim.*
(David Underwood, Graphic Design, CU-Boulder)

known black players in the major leagues, playing for the American Association's Toledo Mud Hens. Their days were numbered, however, for Cap
Anson spearheaded a white backlash against them. He simply refused to
play against "brunettes" or protested when African Americans took the
field, thereby effectively barring them from professional baseball. Walker
got a temporary reprieve that permitted him to play for Buffalo, yet a
month before the Spalding tourists left Chicago, on September 27, 1888,
Anson barked "get the nigger off the field" when Buffalo faced his White
Stockings in an exhibition game. Buffalo released Walker soon thereafter.

    There was no written National League law against integration, just a
"gentleman's agreement" among officials, owners, and players that suffi-
ciently prohibited African Americans from white professional baseball. A
few played in organized baseball in the 1890s, and a handful, especially
light-skinned Cubans, tried to "pass" as white. Baseball eventually moved
progressively ahead of other U.S. institutions and erased the color barrier
in 1947, when Jackie Robinson debuted with the Brooklyn Dodgers, but it

took a half century to do so. At the time of the Spalding tour, the national pastime drew a bold color line that prohibited racial equality and integration.[1]

Anson might have been the loudest ringleader of racism, but his views were not at all out of sync with white America, which adopted both informal customs and formal practices to separate the races at the time. On occasion, black Americans could overcome racist laws. For example, in 1888, a black woman in Chicago successfully sued a white manager of a theater for refusing her entry to a first-balcony seat. But more often than not, minorities ended up on the losing side. For instance, other sports witnessed the scourge of racism. Peter Jackson, the most famous black athlete of the late nineteenth century, won the heavyweight boxing championship in Australia in 1886 and then sailed for San Francisco in 1888 to take on John L. Sullivan for the world title. The American public clamored for the match, yet, like Anson in baseball, Sullivan refused to fight.[2] The color barrier climbed higher than ever before. The post–Civil War system of "Jim Crow laws" instituted legal racism, while lynchings of blacks who did not obey the oftentimes arbitrary rules of segregation became commonplace. Discrimination and violence against blacks and other people of color allowed whites to assert ideas and practices of racial superiority. This was as true abroad, in imperial holdings, as it was at home.

White attitudes toward race shaped globalization and imperial imaginations. In 1888–1889, the United States stood on the brink of joining Britain, France, Germany, Italy, and Russia in the pursuit of empire; at this moment in history, the new paradigm of imperialism was forming but was not yet complete. Like Europeans, Americans trampled on indigenous peoples and engaged in the civilizing mission, itself grounded deeply in the creation of racial hierarchies. Worldwide expositions presented anthropological displays that characterized blacks as childlike or not fully human, Indians as savages, and the Chinese as peculiar, deceptive, and inassimilable as a people into American culture. In short, all were barbarians. Comparing the "fetal, infantile or simian traits" of colored people to Caucasians, for example, one scholar commenting on the science of anatomy wrote just a year after the baseball tour that "the European or white race stands at the head of the list, the African or negro at its foot."[3]

The Spalding tourists also brought with them notions of superiority that typified norms of late nineteenth-century imperialism. To be sure, their role in U.S. empire-building should not be exaggerated, for unlike missionaries and other permanent overseas settlers, the baseball entourage moved through foreign lands quickly and for pleasure. Yet taking part in the process of globalization, which itself aided the creation and maintenance of empires, they certainly carried with them and even

communicated—however unwittingly—ideas of identity and power relationships critical to the projection of America's brand of empire. The tourists traveled in the context of race, a context that shaped their views of
and experiences with the nonwhite domestic and foreign cultures to
which they were exposed.

## RACISM AT HOME

The baseball trip into the Pacific and beyond showed the attitude of superiority of white America to people of color. Hawaii turned out to be the
first place outside of the United States that exemplified the tourists'
Anglo-Saxon doctrine of superiority as part of the nascent impulse of
imperialism. Yet while traveling within America, they had also expressed
their prejudiced views on race and culture.

For instance, the players had spent significant time in San Francisco's
Chinatown, some of the players returning for two or three visits, usually
with licensed guides and, at nighttime, with police escort. The quarter
offered a contrast of wealth and poverty, and a lesson in the cultural
divide that race provided during the era. The sights, according to tour
chronicler Harry Palmer, were both "revolting and yet fascinating," with
vice and crime supposedly so prevalent that newspaper coverage and
illustrations did no credit to "the horror" of the six-by-three-block area.
The "Celestials," as Palmer referred to the Chinese in his more gracious
moments, had "crowded all the white people out of their district" and put
in place their own government, businesses, utilities, and even courts, to a
great extent. That the tourists had trouble comprehending that their
impressions arose from unwarranted racist preconceptions was not surprising for whites at the time. Thus, "John Chinaman," assumed Cap
Anson later, "is a natural born gambler," who, if he murdered somebody,
would escape San Francisco law but would likely be punished "in some
horrible form" by the victim's relatives.[4]

They also noted the impoverished conditions in Chinatown, but here,
too, the commentary presumptuously placed the burden of responsibility
on the Chinese immigrants rather than on U.S. policies. After the Civil
War, while missionaries continued to try to convert the Chinese to Christianity, Chinese immigrants had flooded into the United States, many
under the provision of the Burlingame Treaty of 1868, which permitted
the entry of contract laborers. They were soon known as "coolies," a
derogatory term meaning "bitter labor," for which whites deemed them
wholly suitable because of their supposed docility and immunity to the
normal pain encountered by other workers. They clashed over jobs with
recently arrived European immigrants, as well as white American

migrants, and violence ensued. Oftentimes, attacks on the Chinese went unpunished. The most blatant brutality occurred when twenty-five "heathen Chinee" were killed in Wyoming in 1885. Yet there were so many incidents of stonings, lynchings, and threats against adults and children, as well as rumors of innocent girls being lured into Chinese opium dens, that the mistreatment these immigrants faced gave rise to the phrase "not a Chinaman's chance."

It was unremarkable, then, that the tourists seemed unaware that the conditions were of their own countrymen's doing. In 1882, pressure to end the inflow of people led Congress to place the Chinese in a special category along with imbeciles, paupers, and prostitutes that prohibited them from entering the United States or achieving U.S. citizenship. This shameful Chinese Exclusion Act, passed just six years before the Spalding tour, remained on the books until 1943. The Chinese struggled against discrimination without much success. They stuck to themselves, creating in Chinatown an almost all-male outpost where they assembled into a bachelor society governed by family rules, ancient rituals, and crime bosses.[5]

To their credit, the tourists seemed shocked by what they saw, but disgust betrayed whatever sympathies they had. White officials considered the Chinese to be filthy, incurable medical menaces who were just too different to be assimilated into American society. Indeed, journalist Palmer remarked that living conditions were "simply beyond the power of human conception until seen." American tenement houses, added Anson, were "a disgrace to modern civilization," but the Chinese versions were "much worse than any of these as can be imagined" because the buildings were so crowded. Landlords often leased a building four stories high, then deepened the foundation to add two floors, and partitioned off quarters so that six hundred people could live in apartments that could accommodate no more "than thirty or forty Americans comfortably." Into these rooms they jammed clothing, eating utensils, and "their opium outfit, without which no Chinaman could exist." As they threaded their way through the streets, the travelers snatched nervous glances at "hordes of almond-eyed, villainous-looking, and at times murderous faces peering at us from every nook and corner." Exiting the quarters, Palmer was anxious "to again breathe the air of a Christianized and civilized community." He unintentionally summed up the experience as a lesson in the superiority of whites. It appeared evident to him that the Chinese had no religion "save idolatry," having "brought their heathenish customs and horrible practices of their barbarous country with them to San Francisco." Because "virtue is unknown," he was convinced of "the hopelessness of converting them to our views of life and religion and of their ever becoming desirable citizens."[6] Thus, encouraged to join the world labor pool and allowed to cross borders as global migrant workers, the Chinese were, nonetheless, targets of racist sentiment in America and, for that matter, wherever they landed.

Although more sympathetic to the Hawaiians than to the Chinese, white Americans like the baseball tourists held similar prejudicial views toward these islanders. In fact, the ongoing urge among the more imperial-minded policy makers in Washington, D.C., to annex the Sandwich Islands stemmed, in part, from the fear that white Americans were vastly outnumbered by other racial groups there, including native Hawaiians, Japanese, Chinese, and Portuguese.[7] The tourists saw this firsthand and told of their experiences in terms quite jarring for modern tastes.

## A PROTECTORATE OF PREJUDICE

The main accounts of the tour by Anson, Palmer, and outfielder Jimmy Ryan all alluded to color even before the tourists landed on Honolulu's docks. Welcoming the Spalding party to the "Paradise of the Pacific" waited a crowd of dignitaries and baseball fans of all colors. Ryan noted the "dark skinned natives" on shore, while Palmer and Anson gazed down on "dark-complexioned, straight-haired fellows, with regular features and bright, intelligent faces." Such traits distinguished the native Hawaiians from the white entrepreneurs who had built their sugar mini-empires in the islands. While we should not apply contemporary standards to people who lived more than a century ago, the tourists implicitly recognized that they were racially ordering those they met on their trip.

The Hawaiian Islands had long been the crossroads of trade and shipping in the Pacific, an outpost for white missionaries, and recently, a source of political intrigue by investors and plantation owners bent on having the United States absorb the territory into the Union. Overcoming opposition from the U.S. domestic sugar lobby to the duty-free entry of Hawaiian sugar, American officials signed a sugar reciprocity treaty with King David Kalakaua in 1875. Hawaiian production of sugar, unrivaled in quantity anywhere else in the world, rose into the late 1880s, but the favorable trade treatment came at a price. Under the treaty, the monarchy could not make economic or territorial concessions to a foreign power. This restriction converted Hawaii into an American domain in all but the legal sense; the king was so dependent on U.S. consumers, investors, and protection that when the special sugar tariff arrangement ended in 1890, the Hawaiian economy fell into depression. Kalakaua, therefore, encouraged annexation as the sole way for native Hawaiians to survive a worse fate under white imperialism.

Thus, white Hawaiians of American and European descent dominated the islands. Such businessmen as sugar magnate Charles Spreckels—owner of the Oceanic Steamship Company, which controlled the sea lanes between the United States and Hawaii and under which the *Alameda* sailed—as well as religious groups, shared power. They tightened the U.S. hold even more by renewing the reciprocity treaty in 1887 under terms that gave the United States exclusive rights to the strategic Pearl Harbor base. Naval officials coveted the port, and President Grover Cleveland admitted that its acquisition was the only way to persuade a protectionist-minded Congress to continue the duty-free sugar deal for Hawaiian producers. The naval base ensured that Hawaii would remain in U.S. hands as a stepping-stone to exploiting other Asian markets. Indeed, a British traveler noted in 1888 the pervading "American element" in Honolulu; geographically, this was the tropics but "you are morally in America" because the legal system, economy, and customs were governed by the United States.[8] As Secretary of State Thomas Bayard remarked, America could "wait quietly and patiently and let the islands fill up with American planters and American industries until they should be wholly identified with the United States. It was simply a matter of waiting until the apple should fall."[9] It took a decade before the apple would drop into American hands, but as the Spalding tourists landed, the new Harrison administration planned to make Hawaii a protectorate.

In their day in Hawaii, Spalding and company benefited not only from imperialist plans but also from a long history of baseball in the islands. The game was played there well before the so-called Father of Baseball, Alexander Joy Cartwright, settled in Honolulu in 1849. Cartwright receives the lion's share of the credit for codifying the rules of the sport when he played for the New York Knickerbockers in the 1840s. Caught up in gold rush fever, he had departed from the hotbed of baseball for California, but after contracting dysentery, doctors advised him to recover in Hawaii. He promoted the game there while also managing the finances of the royal family by drawing on his expertise as a former bank clerk, until he died and was buried in Hawaii in 1892.[10] There is no indication Cartwright met the tourists, but his influence over their game had been sizable. Baseball was popular in the islands; a bitter rivalry, for instance, existed between two local white Honolulu clubs that stirred the fans and stimulated interest in the game.

Upon docking, the Spalding party drove quickly through streets lined with palm, banana, and coconut trees and American flags, past King Kalakaua's palace, to the sumptuous Royal Hawaiian Hotel, a place fit for "some Sandwich Island or Cuban sugar king," where they listened to the king's band play the welcome song, "Aloha Oe." They then ate a breakfast of tropical fruit and the native pink-colored poi, a pasty mush, with their fingers. The white reception committee and U.S. minister in the islands,

George Merrill, informed Spalding that the king had requested him at his palace later that morning. A parade of players, ladies in carriages, the band, and other members of the entourage fell in behind Clarence Duval, who tossed his baton in the air and led the group to the Royal Palace. Festivities would have to do, for the tourist's overdue arrival prohibited an exhibition game. Despite a petition from fans, the local Sunday statute (a holdover from missionary influence) banning all amusements remained in force, to the disappointment of a crowd of fans. Spalding was tempted to defy the law and grab the $1,000 bonus purse and the promise of a percentage of the gate receipts. The king, moreover, would have been present with his household and army officers of sixty men, nobility would have filled the boxes, and subjects the bleachers. But Spalding honored local rules throughout the tour, including the Sunday blue laws.

In any event, although the scenery that the party then saw was spectacular, just as striking were their views of these people of color, for race was ever-present in their minds. Sunlight warmed the tourists as they explored the magnificent mountain scenery of the Pali, boarded the U.S. warship *Alert* for a look around, saw the Royal Mausoleum, and drove past broad-porticoed mansions of wealthy sugar barons. They actually stopped at John Cummins's estate for music, song, and refreshments on a verandah festooned with U.S. flags. These were wonderful sights, but the people were most fascinating. Descriptive chronicles were destined for readers who reveled in the exotic, but the tone and substance of the commentary reveals certain prejudices. For example, the tourists had eaten breakfast with crowds of "dark-skinned, dark-eyed Kanakas [native Hawaiians]," the same supposedly "hot-headed Kanakas" who had expressed their disappointment that baseball would not be performed that day, wrote Harry Palmer.[11]

Spalding cared less about the canceled game than about the promotional coup he had scored by getting into the palace to meet King Kalakaua, who was a survivor of intrigue and changing times. The first-ever elected king, he had won the throne in 1874 only after British and American marines put down a revolt by the queen dowager. A product of sorts of globalization, Kalakaua had then traveled to the United States, the first king of Hawaii to do so, and had become the first monarch ever to address Congress. A few years later, in 1881, he set out on his own world tour, visiting Tokyo, Hong Kong, London, Lisbon, and other cities. Known as the "Merry Monarch," he cherished Hawaii's native heritage, which was gradually disappearing, while he gave land to sugar barons like his poker-playing friend Spreckels and repealed prohibitions on lotteries, opium, and liquor. In 1887, antimonarchists and the business community, appalled by his loose morals and embrace of foreigners, stripped him of most of his powers under a new "Bayonet Constitution." As a figurehead,

Kalakaua merely played at being king; in fact, he was Hawaii's last ruling monarch. Yet his extensive world travels also provided useful diplomatic ties for Hawaii, and some believed him to be farsighted as he negotiated between modern ways and the preservation of native culture.

Wearing plain civilian clothes, Kalakaua welcomed the tourists, surrounded by his cabinet and courtiers and standing in front of his large throne at one end of a long room hung with ancestral paintings. He was not descended from the Kamehameha line of rulers that preceded him, but he played the monarchical part nonetheless. After chatting lightheartedly, talking baseball with Spalding and Merrill, this "King of the Cannibal Islands," as excited players referred to Kalakaua, dismissed the party. The players signed the court register and exited past full-size photographs of King Kalakaua wearing Masonic regalia; the monarch, like his predecessors, had embraced Freemasonry. The baseball tourists then returned to the hotel.[12]

Although the king's palace was stupendous, Kalakaua himself had undergone microscopic anthropological description and a bit of ridicule. Anson thought him "not a bad-looking fellow, being tall and somewhat portly, with the usual dark complexion, dark eyes and white teeth, which

*Foreground: King David Kalakaua (left) and the Queen (right) of Hawaii.*

(Harry C. Palmer, *Athletic Sports in America, England, and Australia.*
Philadelphia: Hubbard Brothers, Publishers, 1889, p. 211)

were plainly visible when he smiled, that distinguished all of the Kanaka race." Contrast this to the remarks of a British visitor, who focused not on physical traits but on the king's mastery of diplomacy and impressive ability to speak English. As Anson gazed at the king during the audience, a child's song about cannibalism came over him, although such silliness had not occurred to him when meeting President Cleveland. Likewise, pitcher John Tener related more denigrating nonsense, when he wrote that Jim Fogarty had wagered that he would "go up, slap Kalakua [sic] on the back and say, 'How are you, old man.'" Fogarty's "courage" failed him.[13] Such treatment spoke to the antics and lighthearted mores of young male Americans, but it also reflected the belittling nature of their perspectives of nonwhites, even if such disparagement was not conscious.

The special luau called by the king that evening offered more insights into island anthropology. This feast, which Palmer deemed the most beautiful event of the tour, took place at the illuminated grounds of the queen's residence. A tree-lined avenue led to a fruit grove, lit by multicolored Japanese lanterns. Two hundred guests had been invited, including the U.S. minister, officers of the *Alert*, and sugar magnate Cummins, who stood with King Kalakaua, the king's sister, Prince Kawanonakoa, and the royal cabinet. Dressed casually in a suit of white linen and a hat, Kalakaua greeted the players under a tree planted to commemorate the monarch's birth. He impressed the patronizing Palmer as a man "in the prime of life and full vigor of manhood," but equally stunning were the half-dozen pretty girls with "Italian-like complexions" who placed leis on the visitors. The latter were astonished because these "dusky beauties" exposed their arms and shoulders in their affectionate welcomes. At the luau table, laden with poi, meat, fruit, and wine in the center of the grass-covered grove, a hundred "white-clad Kanaka women" waved bright-colored fans to ward off mosquitoes. The guitars and songs of the native boys, perfume of the tropical foliage, and lanterns and oil flames of torches made for an "intoxicating" atmosphere. Palmer wondered where the Kanaka women had learned their "table etiquette" when they plunged "two rosy fingers" into the poi.[14]

The banquet proceeded to toasts and entertainment. His Majesty's attorney-general welcomed the tourists, and Spalding replied with a tribute to Hawaii. Frank Lincoln got the king laughing with a satire on after-dinner speeches, while the players mingled with "scores of dark-eyed Hawaiian beauties." But the king had one more request; he wanted to witness a plantation "breakdown" by Clarence Duval. Just before departing for the ship, the black mascot performed to the clapping hands of Tommy Burns, Fred Pfeffer, Jimmy Ryan, and Ed Williamson. The plantation atmosphere could not have been more suitable, but the irony of Kalakaua, a man of color, laughing at "the little darkie's 'pigeon-wings' and 'walk-arounds'" before rewarding "the little coon" with a ten-dollar gold piece, showed the king was steeped in the ways of white imperialism.[15] If Hawaiians were interesting human specimens, American blacks occupied an even lower rung of respect in a global hierarchy of race.

For that matter, the diminutive Duval knew his place and how to make a livelihood, but he also was a survivor of the vicious racist times of the late 1880s. Degradation was commonplace, even for those times. For instance, the braid, lace, and brass-buttoned red outfit, with white pants and high-topped boots, that he wore—the "paraphernalia of a drum-major's make-up," wrote Palmer—signaled his status as a lowly mascot, an item of interest ranking among the curiosities at a circus. Marching with his silver-tipped baton, or dancing to rhythmic clapping by "expert members of the party"—experts supposedly in the denigrating black entertainment of the old plantation—Duval had to perform or seek employment elsewhere. If his public image and treatment were not brutal enough, the derogatory epithets and plain racist nicknames kept him in his place. Thus, this "impish-faced negro" cavorted for the king, to the delight of all.[16]

Duval was a black man whose sole value lay in his ability to play the

*Duval's "pigeon-wings."*

(Harry C. Palmer, *Athletic Sports in America, England, and Australia.*
Philadelphia: Hubbard Brothers, Publishers, 1889, p. 227)

stereotypical role of an infantile, simple, and wholly physical person of color who occupied the menial ranks of American imperial fantasies. The entourage, for instance, mimicked his accent. When Anson gruffly had asked "the little coon" where he had been after he had shown up in Omaha, Duval had responded, "Miss Jarbeau don gimme my release dis mawnin," and went on to plead his case for reinstatement as if he were a runaway slave returning to a plantation.[17] Spalding had nothing but contempt for Duval, although he recognized his entertainment value, and the rest of the tourists viewed him as "so utterly worthless and so trifling that, despite his dancing powers, we should not have been sorry had he been left in America."[18] But why not take him along as an exemplar of white superiority or, better, of colored inferiority? During the tour, Clarence Duval was a constant reminder, but not the only sign, of the racial pecking order in white American global standards.

Duval's exhibition ended, the tourists boarded the *Alameda* at ten o'clock that night and departed Honolulu for New Zealand, some 3,900 miles away. Their fond memories of their happy day in Hawaii included the "dusky" women and interest in, more than true respect for, King Kalakaua. One commentator on the tour summed up that the islands were "no longer in need of missionary rule," for they now enjoyed "a state of civilization and advanced progress which many an older kingdom might well feel proud." All that was needed was a Honolulu-to-San Francisco cable, and "fast rising" trade and commerce of "public spirited citizens in Hawaii" would tie the islands to the United States permanently and shut out Britain and other imperial powers.[19]

When it came to Hawaii, trade, investment, and technology melded profitably, but race also mixed with imperial aspirations. Although the coup against Kalakaua's successor, Queen Liliuokalani, four years after the tour would fail to convert the islands into U.S. territory, in 1898 America formally annexed Hawaii. The reasons given are many and varied, including the desire to curb the influence of Japanese and other Asian residents from Asianizing Hawaii. Even the quite significant congressional opposition to annexation, moreover, was based on racial considerations. As anti-imperialist senator Richard Pettigrew proclaimed, Hawaiians were "the scum of the world" and "little less than slaves."[20] Racial denigration by residents and transnational visitors alike, however, in a claim to superiority that was implicit in the baseball tourists' inappropriate views of King Kalakaua, also laid the groundwork for the imperial seizure of power.

## COMMONWEALTH COUSINS

The voyage to New Zealand, begun upon departure from Honolulu on Sunday, November 25, took nearly two weeks. Sailing southwest through stifling hot weather, cooling squalls, and the crossing of the equator early in the morning of December 1, the tourists amused themselves with antics, mock trials, music, slumbering on deck, watching Captain Morse box or listening to his sea-dog stories, and cricket practice. Spalding expected to play as much of this British game as baseball, particularly in Australia, and so an old cricket master, George Wright, supervised a half-dozen sailors in building a canvas-covered alley to prevent the balls from going overboard. Then the players took bowling and batting practice—Anson showing an affinity for the sport—and thus remained in shape during the long trip.[21]

During the night of December 3, they made their only sighting of land between Hawaii and New Zealand when the *Alameda* docked at a mailing station at the northern island of the Samoan group. Coincidentally, Samoa was recently witness to jostling between the United States, Imperial Germany, and Great Britain. Since obtaining the excellent harbor and naval port at Pago Pago in 1878, the United States vied for the favor of Samoan native chiefs, who played the three powers off of one another. All three nations had promised to preserve the sovereignty and independence of Samoa. The tourists were well aware of the conflict that was reaching a climax as they approached the port of Tutuila. Revolution was ninety miles to the south and had been headline material. As well, the Cleveland administration's tough stance had upset German Americans, who turned against the president and helped unseat him in the 1888 election.[22]

On this Monday, race consciousness surfaced again. The *Alameda* anchored a half-mile offshore for an hour and picked up the foreign-bound mail and two New Zealand passengers from two small boats. Uneasy with the unstable situation, the tourists surmised that had it been daytime, "our ship would have been surrounded with canoes filled with natives" from which they would have gotten souvenirs, or, perhaps, have been attacked. Samoans did not come close by, except, wrote Anson, for "a red-headed and stalwart specimen of his race" with "copper-colored skin" who climbed up the side of the *Alameda*, took the purser's receipt for the mail sacks, and tossed down a large cup of gin before jumping back in his dory.[23] There was only this opportunity to gaze upon a light-skinned Polynesian. The Spalding tourists could not attest to the Samoans' supposed "charm of appearance and manner, combined with greater mental capacity" than other Pacific islanders, such as the Fijians, especially because the man lacked his native costume. How they could discern intelligence is impossible to know, although they satisfied their scientific observations that the bronze of the Samoans had a copper tinge to it.[24] In any case, the tourists headed back out into the foaming, rough seas for Auckland.

Losing a day as the *Alameda* crossed the International Date Line, the entourage labored through cold weather, boredom with shipboard life despite cricket practice and the nighttime views of the Southern Cross, arriving in Auckland's picturesque harbor on December 9. Again, the fans and players suffered from bad timing; the Sunday arrival brought the tourists to New Zealand a day later than scheduled, and hence the crowd of an estimated ten thousand people remained in church rather than at the wharf to greet them. Still, a nephew of Leigh Lynch, Spalding's overseas planner, presented flowers to the travelers and then introduced several journalists, who had also spread news of the ballplayers' visit in their newspapers during the previous weeks.

Because the *Alameda* required a double load of coal to compensate for a labor strike in Sydney, it would take until the following day for refueling, and thus the tourists scrambled off the ship into the quiet town. After buying strawberries at the few open fruit stands, they went to the Imperial Hotel for a midday banquet and then either toured the seaport or climbed up the extinct volcano, Mount Eden, in a drizzling rain. Cultural sights supplemented the natural beauty. The party met a Maori chief, "a big, broad-shouldered man with an intelligent face and curves tattooed fancifully over his nose, on his cheeks and over his eyebrows."[25] With newsmen in tow, the players returned to the hotel.

The next morning, they attended a reception with the mayor of Auckland before readying for their game. Journalists had advertised baseball, noting that the tour had "caused perhaps the greatest amount of interest and curiosity ever manifested concerning the advent of any sporting or athletic combination" in the colony. Before explaining the rules, they reminded readers that cricket played by the "knights of the willow" would be suspended so all could travel to the grounds in special tramcars to watch "their brethren of the club and diamond." For those who might still balk, the papers announced that Professor Bartholomew would ascend in his balloon and fall back to earth in his parachute.[26]

At noon, a local band marched behind Clarence Duval at the head of a procession of carriages to the *Alameda* and escorted the players into the Tramway Company's grounds at Epsom, a field of level ground and velvety grass. The teams played in a blustery wind in front of 4,500 mostly bewildered spectators, who sat in a pavilion decorated with U.S. and British flags. It was the tourists' first game in a month, and the pitcher's showed their rustiness as Chicago won a laughably unscientific game, 22–13. The heavy batting appealed to the New Zealanders, who were surprised when the White Stockings took a 10–0 lead after two innings, then added another ten runs, while All-America could not score enough in batches. The only negative of the day came when high winds forced the cancellation of the Proff's leap from the balloon.[27]

Like other British subjects, New Zealanders seemed primed for the gospel of baseball. International sports had flourished from the 1870s. Travel became easier, financing sports was not as expensive as before, professionalism emerged, and the media publicized a new culture of sports. American baseball followed suit. Yet in this globalized era of transport, the British especially played sports farther from home, and modernizing nations adopted new forms of recreation in response to England's lead. Part of Britain's imperial strategy depended on acculturating colonial subjects, as well as the British middle class, to the "games ethic" of fair play, order, and elite-led rule making. In essence, American baseball, like other sports, arrived abroad (in baseball's case, in Cuba and Japan) as a function of Victorian-era imperialism. It did so, in part, by trumpeting national ideals and ideas of culture. An international baseball league emerged in the 1880s, while several countries, particularly Britain and its colonies and commonwealth, established franchises as the basis for forming leagues and championship series.[28]

Into this milieu entered Albert Spalding. In the colonies and nations his world tour targeted, he did not hesitate to provide cultural reasons why he was there. He set out, in short, to internationalize baseball, believing the sport was destined to become "the universal game of the world." Spalding thought his tour made headway toward that goal, although he claimed that the sport's adoption was impracticable in many places because of their distinct customs. Yet he posited that devising global contests between the United States and other "English-speaking countries" would "cement a friendly feeling between these nations." Baseball served as a cultural diplomatic emissary.[29] The rest of the world might be dragged along by the modern Anglo-Saxons. Hence, the importance of traveling the civilized world of the British Empire and Europe.

Spalding was as convinced of the supremacy of baseball as British empire-builders were of their national superiority, but he faced a major challenge in convincing foreigners to accept the American pastime. Thus, he looked forward to the Australian leg of the trip. Cheered by two thousand locals, the tourist's ship sailed from Auckland at 5 P.M. on December 10 and headed for Sydney, Australia, some 1,240 miles distant. Spalding could be heartened by the verdict from New Zealand, that baseball improved upon English rounders and that the people of Auckland wished the Yankee ballplayers the best of luck in Australia.[30]

At long last, Spalding's tour was in its original destination, the Antipodes, to play the American game alongside the revered English sport of cricket. This part of the Spalding mission—of showing that baseball was equal to cricket—would therefore reveal Americans to be part of the "civilized world," as well as exemplars to the nonwhite world of "refinement," trumpeted revered journalist Henry Chadwick.[31] With such a foundation of racial hierarchy in place, economic globalization could proceed in an orderly and expansive fashion, and empire could be justified in the end. In sum, if baseball were played and accepted alongside cricket, it would be another way to solidify white preeminence in the global racial order.

## AUSTRALIAN ANGLO-SAXONS

Four days later, on Thursday, December 14, the tourists thankfully sighted the Australian coast after a rough voyage in heavy seas that sent many players to their cabins with seasickness. The headlands of Sydney grew more distinct as a pilot's tug made its way to the *Alameda*. On board was Leigh Lynch, the business manager, who informed the voyagers of the large reception awaiting them. He was true to his word, as several steamers, each with a band playing music and laden with spectators, escorted the ship into Sydney's beautiful harbor, set amid hills and parkland. Red, white, and blue bunting draped the port—even the lighthouse was covered—and the ship sailed under bunting strung between thirty miniature barques. The Stars and Stripes mingled with Union Jacks and hundreds of waving handkerchiefs, the "storms of cheers" and boat signals deafening. To enter the lovely port, a seat of British imperial power, was "glorious! It was soul-stirring!" recalled Henry Palmer. Anson thought it like a "fairyland," the grand residences topped with towers and turrets glistening in the sunshine.

The tourists disembarked to cheers at the wharf in Woolloomooloo Bay and four-horse coaches took them to the elegant Oxford and Grosvener hotels. American Consul G. W. Griffin issued a hearty welcome, and the tourists then retired to their rooms to ready for a performance at the Royal Theater that evening.[32]

They were "among friends," wrote Anson, and not just because of the reception, for Anglo-Saxon ties bound Americans to Australians, including shared racial beliefs, cultural backgrounds, nationalistic longings, and affinities for sports. Australian visitors to America applauded U.S. political traditions and noted the similarities between these developing settler nations. It did not hurt that the two helped each other economically, too. Trade between the Australian colony and the United States had multiplied since the 1876 Centennial Exhibition in Philadelphia, and ambitious advocates for U.S. commercial expansion and Anglo-Saxon unity called for even more.[33] To the delight of Australian ranchers, Consul Griffin had worked hard since early in the decade to reduce the 100 percent U.S. wool duty. American imperial observers also noted that Australia stood as a white, civilized outpost among the "multitudinous Asiatic races." Looking into the south seas toward the fruit and spice riches of Samoa, Fiji, and New Guinea, which imperialists claimed would be "peopled by the Anglo-Saxon race, and will no doubt become tributary to the new Commonwealth of Australia," Australians pushed for the shutting out of "aliens of inferior races" from its shores. Australia and the United States could embrace in a fellowship of common economic drive, political aspirations, and race.[34]

The displays of welcome and commonalities were abundant. For instance, the Royal Theater was decorated with U.S. flags and the ballplayers were applauded as they sat in their box seats before the performance of Americans James Cassius (J. C.) Williamson and his wife, Maggie Moore, in *Struck Oil*, a show they had first performed in 1874 on a tour of Australia. The tourists then went down to the stage to be received again by the audience. Cheers went up for "Baby Anson," and then a popular member of Parliament, Irish-born Daniel O'Connor, welcomed the Spalding party by noting its pluck in traveling so far from home without any guarantee against financial or artistic failure except the confidence in the genius of baseball and in the "sport-loving spirit of the Australian people." He closed by emphasizing that Americans and Australians "were members of the Anglo-Saxon race and sprang from the old English stock, and their games were not really very different." Spalding graciously responded by also linking the common heritage of baseballers and cricketeers. Returning to their seats, both nationalities could well appreciate a brief afterpiece on "the evils of Chinese Immigration," a farcical performance but also a reminder of the whiteness of the current and former British colonists: the American and Australian "cousins."[35]

From all reports, including some by the tourists, the vast Australian colonies in 1888 were full of ambitious citizens who were loyal to the British Crown, many of whom had left Britain to exploit the rich resources of the continent but had retained, and cultivated, their affection for the mother country. The colonists had grown up under British tutelage as part of "the English race," adopting the two-house parliament, free elementary education, roast beef and plum pudding on (in Australia, hot) Christmas days, well-watered gardens, and other English traditions. They proudly assumed the reigns of democracy and strived to live up to their motto of each generation, "Advance Australia." Advancement meant a good standard of living and pleasure-seeking for the people, relatively little social strife, and modernization of institutions. Although most of Australia was barren wasteland, the energy, relentless laboring, and the discovery of gold adapted them to the hardships. By the time of the world tour, life was not too arduous for most, though John Tener and other observers wondered how this "truly wonderful place" could have flourished with just three million souls, one good river, and railroads running through "a great barren country" larger than the United States.[36]

Like Americans, Australians were builders, determined to forge a viable economy and thriving culture. Aussies, like Americans in the West, were subject to boom-and-bust cycles of nature; a punishing drought had just given way to a wet season of revival. Unlike measuredly polite New Englanders, however, the Australasian adventurers were strikingly unrestrained in manners, delightfully generous to each other and to tourists. In general, wages were decent and prosperity widespread, so much so that the cities of Sydney, Melbourne, and Adelaide, like many communities in the United States, endowed new colleges, galleries, and libraries and promoted a growing leisure class of modest means. The growing middle class of young professionals born in Australia, as well as the well-to-do, welcomed cultural refinements, including ballroom dancing, theater, and sports. Indeed, Australians of all classes loved outdoor amusements, with football and regattas attracting tens of thousands of spectators. Cricket was a very popular game but it competed for attention with football, rowing, horse racing, and other sports. Men in particular prided themselves on their athletic abilities, as they did in the United States. Such lovers of the outdoor life were prime targets for Albert Spalding.[37]

Yet this very sporting tradition, as well as British cultural unity campaigns, also confronted Spalding. Australians weighed the merits of the American pastime, but they also maintained their loyalty to the British Crown and boosted their national self-esteem by promoting cricket. Tours of British cricketers to Australia—and Aussies returning the favor—had multiplied over the past decade and shown the sport's effectiveness as a tool of imperial accord. In fact, cricket knitted the empire together by colonial victories over the mother country; the British were, simply, well ahead of Spalding when it came to imperial promotional efforts through sports. In 1877, Australia won the first international test match in Melbourne, and then whipped the British in London five years later. British journalists sounded the death knell for their nation's supremacy in the imperial game.[38] If the British were so treated, baseball faced an even bigger hurdle of acceptance. In the end, only Spalding's tireless advertising machine and a feeling of Anglo-Saxon unity, rather than a love of baseball, brought out crowds to the exhibition ball games.

That unity was founded on a kinship of racial discrimination. Captain Morse of the *Alameda* had firsthand experience. In July, his ship was refused a berth in Sydney by the Federated Seamen's Union of Australia, which forbid its members to assist vessels carrying the English mails that employed Chinese labor. Many British and U.S. steamship companies benefited from the reliable and inexpensive work of Chinese seamen who faced prejudice from white union workers. Transporting the mail and cheap Chinese crews compelled Morse to anchor in the harbor and issue a protest through U.S. officials. He faced a threatening situation, and, moreover, he could not recoal. The Seamen's Union and the ship's owners, through the offices of Consul Griffin, struck a deal in which Morse would transport a group of Australian firemen and coal passers to San Francisco and back, in place of the Chinese, and pay them accordingly.[39] The matter was resolved in the name of maintaining wages in Australia, but it also carried the obvious racist overtones perpetrated by U.S. restrictions on Chinese laborers.

The Spalding party understood this racial sentiment, and, in fact, endorsed it by engaging in thoughtful displays of camaraderie and warmth. Crowds cheered the party as it rolled in carriages to meet Mayor John Harris, who wore his official purple and ermine robes at the Sydney Town Hall. He predicted Australians' adoption of baseball as they had American horse-trotting and rowing, the latter a reference to All-America's Ned Hanlon, a Canadian ex-champion sculler. Australian dignitaries also marketed the importance of sports to the masses by having popular leaders like O'Connor and Harris meet the party. Sports enhanced nationalism but also joined the Anglo-Saxons across the world into a band of brothers. Typically, Australians linked with countries that spoke English, inherited English laws and customs, adopted English religion, and read English literature. As the Australian premier Sir Henry Parkes announced in honoring Consul Griffin in 1888, notwithstanding the "German element," a "negro element, which will be one of the problems of the future," and "the many foreign elements" in the United States, Americans "are in their heart and soul" Australian kin, descended from the same mother country. They were even more than "American Cousins"; they held the possibilities of reuniting the English-speaking race into "one world-embracing empire."[40] The tourists understood such thinking, on and off the ball fields.

After absorbing the Anglo-Saxon unity theme at the mayoral meeting, the Americans entered the Association Cricket Ground to play their first game. The tourists noted that "in whatever other respects the Colonies might be inferior to the United States," the silky green and level athletic grounds were unparalleled in America by their lush appearance, convenience, or comfortable clubhouse. More than 5,500 appreciative and respectful spectators watched an exciting match, among them hundreds of ladies, cricketers, and such dignitaries as the governor of New South Wales, Lord Carrington, who received the players during a break after the sixth inning and wished them well on behalf of Australians and Queen Victoria. Cricket players noted the adept throwing, hard hitting, and quick base-running, and the teams played some of their best baseball of the tour in this game. With the score tied 4–4 from the first to the ninth innings, All-America finally pushed across the winning run on a hit, two stolen bases, and a wild pitch to win 5–4. The spectators were satisfied, though many were puzzled by the rapidity of play.[41]

During the fifteen-minute interval with Lord Carrington, Angus Cameron of the Cricket Association also shook hands with Spalding and the teams. Cricketers marveled at the quickness of baseball, the style of play, the game's duration, and the manner contests were decided. But after three weeks of witnessing the matches in Sydney, Adelaide, Ballarat, and Melbourne, they concluded that baseball was no better than a training sport over the winter for cricketers. Indeed, some observers were contemptuous, arguing that baseball merely professionalized the child's game of rounders (it was even played in children's knickers). If not for Spalding's energetic promotional activities and a feeling of goodwill toward America, the games would not have garnered much attendance. Spalding countered that cricket was, and would be, the national game for Britain and her colonies, but he also believed that baseball would attract the masses. Because cricket matches lasted two or three days, only the leisure class had time to master it. And with the thousands of cricketers in the country, establishing a few nines of baseball teams would not be difficult. The "new countries," like Australia, Canada, and the United States, where people were busy, would embrace baseball, he argued.[42]

This was more dreamy marketing, written after the tour had ended, for cricket would not be surpassed so easily. Sydney, Melbourne, and Adelaide hosted cricket associations and several world-traveling teams, and fans predicted that "it may not perhaps be rash to predict that in a few years Australia will be almost as far ahead of the mother country in cricket as she is in sculling," despite a population one-eighth of England's. Furthermore, while the popular Lord Carrington and other "respectable" fans attended cricket games in Sydney, spectators in Adelaide could sit on a nearby hill free of charge. With a proliferation of cricket clubs throughout Australia, the game drew a diverse lot of followers, as baseball did in America.[43]

Furthermore, Spalding got a taste of his own marketing medicine, for cricket had loyal adherents in America. Tourist George Wright won fame as an accurate bowler and a vigorous batsman. He had played throughout New England, where cricket had a foothold at Boston's Longwood Club, and he had accompanied the 1874 baseball tour to England to play the sport. A U.S. Cricketers' Association met annually, represented by teams throughout the East and Midwest, including Philadelphia, its home. The sport had been played in the American colonies and in twenty-two states before the Civil War, and it had a presence from Savannah to San Francisco. Transatlantic cricket tours were common; an English side visited Baltimore in 1886, followed by an Irish tour to America in 1888, and a Philadelphia team traveled to England the following year. West Indian teams visited the States, while Americans played in Jamaica and even more against Canadian clubs. Interest in cricket often seemed as high in the United States as it was overseas. Henry Chadwick wrote routinely about the game from the early 1870s onward by covering international matches, noting its popularity in New York, and urging its rules committee to make the administrative adjustments necessary to increase audiences.[44] There was a substantial international interchange in cricket among those of British heritage; in truth, it was baseball—which developed from cricket—that was the latecomer to transnational travel.

Cricket turned out to be a draw for the Spalding tourists, too. After the good turnout for the first baseball game, the numbers of spectators plummeted to 3,000 for the next game, two days later, which All-America won, 7–5, and to 2,500 for the third and final exhibition in Sydney on December 18, which gave Ward's side its third straight victory, 6–2. These games, however, were played around two cricket matches. The first, resulting in an All-America victory by a score of 67–33, pitted the two tourist teams against one another. The second one involved competition against Australian cricket players, who beat the tourists 115–87 even after allowing the Americans seventeen men to their eleven. Spalding's side sported only two bowlers, George Wright and Spalding himself, and thus was at a decided disadvantage. Spalding, despite his ambitions and pronouncements back home, likely realized he could do little more than educate Australians about baseball, because they were not about to abandon their national game.[45] Anyway, that baseball and cricket could serve as cultural unifiers was more to the point than the sometimes flat reception the U.S. pastime received at games.

The tourists enjoyed their three games in Sydney, but liked even more the surroundings and treatment they received. From Sydney harbor's aquariums to the fashionable Coogee Bay to a delightful concert at the Criterion Theater, they were feted. Tener ran across a relative at the Oxford Hotel, probably not the only instance when the Anglo-Saxons met distant family members who had migrated around the world. A final, two-hundred-plate English and American flag-bedecked banquet at Town Hall, attended by journalists and officials who toasted the queen, president, and governor, ended the Sydney leg. Among other pleasantries, the Australians, ever aware of the empire of race, prophesied a time when English "would be the language of the world, and England, America, and Australia be bound together in closest fellowships as one people."[46]

## IMPERIAL TIES

The next morning, Wednesday, December 19, before boarding the cramped English-style train for Melbourne with sounds of "Yankee Doodle" and

"The Star-Spangled Banner," cheers, and speeches ringing in their ears, the party procured Stars and Stripes buttonhole badges and straw hats with red-white-and-blue ribbon. The tourists had found their home away from home, and even the uncomfortable train car or rousting at 5:30 the next morning by customs authorities at the Victoria border did not dampen the spirits for their "cousins." Rather than complain, they were quick to point out that the roadbed was solid, the countryside beautiful, and the Victorian carriages much more suited in elegance than to those of New South Wales. When they arrived before noon in Melbourne to a waiting group of five hundred at Spencer Street station, the players could not but conclude that they had tightened the bonds of American–Australian relations.[47]

Melbourne matched, if not exceeded, Sydney's welcome. The city held a special place for the tourists as their original destination, and thus Spalding considered it home until he scheduled the tourists onward. The colony of Victoria had boomed during the gold rush after 1851, attracting a higher percentage of Scots and Irish than the other colonies. The capital's familiarity to the baseball tourists also stemmed from its rather exhilarating pace of growth and dynamism; many American firms and businessmen were active in the commercially oriented city of Melbourne. For their part, the residents knew a bit about baseball, having witnessed a whisky-laden exhibition by cricket clubs against the Georgia Minstrels some years back.[48] The tourists promised a more scientific, skilled, and serious exhibition, just as the great world exposition then occurring in Melbourne displayed the wonders of American wares and ingenuity.

By the 1880s, a maturing of overseas consular services aided U.S. travelers and businessmen, and thus Spalding's promotional ploy did not step into virgin territory. Going back to the Crystal Palace Exhibition in London in 1851 and moving forward to big international expositions in Paris and smaller ones in Sydney, Melbourne, Vienna, Germany, and elsewhere during the next three decades, Americans had readily displayed their gold-medal-winning wares, aided by Congress and the State Department. These venues provided another impetus to globalization by marketing goods, services, and ideas worldwide. Europeans, Asians, and British colonial subjects had seen the McCormick reaper, Goodyear rubber products, and American false teeth years before. In Paris in 1881, Edison's incandescent lamp had made a sensation. Soon legions of U.S. consuls had distributed handbooks describing the best sea and land routes to capital cities, as well as transportation schedules and hotel information for American travelers. A corrupt patronage system did not detract from the flow across the oceans of Americans who sold products. And all was not rotten, as U.S. officials took part increasingly in international conventions and congresses in the 1880s to set standards for shipping, exchanges of money, and even for peaceful resolutions of conflict.[49]

The Melbourne show, therefore, provided a familiar backdrop for entrepreneurs like Albert Spalding. Meeting the tourists at the train station, a reception committee made up of the U.S. consul-general of the Exposition, some U.S. residents, and the Victorian Cricket Association put the players in carriages and sent them up Collins Street to Town Hall. There, the mayor and members of the City Council stood before three thousand people and beneath a booming pipe organ that spilled out American and British songs. Lunch and speeches ensued, as Mayor Benjamin proclaimed the greatness of the United States, and Spalding stressed the affection Americans held for England, the Queen, and cricket. Then all retired to the Grand Hotel, known as the "Coffee Palace," which was situated near the Exposition and Treasury and Parliament buildings.

The players might roll their eyes at such high-falutin' talk, but they knew who buttered their bread. The hotel surpassed in luxury any accommodations thus far encountered on the trip. As in Sydney, the travelers attended the theater on the first night, seeing *The Princess Ida* at the Princess Theater. The owner, a partner of J. C. Williamson at the Royal Theater

*Melbourne Exposition building.*
(Harry C. Palmer, *Athletic Sports in America, England, and Australia.*
Philadelphia: Hubbard Brothers, Publishers, 1889, p. 264)

in Sydney, toasted the party after the third act in a special reception room. Topping off the evening, journalists from the major area newspapers expressed their hope that baseball would be established in Melbourne and throughout the colonies.[50]

The games that followed took place at the Melbourne Oval, the well-kept home of the Melbourne Cricket Club. The grandstands were packed on Saturday, as were the balconies and rooftop of the clubhouse. Nearly twelve thousand spectators appeared to see a good game pitched by Baldwin and Crane, with some excellent exhibitions of base-running and throwing, as Chicago broke its losing streak, 5–3. The locals had a good chance to see the attributes of their fellow Anglo-Saxons and "the splendid physical development of the boys and their skills as athletes—qualities of manhood which are not valued higher anywhere than in Victoria, and, in fact, throughout Australia," wrote Palmer.[51] Melbourne papers were even more effusive as they touched on the theme of the cultural and racial connections. One reporter hoped that the games would be the "first link of a mutual friendship between two island continents," and that Australia's acceptance of baseball would ensure that the United States "will always be on our side helping us on the onward path." Spalding later dedicated a special edition of *Spalding's Official Base Ball Guide* to the "sportsmen of Australia" who, like baseball players, displayed "all those essentials of manliness, courage, nerve, pluck and endurance, characteristic of the Anglo-Saxon race."[52]

Christmas Day found the tourists departing for Adelaide in ninety-degree weather, having played a 15–13 contest in front of six thousand fans the day before that saw All-America celebrating after both pitchers, Ryan and John Healy, took a pounding. To the thrill of the crowd, the "Proff" followed with his first ascent and parachute drop on Australian soil. That evening, a baseball farce played at the St. George's Theater, with a performance by "the little darkey" Clarence Duval to great applause and a significant shower of money. *The Age* of Melbourne had noted the "bright little black boy" at the game; "gaily attired as a courier," he delighted the crowd.[53]

The overnight trip to Adelaide, made in the comfort of a Mann Boudoir sleeper, whisked the entourage past sparse countryside full of farmers, fruit stands, and rabbits and into a depot of excited crowds. All the women and Ed Crane stayed behind in Melbourne due to the hot weather, which was unbearable in Adelaide. Peopled by a large proportion of English, as opposed to Irish or Scots, the colony of South Australia had seen hard times. Copper mining in the 1840s had drawn settlers, but the gold rush in Victoria during the next decade had lured many away. By the mid-1880s, South Australia's population dipped under 320,000 while New South Wales and Victoria attracted a million people each. Harsh, sweltering weather was a bane. Adelaide did not rate as a city on the scale of Melbourne or Sydney, and the people seemed more calm and quiet than in those places, more likely to enjoy the natural environment than fabricate cultural distractions.[54]

The mayor and the U.S. consul provided a lunch of champagne and sandwiches at town hall (their fifteenth reception in ten days), escorted them to their hotels after another "shake-down" by an overheated Duval, and then drove them out to the beautiful Adelaide Oval for their game. All-America won again, its fifth victory in six games in Australia, in a bat-cracking 19–14 game in front of an enthusiastic but largely confused crowd of two thousand who braved the heat and exempted themselves from the opening day at the racetrack. That evening included a play at the Royal Theater followed by a cool nighttime coach drive near the beach to the vineyard of Thomas Hardy & Sons, the largest grape and fruit growers in Australia. Wine making was a growth industry, and the Hardy family, and other South Australians, found their vast stretches of worn-out wheat land ideal for grapes and profits from the English market for Rieslings.

John Ward could have used a drink, although Australians preferred to toast the Americans rather than argue. Slightly more people witnessed a Chicago exhibition of base-sliding the next day in a 12–9 win, and unfortunately also saw Ward pitch for the first time in five years. Cap Anson and Tener both umpired the match and questioned the legality of his throws, in which Ward turned his back to the batter during his delivery. The Australians agreed with Anson that the style was deceptive and unsportsmanlike. Offering to step in behind the plate for Tener to pass judgment, Spalding angered Ward even further in front of the Australians, who were used to seeing better sportsmanship. On Friday morning, the tourists played their last game in Adelaide, a second consecutive win for the White Stockings, 11–4, and one seen by the governor of the colony, Sir William Robinson. He complimented the players on their "manly" prowess and reiterated an imperial sentiment he had heard from one of the tourists that "both in physical and other features Australia reminded you of your own great country at home."[55]

Then the party left overnight for the gold-mining town of Ballarat, awakening with a trip to the botanical gardens, a bath at the Swimming Aquarium, and breakfast at the Craig Hotel. Attired in overalls, boots, and slouch hats, they descended more than 1,100 feet to the slimy and wet bottom of the Barton Gold Mines. Gold had been discovered in Ballarat in 1851. Meeting the mayors of both West and East Ballarat, the tourists were taken to an orphanage, where they threw shillings into the bathhouse waters for the boys to dive after and then invited two hundred of them to the game that afternoon. For a small town, Ballarat turned out in impressive numbers for the match. Nearly 4,500 spectators saw All-America consistently hit its way to an 11–7 victory, but the sensation of the day was Professor Bartholomew. The Proff rose into the air in his balloon but plummeted back to Earth too fast in the high altitude, hitting an iron spike, part of an ornamental railing on the roof of the Buck's Head Hotel in the business district, and injuring both of this legs. The balloon landed in East Ballarat, and the Professor landed in the hospital, from which he departed a few days later to rejoin the tourists in Melbourne.[56]

Back in Melbourne, the welcome continued for several days. Clarence Duval did an "Alabama shakedown" and other plantation dancing before the colonists; he was the tourists' most interesting representative of U.S. culture. A contest of Australian-rules football took place between twenty baseball players and the St. Kildas squad, and then two thousand spectators watched Chicago double up their opponents, 14–7, on New Year's Day 1889. Considering that forty thousand residents were attending the races on that Tuesday at the Flemington horse track, and others went to cricket matches, this was a decent showing.

The day also offered a look into Australia's unfortunate minorities. A lunch hosted by cricketers gave way to a boomerang and rope-skipping demonstration by several aborigines, "black-faced, bushy-haired Queenslanders" who, Palmer, Anson, and others marveled, had attained a remarkable level of skill. Like the Americans with their indigenous Indians, the Australians had subjugated the aboriginal people on the continent to a place of distinct inferiority. They were laborers or, at best, curiosities, to be carted out and displayed for their prowess with boomerangs or simply for their "Neanderthal" appearance. In addition, other people of color suffered in the colonies, or were simply barred from them. These natives had shown prowess in boxing and cricket, but faced severe discrimination and segregation in both sports until the 1960s. Now, in 1889, they impressed with the boomerang, although the tourists implicitly viewed them as heathens and primitives. The boomerang proved impossible for the players to master; the rope-skipping, "which the natives are wont to amuse themselves, was a quite grotesque and yet clever performance" of squatting postures, wrote Palmer.[57]

In the interval between New Year's and January 7, the date set for departure from Australia, the tourists bought exotic souvenirs, visited the U.S. exhibit at the Melbourne Exposition, and played their final game, on Saturday, January 5. More than eleven thousand spectators appeared on a beautiful day, lining the Oval to see several exhibitions but really coming out in hopes of seeing Professor Bartholomew try to parachute again. He would not, hobbled as he was on crutches. First, All-America played a two-inning baseball game against a team of cricketers who hailed from the Melbourne Baseball Club, formed in the months prior. The Americans

*The flying "Proff" Bartholomew.*

(Harry C. Palmer, *Athletic Sports in America, England, and Australia.*
Philadelphia: Hubbard Brothers, Publishers, 1889, p. 161)

routed them. Then, a rugby game between Port Melbourne and Carleton took place, followed by a five-inning baseball matchup in which not one error was committed. Anson's side led 5–0 on superb batting and skilled base-running, with just one hit given up by Baldwin. The crowd appreciated the play, but they enjoyed even more the long-distance throwing efforts of hurler Ed Crane, who beat the cricket-ball record of 126 yards, 3 inches by more than $2^1/_2$ feet. Demonstrations completed, the tourists fanned out over Melbourne for their last day with their Australian cousins.[58]

While reminders of Anglo-Saxonism continued, others of racial separation persisted as well. That night, a fire alarm caused Fred Pfeffer and Clarence Duval, who was curled up in a blanket on the ballplayer's floor (a common arrangement because hotels did not allow blacks to register), to flee their room yelling "Fire!" down the hallways. It turned out to be a drunken prank perpetrated by some young travelers on the top floor, who also knocked out Manning by dropping an empty whisky bottle on his head as he gazed out his window. Duval was finally found, crouching behind a water cooler "trying hard to cover his black legs with a floor-rug," noted Harry Palmer.[59] Yet foreign natives also came in for similar derision. A cartoon showing the "results of the Spalding Tour" pictured excited natives running up to a shipwrecked sailor, asking for a pointer on baseball. The tribe wore comical skirts and hairpieces and begging looks on their faces, which were occupied by huge, out-of-proportion lips. Such racist caricatures were prevalent in the press and theater (such as minstrel shows) of the times, and they contributed to the rhetoric of both discrimination and race unity.[60]

On Monday, January 7, the party boarded the *Salier*, a ship commanded by a veteran of Indian Ocean crossings, Captain Thalenhorst of the German Lloyd Steamers company. As the tourists left, Australian newspapers had mixed reviews of the visit. Many delighted in the performance of baseball, but a handful claimed that the tour's success was due primarily to the puffery of the preliminary advertising and the drumming of journalists accompanying Spalding. Yet the receptions reproduced in Melbourne and Adelaide convinced Spalding that Australians might latch onto baseball—so convinced him, in fact, that he left behind in Melbourne his willing assistant Henry Simpson to teach the game. Within weeks, on January 18, 1889, Royal Theater director J. C. Williamson's Thespians took on Simpson's team in East Melbourne. In addition, Adelaide's several teams planned to use suburban cricket ovals as grounds, while Melbourne possessed six clubs with hundreds of paying members. Simpson, meanwhile, reported that a roving African-American troupe called Hicks-Sawyer's Minstrels played the Victoria club, beating them by one run on February 14 before a large turnout. Some months afterward, three games in Melbourne between a squad of cricketers from South Australia and one from Victoria represented the first intercolonial matchups. Sydney followed that August with a Sydney Baseball Club contest against the Union Club. Most teams fell prey to a lack of organization and interest or nationalistic discouragement by threatened cricketers.[61] Still, baseball emerged in Australia next to cricket, thanks to the Spalding tour.

Leaving the New Jerseyite Simpson and much goodwill behind, the tourists got ready for the next leg of their journey. They came down to the Melbourne docks, which were peopled, recalled Anson, by "Turks and Hindoos, with their dark skins, red turbans and bright costumes" who also waited to sail. They left Australia on the comfortably equipped ship with many of these "strange" people residing in steerage, and they departed with regrets. Having not shot a kangaroo or met a dangerous "bushranger"—who, like the outlaws of the American West, "had been wiped out by the march of civilization"—they felt slighted by not experiencing these two symbols of Australia.[62]

## THE UNCIVILIZED WORLD

The tourists soon believed they had entirely missed civilization as they circled the south of Australia, stopped to pick up a load of wool at Port Adelaide, and then crossed the Indian Ocean to the Suez Canal, planning to stop in Ceylon and India before reaching Egypt. Done for the moment with binding up the ties of empire with their Australian kin, the tourists returned to denigrating the colored subjects of the white imperial domain.

The two-week crossing was uncomfortably cool and rough at first, then sultry as the *Salier* crossed the equator. The distractions were few except for occasional schools of sharks. The tourists amused themselves by walking through the quarters of the 150 Hindu, Chinese, Cingalese, and European emigrants on board, fascinated by their "babble of tongues." Jim Fogarty nicknamed the forward steerage compartment the "Zoo" and even ran tours to show his fellow white passengers the "origins of the different animals and the different races of people." The "Hindoos" garnered the most interest because they cooked for themselves, refusing to let infidels defile their food, and also because they raffled their embroidered textiles (Anson won a silk pillow). After the body of an Indian was thrown overboard with no funeral services, Jimmy Ryan explained it was "because he was not a Christian." Meetings with the other white passengers also provoked curiosity. Two Australians, for example, headed for Zanzibar in "the dark continent." Imagine "facing the wild beasts and still wilder savages of Central Africa," wrote Harry Palmer, while "cut off from all connection of any and every kind with civilization." The Aussies would subject themselves to "savage tribes, who would be as likely to murder them for their weapons as not."[63] The racial pecking order was clear once again.

The tourists had their own "savage" on board in Clarence Duval, and they made him pay. Because the German waiters treated him kindly, perhaps to irritate the tourists, Anson mocked him as an "Indian Prince." Taking umbrage, Spalding suggested to Captain Thalenhorst that Duval be put to work, and the captain obliged by having him pull the punka rope that swung the big tapestry fans suspended over the saloon tables. This offended Duval, who was further humiliated when players threw biscuits at him. Such treatment did not end there. During a torpid "insufferably stupid" day, Fogarty and some others held a mock trial in which they sentenced "Clarence Duval, our chocolate-colored mascot" to a bath. Mark Baldwin recovered Duval from his hiding place in steerage and hosed him down until the saltwater tank was empty. "A madder little coon than he was when released it would have been difficult to find," wrote Pop Anson. In rage, Duval wielded a baseball bat but soon calmed down, rescuing his dignity by introducing the "negro game" of craps to the passengers. Still, all made fun of his calls of "Come, seben" and "come along dar eight," expressions without which, Palmer and Anson claimed, "no American negro ever engaged in his favorite method of gambling."[64] To deal with a large shark that followed the ship, Anson pondered offering Duval as bait to catch it. The "pickaninny" objected so forcefully, that the tourists "chose salt pork instead."[65] That the white tourists gave hardly a thought to such prejudice was evident.

Fortunately for Duval, Ceylon was sighted on January 25 after a night of gales and lightning, and the tourists could turn some of their attention back to the foreign people of color. Surrounding the ship as it steamed into the harbor of Colombo in the afternoon were bands of "natives," dark-skinned boatmen in skimpy or no clothing. Dropping anchor, the harbormaster came out on a boat sailed by native Cingalese, their long hair rolled into a knot in back and held with big tortoise-shaped combs. Palmer found that they "chattered and gesticulated like a lot of monkeys," but he and the tourists also were occupied with others, such as the young boys who dove "like otters" for coins. The waters were full of multicolored, odd-shaped fishing boats and the docks swarmed with Cingalese, Malays, and Hindus as the entourage made its way to the elegant Grand Oriental Hotel to await word whether they would continue on with the *Salier* to India, or if Spalding's advance agent had made other plans. That evening, after lounging on Turkish divans and eating dinner under punka fans, they learned from the U.S. consul that Calcutta was

*Duval punished.*

(Harry C. Palmer, *Athletic Sports in America, England, and Australia.*
Philadelphia: Hubbard Brothers, Publishers, 1889, p. 291)

just too unhealthy and the steamship and railway connections too inconvenient for travel to India.

Thus, they spent a day in the ancient British colony of Colombo in Ceylon (today, Sri Lanka), which proved to be a laboratory of racial differences. Americans had first made contact with Ceylon in 1788 in order to gain access to the East Indies, and since then, missionaries, traders, and educators had expanded their presence. The tourists rode in jinrickshaws, pulled by "sinewy" Cingalese who trotted "as easily and rapidly as a horse could draw you." Spalding was particularly infatuated with this mode of transport, imagining himself relaxing in one as he circled the ballpark in Chicago. The market and business quarters were unforgettable, peopled more thickly than Chinatown by "dusky inhabitants," cows and carts filling the streets and noisy crows fluttering about. Buying white suits with bright-colored sashes draped around the waist, and topped off with a cork hat with a silk scarf to protect the neck from sun, the tourists took on an "Oriental appearance" as they donned the dress worn by the "higher classes and by all Europeans living in Ceylon and India." Then they made their way down a beautiful beach road past Buddhist temples to a shipboard visit on the U.S. corvette *Essex*, along the way fending off cries of "mastah, mastah" from beggars who had perfected their professions "to a fine art" and stopping to see a snake-charmer mesmerize a cobra. They were not allowed in the temples, which they might have desecrated anyway to their peril; Ceylon was the most revered place of Cingalese Buddhism in India. On board the *Essex*, the sailors cheered particularly at Clarence Duval's plantation shakedown routine.[66]

By afternoon, it was time to suit up in baseball uniforms. The procession moved by heavy-wheeled covered carts pulled by humpbacked bullocks, with whites sitting in chairs and natives on the floor, cross-legged, out to the Colombo Cricket Grounds under the awed gazes of the "howling, chattering, grotesquely-arrayed" Cingalese, who were stunned by the circus atmosphere. The tourists were just as surprised by the wild confusion, but impressed by the elegant cricket lawns surrounded by coconut trees and stretched away to the ocean sands on one side. A crowd of five thousand people encircled a baseball diamond, with the crew of the *Essex* and English residents—spectators of cricket and lawn tennis—joined by enthusiastic Cingalese. The five-inning, 3–3 tie game met the approval of the Englishmen and seamen. The Americans loved the military band on the clubhouse balcony, along with Scottish Highlander bagpipers below, who gave a colonial meaning to "picturesque." The natives enjoyed the

*Clash of cultures: Business in Colombo, Ceylon.*
(Harry C. Palmer, *Athletic Sports in America, England, and Australia*.
Philadelphia: Hubbard Brothers, Publishers, 1889, p. 298)

batting most of all; when a ball zoomed toward them, they tumbled out of the way, "chattering like a lot of magpies," reported Harry Palmer.[67]

Colombo offered up such an alien culture that the tourists were ready to leave that afternoon; they journeyed back to the hotel and out to the waiting ship by five o'clock. Beggars and peddlers watched carefully, joined by "blacks, bullock carts, and jinrickshaws" and "hordes of natives" who saw off the party. John Tener, speaking for the tourists, had had enough of the people. "They are nearly all darkies and after awhile, you get tired of looking at them and hearing their funny talk," he wrote home. "The first thing they are taught is to beg and most of them do nothing else all their lives."[68] John Ward summed it up as a "queer sort of a place inhabited by a queer sort of people."[69]

The sun sank as the *Salier* left the harbor and out to sea on that Saturday, January 26, to sail under blue skies in balmy temperatures to the Gulf of Aden. The second day out, the ship fired its cannon in honor of the German emperor's birthday, but a few tourists pulled a prank by scampering around the decks claiming pirates were nearby. Anson placed his wife's diamonds in his mouth and wielded a bat. Playing his plantation boy role, a terrified Duval became the brunt of the joke and disappeared in shame until the evening.

After watching the boatloads of "chattering, black-bodied fellows" and scantily clad Arabs in the port of Aden, and whipping through the town's curio shops in just an hour, the ship proceeded into the Red Sea. The air seemed not as sultry as predicted, and the sights of rock formations arising from the sea, beautiful islands, and occasional boats of "Mohammedans" making for Mecca made for a pleasant trip. The *Salier* sighted Mount Sinai and then entered the harbor of Suez on Thursday, February 7, anchoring among an English troop ship, an Italian man-of-war, and dozens of small Egyptian vessels noisy with the "unintelligible chatter of a new race of people."[70]

## BARBARISM IN PHARAOH'S LAND

So began a four-day visit to Egypt, notable for offensive behavior indicative of the tourists' profound racism. Rushing past camels, donkeys, and white-turbaned, shoeless Arabs, the party immediately boarded a train for Cairo, the Egyptian capital. It was a relief to pull out of Suez, with its dirty structures and the "general shiftlessness" that made its people "the most thoroughly antique of all the antiquities of this nineteenth century," Palmer and Anson agreed. Traveling through a countryside of dilapidated mud huts did not improve their opinion, but the view of the Suez Canal and then the rich Nile River Valley, its fields of grain and clover dotted with groves of palms and acacias and flocks of sheep and goats, impressed them. When seeing a waterwheel used as an irrigation pump, instead of an efficient motorized American one, they got a dim but definite understanding that this ancient land had ways different from theirs.

Still, the clash of cultures was evident. Each train station revealed Bedouins and other locals, the men muscular "but servile of manner," the veiled women "disfigured" by the Egyptian brass ornaments hanging from their heads and their figures "thick-set without the faintest suspicion of contour." The Egyptians took fright at a station twenty miles from Cairo when Jimmy Ryan dressed Clarence Duval in his drum-major suit, put a catcher's mask on his face, and fastened a rope around his waist. He had the mascot jump around like a monkey, scaring the "unsophisticated natives," who thought he was a great ape. Nobody could blame them, wrote Palmer in an unmistakable revelation of race-ordering, "for could a disciple of Darwin have seen the mascot in his impromptu make-up, his heart would have bounded with delightful visions of the missing link."[71]

Journalist Palmer typified the American views of the nineteenth-century traveler to the Near East, who gazed enviously on the work of colonialism. Like others, he found stark contrasts in customs and conditions, and everywhere the racial stereotypes seemed evident. In Egypt, the people were either exotic inhabitants of a beautiful and historical land, or barbarians existing in backwardness. Sometimes they seemed to climb to the stature of Westerners in modernity; oftentimes their odd ways and squalor perplexed tourists, and they emphasized the strangeness of these diverse people. "It is a strange land and a still stranger people," followed Palmer.[72] A sophisticate like Mark Twain had wondered, too, about the ways of the Levant in *Innocents Abroad*, alternating between bemused irony, bewilderment, and occasional hostility. Like many travelers, he fell into the common trap of stereotyping the Muslims and Arabs as indolent, stupid, or barbaric. Little did they comprehend the cultural complexity of Egypt.[73]

For example, there was Cairo. Known as the Paris of Africa—though a sunnier version—it was a cultural, government, and economic center in which people from east and west converged. Englishmen in frock coats jostled trousered Turks and turbaned Egyptians, and a babble of Arabic, French, German, and Greek could be heard amidst the rush of cabs, carriages, camels, and donkeys. From the tourist's Hôtel d'Orient, they ogled at the diverse number of nationalities smoking, drinking chocolate, and spinning roulette wheels at bars and cafés in the area. The French brasseries never seemed to close, and the night, concluded Cap Anson, hid the squalor and filth that seemed typical of "all oriental cities and towns."

Yet while it retained vestiges of the "Arabian Nights" in its palaces and bazaars, and a biblical hold on the imagination, by the time the tourists arrived, Cairo had been Europeanized. Cafés and casinos proliferated, as did electricity, hotels, and theaters. In its cosmopolitanism, Cairo had lost some of its picturesque character while enjoying such modern amenities as telegraph service and even telephones. The wealthy had moved out to suburbs, often breaking with the Koran and sipping cognac and wine, leaving the center to travelers, peddlers, and the poor who drank the unhealthy water from the Nile. The new Cairo was split between the Oriental side—narrow streets, mosques and minarets, and veiled women— and the booming French section's paved streets lined with large, European-style homes, modern stores, and Westerners who wintered in the pleasant climate. Even the band of the figurehead *khedive*, whose barracks now housed English troops who enforced Britain's "veiled protectorate" over the Suez Canal, dressed in European uniforms and played Western music.[74]

Indeed, the next day, Egypt looked more civilized to the tourists. With no game scheduled and Friday being a holy day for Muslims, Spalding set the players free to wander the Arabian, Moorish, Turkish, Algerian, and Greek quarters and to cross the Nile to the Khedive's Gardens to witness the splendor of the wealthy, elites, and government officials of Cairo. Regal carriages swept down the avenues, liveried coachmen clearing the way for elegant ladies and their courtiers. That evening, the tourists split up between the French opera, Algerian dances, and the well-lighted bazaars and then returned to their hotel to prepare for the next morning's visit to the Pyramids. Not only was sightseeing in store but they would play baseball in the shadow of the Sphinx. That it did not dawn on them that these were revered sites spoke volumes about their cavalier attitude toward non-Western cultures.

With the All-Americas mounted on camels and the White Stockings sitting on donkeys, then switching halfway out, the tourists made their most famous side trip of their world travels on Saturday, February 9. The large procession stopped for cheers at the U.S. minister's residence and then moved past the Khedive's Gardens into the desert on a seven-mile, acacia-lined smooth road. Some in the entourage, like sporting goods dealer Irving Snyder, perched precariously on the beasts before tumbling to the ground. Passing the huge Pyramids, they arrived at the Sphinx, an incredible seven thousand years old and worn out by the thousands of tourists who had scrambled over it. Grouping the party on its shoulders and around its base, with local Bedouins and beggars in the foreground, a photographer took the most renowned picture of the tour. But insensitive to the last, many of the players tried punching at the Sphinx's eyes and also attempted to throw baseballs over it, as well as over the Pyramids. Spalding later commented that "the native worshippers of Cheops and

*The Khedive's Palace in Cairo.*
(Harry C. Palmer, *Athletic Sports in America, England, and Australia.*
Philadelphia: Hubbard Brothers, Publishers, 1889, p. 341)

the dead Pharaohs" were mortified, but it was all done in fun, regardless of the distasteful behavior.[75]

What they did know was baseball, and they played a game alongside the Pyramids on a diamond cut from the hard sands of the desert. The atmosphere had to be a bit disappointing, for civilization intruded. Railroad whistles from the Alexandria train could be heard and a lawn tennis court had been built at the base of the Pyramids. The spectators were a bit unorthodox to boot. Ward, awed by the backdrop of the game, led his team to a 10–6 victory in five innings of error-filled play. Sliding into base, players plowed up sand and ground balls dug into the diamond. While Bedouins with long rifles gazed down from the Pyramids, the 1,200 spectators behaved like the Cingalese by chasing after batted balls and then gathering around them for inspection. At game's end, the crowd ran to the tourists demanding *baksheesh*, a payoff, for watching the entire event! The teams then dallied around the tourist sites, again throwing baseballs two-thirds up the sides of the Pyramids, before returning to Cairo that evening, this time by carriage and donkey and not by the ornery camels.[76]

By that time, Spalding's group were ready for Europe and "civilization." The khedive had left the city, but, having heard through the U.S. consul general that Spalding wished to play a game before him, His Highness

*Baseball tourists at the Sphinx.*
(Bill Sear Collection, reprinted with the permission of Stephen Wong)

had invited the party out to his Nile palace. Spalding, regrettably, had to refuse because it would have delayed the tour by a week or so. According to Tener, there had also been talk of travel to the Holy Land and playing in Jerusalem, but that, too, was quashed. They occupied themselves during their final day, Sunday, February 10, by shopping and climbing to the mosques and citadel above Cairo, and the next day, they took a train to Port Said. There, a small steamer took them the forty-three miles to the other end of the Suez Canal, where they would board a ship and cross the Mediterranean Sea. Halfway to Port Said, they stopped at the depot at Ismalia and were assailed, once again, by natives. A bold youngster urged on the crowd to steal from the players before pitcher John Healy pegged him with a big orange and knocked him off his feet. He might have thought he had been kicked by a donkey.[77]

In reality, however, he was flattened by Anglo-Saxons. The tour had not run in a north–south direction, thereby creating the possibility of promoting an enlightened racial view of the world. Instead, on its east–west course, it had overrun people of color over the past month and a half. Both at home and abroad, the Spalding tourists had exhibited the traits of racial superiority in their thinking, words, and deeds. Whether encountering Chinese immigrants, Clarence Duval, Hawaiians, or Hindus—or white British colonists held in high esteem—the tourists engaged in the late nineteenth century's hierarchy of race. This usually translated into denigrating people of color as a means of asserting the white man's place at the top of the human pyramid. It was all a part of globalization, by which empires were built by the fittest competition—that is, by white men.

Baseball players, like other white Americans, drew the color barrier inside and outside of the United States, as they dreamed of imperialism. That the Americans moved on from the developing world to encounter their cultural equals in Europe turned out to be the tourists' next chance to compare notes on the issue of cultural superiority. They discovered some surprising things, however. Unlike the British colonials who talked of kinship, the Italians, French, and British thought of Americans as social climbers who occupied a rung of the ladder of civilization below the Europeans. Discrimination could cut both ways.

## NOTES

1. Light, *Cultural Encyclopedia of Baseball*, 373–74, 486; Zang, *Fleet Walker's Divided Heart*, 55–56; Peterson, *Only the Ball Was White*, 21–46. Other minorities faced problems, too. Around the time of the world tour, a Native American named James Madison Toy played in the American Association from 1887 to 1890,

but Indians, like other ethnic groups, suffered indignities such as being called "Chief."

2. For the theater suit, see Dale, "Social Equality Does Not Exist"; for Jackson, see Wiggins, "Peter Jackson."

3. D. G. Brinton, *Races and Peoples* (1890), quoted in Jacobson, *Barbarian Virtues*, 139. See also Nugent, "Frontiers and Empires"; Rydell, *All the World's a Fair*, 25–30; Crapol, "Coming to Terms with Empire"; Krenn, *Race and U.S. Foreign Policy*; Love, *Race over Empire*; and Chang, "Whose 'Barbarism'?"

4. Palmer, *Athletic Sports*, 194–96; Anson, *A Ball Player's Career*, 166.

5. Schaller, *United States and China*, 19–20. See also Harris, "Cultural Imperialism"; Chin, "Beneficent Imperialists"; McClain, *In Search of Equality*; Gyory, *Closing the Gate*; Lee, *At America's Gates*; Aubertin, *A Fight with Distances*, 161; and Daniels, "Asian Americans."

6. Palmer, *Athletic Sports*, 196–97; Anson, *A Ball Player's Career*, 167–68. See also Shah, *Contagious Divide*.

7. LaFeber, *The Clash*, 55.

8. Aubertin, *A Fight with Distances*, 164–65, 177. See also Adler, "The Oceanic Steamship Company."

9. LaFeber, *New Empire*, 53–54, quote on 53. See also Mark and Adler, "Claus Spreckels in Hawaii"; "A Kanaka Royal Family," *All the Year Round*, April 9, 1887, p. 278.

10. Ardolino, "Missionaries, Cartwright, and Spalding"; Light, *Cultural Encyclopedia of Baseball*, 136–38.

11. Palmer, *Athletic Sports*, 210, 216.

12. Anson, *A Ball Player's Career*, 179; Palmer, *Athletic Sports*, 214–15; David Kalakaua, http://www.des-chico.com/~star/Hawaii/h_monarc.html (accessed March 2004); James, "Hawaii's Last King"; Osorio, *Dismembering Lahui*; Greer, "Royal Tourist"; Schweizer, "King Kalakaua"; Karpiel, "Mystic Ties of Brotherhood," 357, 381–82, 385, 392. See also "Our San Francisco Letter," *Pacific Commercial Advertiser*, November 26, 1888, p. 1; Spalding, *Baseball*, 255–57; "At Honolulu," *Sporting Life*, December 26, 1888, p. 4; and "Received by the King," newspaper clipping, *Albert Spalding Scrapbook*, vol. 8, Albert Spalding Collection, Society of American Baseball Researchers Lending Library, Cleveland, Ohio (hereafter cited as Spalding Scrapbooks).

13. Anson, *A Ball Player's Career*, 180; Tener, "On the Alameda," correspondence to the *Pittsburgh Chronicle Telegraph*, December 1, 1888, John K. Tener Biographical File, National Baseball Hall of Fame, Cooperstown, New York (hereafter cited as Tener File). See also Aubertin, *A Fight with Distances*, 194.

14. Tener, "On the *Alameda*"; Palmer, *Athletic Sports*, 223–24. See also James Ryan, *Tour of the Spalding B.B.C. around the World* [diary] (hereafter cited as Ryan Diary), James Edward Ryan Biographical File, National Baseball Hall of Fame, Cooperstown, New York, entry for November 25, 1888, p. 31.

15. Palmer, *Athletic Sports*, 224–25; Anson, *A Ball Player's Career*, 184.

16. Palmer, *Athletic Sports*, 160.

17. Palmer, *Athletic Sports*, 169. See also Anson, *A Ball Player's Career*, 149.

18. Palmer, *Athletic Sports*, 171.

19. "At Honolulu," *Sporting Life*, January 9, 1889, p. 4. See also Ryan Diary, November 25, 1888, p. 31; Minister George Merrill to Secretary of State, Sub-Marine Cable, September 29, 1888, "Despatches from U.S. Ministers in Hawaii," roll 24, T-30, Record Group (RG) 59, Records of the Department of State, National Archives and Records Administration of the United States, College Park, Maryland (hereafter cited as RG 59, NARA).

20. Love, *Race over Empire*, 122, 123.

21. Palmer, *Athletic Sports*, 228–33.

22. Beisner, *From the Old Diplomacy to the New*, 68; LaFeber, *New Empire*, 55–56, 138–40; Andrade, "Great Samoan Hurricane"; Anderson, "Pacific Destiny." By the mid-1880s, Germany, with the largest economic interest at stake, pushed for dominance. Secretary of State Bayard met with his German and British counterparts in 1887, insisting on America's moral responsibility for protecting the natives as well as enhancing this key strategic and commercial link in a trans-Pacific communication and transportation system. No agreement on dividing power was reached, however, and the tourists sailed into Samoan waters with tensions at a high level. A native war, inspired by the imperial rivalries, wracked the islands from spring 1888 onward. The pressure cooker had eased somewhat after a hurricane, just months before, had destroyed U.S. and German warships in Apia harbor and killed 150 men. This led to a settlement in early 1889, and a decade later, Germany and America divvied up Samoa, leaving Britain with nothing.

23. Anson, *A Ball Player's Career*, 189; Palmer, *Athletic Sports*, 234. See also DeConde, *Ethnicity*, 149.

24. Trotter, "Among the Islands," 797; Whitaker, "Samoa."

25. "Auckland, N. Z.," December 9, 1888, newspaper clipping, Spalding Scrapbooks, vol. 8. See also Palmer, *Athletic Sports*, 235–36.

26. "Baseball and Ballooning," *New Zealand Herald*, December 8, 1888, p. 6.

27. Mayor Devore to Spalding, December 10, 1888, Spalding Scrapbooks, vol. 10; Anson, *A Ball Player's Career*, 191–92; "The American Baseball Teams," *Wellington Evening Post*, December 11, 1888, p. 2; "The Balloon Ascent," *New Zealand Herald*, December 11, 1888, p. 6.

28. Van Bottenburg, *Global Games*, 5–9, 46–55; Perez, "Between Baseball and Bullfighting," 494; "International Baseball League," *New York Times*, January 10, 1889, p. 2; "To Teach England Baseball," *New York Times*, October 14, 1888, p. 1.

29. Spalding, "Field Papers,"

30. Ryan Diary, December 10, 1888, p. 36.

31. Mitchell, "Sporting Traditions," 4.

32. Palmer, *Athletic Sports*, 240–41, also 242. See also "Ward's Base-Ball Gossip," newspaper clipping, Spalding Scrapbooks, vol. 8; "Arrival and Reception of the American Base Ball Players," *Sydney Morning Herald*, December 15, 1888, p. 15.

33. Hoffenberg, "Colonial Innocents Abroad?"; Spillman, "Neither the Same Nation."

34. Anson, *A Ball Player's Career*, 193; Cameron, "Commonwealth of Australia," 250, 256–57. See also Kramer, "Empires, Exceptions, and Anglo-Saxons."

35. Palmer, *Athletic Sports*, 243–44; Mitchell, "Sporting Traditions," 6; Bartlett, *Baseball and Mr. Spalding*, 183. See also "Base Ball: The Great Trip," *Sporting Life*,

February 6, 1889, p. 4; and Banham, *Cambridge Guide to World Theatre*, 1075. J. C. Williamson, born in Pennsylvania, became an actor and dancer in New York and Pennsylvania before permanently settling in Australia in 1879. From that point, he changed the market for global theatricals by developing a traveling theater route from Honolulu, through Sydney, to Cape Town that competed with the San Francisco-to-British colonies itinerary. Williamson formed a firm that dominated the Australian theater until 1976. When he died in 1913, all theaters in the country remained dark for a night.

36. Tener to Steve, January 16, 1889, Tener File.

37. Carnarvon, "Australia in 1888"; Dale, "Impressions of Australia"; Moon, "Some Aspects of Australian Life"; Royce, "Impressions of Australia," 76. See also Consul in Sydney G. Whippie to Assistant Secretary of State George Rives, April 17, 1888, Report on the Australian Railways, M173, reel 13, "Despatches from U.S. Consuls in Sydney, Australia, 1836–1906," RG 59, NARA.

38. Cashman, "Symbols of Unity"; Ferguson, *Empire*, 261.

39. Consul G. W. Griffin to Assistant Secretary of State George Rives, cables, July 2–9, 1888, M173, reel 13, "Despatches from U.S. Consuls in Sydney, Australia, 1836–1906," RG 59, NARA; Schwendinger, "Chinese Sailors."

40. "Banquet to Consul Griffin," undated, M173, reel 13, "Despatches from U.S. Consuls in Sydney, Australia, 1836–1906," RG 59, NARA.

41. Dale, "Impressions of Australia," 833–34; "The American Baseball Players in Sydney—The First Match," *Sydney Morning Herald*, December 17, 1888, p. 4; Palmer, *Athletic Sports*, 245–46. See also Mitchell, "Sporting Traditions," 8.

42. Spalding, "Field Papers," 609. See also Tener to Steve, January 16, 1889, Tener File; *New York Times*, December 5, 1888, p. 4.

43. Gossip, "Cricket in Australia," April 1889; Gossip, "Cricket in Australia," June 1889.

44. "George Wright," *American Cricketer* 14 (May 13, 1891): 1; "In the Athletic World," *New York Times*, April 15, 1889, p. 5; Wharton, "Inter-City and International Cricket"; "Cricket in 1886," *Outing* 14 (January 1887): 388; "Cricket in America," *Outing* supplement (1889): 47–51; Chadwick, "Cricket in the Metropolis"; "Cricket," "The Cricket Centennial," "International Cricket Games," and "Brooklyn, July 5, 1904, Special Correspondence," all in Henry Chadwick Scrapbooks, Society of American Baseball Researchers Lending Library, Cleveland, Ohio, vol. 17, reel 3. See also Melville, "Our First National Pastime"; Kirsch, "American Cricket"; Melville, "Aspiration to Cosmopolitanism"; Melville, "From Ethnic Tradition"; Lockley, "The Manly Game"; Lewis, "Cricket and the Beginnings"; Park, "British Sports and Pastimes."

45. Mitchell, "Sporting Traditions," 9–11; Palmer, *Athletic Sports*, 249–50; "The American Baseball Players in Sydney—The Second Match," *Sydney Morning Herald*, December 18, 1888, p. 5; "The American Baseball Players," *Sydney Morning Herald*, December 19, 1888, p. 11; Mandle, "Cricket and Australian Nationalism."

46. Newton MacMillan, "The American Base Ball Tourists Royally Entertained before Their Departure," newspaper clipping, Spalding Scrapbooks, vol. 8. See also Tener to Maud and Will, December 23, 1888, Tener File.

47. "Base-Ball: The Great Trip," *Sporting Life*, February 13, 1889, p. 4; Palmer, *Athletic Sports*, 251–53.

48. "The American Game of Base-Ball and How To Play It," *The Age* (Melbourne), December 22, 1888, p. 14; Dale, "Impressions of Australia," 832–33.

49. Beisner, *From the Old Diplomacy to the New*, 32–71; Plesur, *America's Outward Thrust*, 44–49.

50. "The American Baseball Players," *The Age* (Melbourne), December 21, 1888, p. 7; "Base-Ball: The Great Trip," *Sporting Life*, February 13, 1889, p. 4; Palmer, *Athletic Sports*, 253–59; "Baseball in Australia," *New York Times*, February 10, 1889, p. 4.

51. Palmer, *Athletic Sports*, 261.

52. Levine, *A. G. Spalding*, 103.

53. "The American Baseball Players," *The Age* (Melbourne), December 24, 1888, p. 6. See also Palmer, *Athletic Sports*, 265.

54. Dale, "Impressions of Australia," 835.

55. Quoted in Joe Clark, excerpts from *The History of Australian Baseball: Time and Game*, author's possession. See also Dale, "Impressions of Australia," 846–48; Di Salvatore, *A Clever Base-Ballist*, 233–34; Stevens, *Baseball's Radical*, 75; "Baseball," *Adelaide Observer*, January 5, 1889, p. 19.

56. "The Baseball Team at Ballarat," *The Age* (Melbourne), December 31, 1888, p. 7. See also Rash, "Discovery of Gold."

57. Palmer, *Athletic Sports*, 275. See also Mitchell, "Sporting Traditions," 11–12; Tatz, "Racism and Sport."

58. "Football and Baseball," *The Age* (Melbourne), January 7, 1889, p. 6.

59. Palmer, *Athletic Sports*, 278. See also "A Stupid Practical Joke," *The Age* (Melbourne), January 3, 1889, p. 5.

60. "Results of the Spalding Tour," cartoon, Spalding Scrapbooks, vol. 8. See also Wonham, "I Want a Real Coon."

61. "Baseball in Australia," *New York Times*, February 27, 1888, 4; Henry Simpson, "It Is Growing," *Sporting Life*, April 3, 1889, p. 1; Mitchell, "Sporting Traditions," 13–15; Clark, *History of Australian Baseball*, 18–40. Only the Goodwood team of South Australia and East Melbourne in Victoria enjoyed any longevity. In any case, Australians returned Spalding's favor in 1897, touring the United States in what became known as the Disaster Tour. Spalding and Anson embraced them in thanks for their kind treatment in 1888, but few others did. The tour failed because of the bad play, bankruptcy, and a manager who abandoned the team in the States.

62. Anson, *A Ball Player's Career*, 213–14.

63. Palmer, *Athletic Sports*, 283, 285, 289; Ryan Diary, January 18, 1889, p. 50.

64. Palmer, *Athletic Sports*, 286, 291–92; Anson, *A Ball Player's Career*, 219, 220, 221.

65. Ryan Diary, January 22, 1889, p. 50. See also Di Salvatore, *A Clever Base-Ballist*, 238; "The Grand Laugh," *Sporting News*, February 2, 1889, p. 3.

66. Palmer, *Athletic Sports*, 295–303. See also Sherman, "American Contacts with Ceylon"; Rajapakse, "Christian Missions"; Levine, *A. G. Spalding*, 104; Burrows, "Modern Pilgrimage," 467.

67. Palmer, *Athletics Sports*, 303–4. See also "Spalding's Ball Players," newspaper clipping, Spalding Scrapbooks, vol. 8; "Lawn Tennis in Ceylon," *Overland Cey-*

*lon Observer*, January 24, 1889, p. 89; "The American Base-Ballers in Colombo," *Ceylon Independent*, January 28, 1889, p. 1.

68. Tener to Ll'ee Bec, February 6, 1889, Tener File.

69. Di Salvatore, *A Clever Base-Ballist*, 239.

70. Palmer, *Athletic Sports*, 304–12; Ryan Diary, February 2 and 6, 1889, pp. 56–57; Tener to Maud, February 6, 1889, Tener File.

71. Palmer, *Athletic Sports*, 313, 315, 316; Anson, *A Ball Player's Career*, 232.

72. Palmer, *Athletic Sports*, 318. See also Hopkins, "Victorians and Africa."

73. See Obeidat, "Lured by the Exotic Levant"; Hollenbach, "Image of the Arab"; Warzeski, "Mapping the Unknown."

74. Anson, *A Ball Player's Career*, 235. See also "Changing Cairo," *Littell's Living Age* (January–March 1889): 446–47; Carpenter, "Cairo under the Khedive," 48, 580–82; Ferguson, *Empire*, 233.

75. Quoted in Di Salvatore, *A Clever Base-Ballist*, 240. See also Palmer, *Athletic Sports*, 323–33.

76. Palmer, *Athletic Sports*, 333; Carpenter, "Cairo under the Khedive," 582; Di Salvatore, *A Clever Base-Ballist*, 239–40; "Baseball: The Great Trip," *Sporting Life*, February 20, 1889, p. 4.

77. Palmer, *Athletic Sports*, 336–40; Tener to Maud, February 6, 1889, Tener File.

# 4

# Old and New World Cultures
## Europe

ITALY
> Naples, Tuesday, February 19, 1889—*All-America* 8, *Chicago* 2
> Rome, Saturday, February 23—*Chicago* 3, *All-America* 2
> Florence, Monday, February 25—*All-America* 7, *Chicago* 4

FRANCE
> Paris, Friday, March 8—*All-America* 6, *Chicago* 2

ENGLAND
> London (Kennington Oval), Tuesday, March 12—*Chicago* 7, *All-America* 4
> London (Lord's), Wednesday, March 13—*All-America* 7, *Chicago* 6
> London (Crystal Palace), Thursday, March 14—*All-America* 5, *Chicago* 3
> Bristol, Friday, March 15—*Chicago* 10, *All-America* 3
> London (Leyton), Saturday, March 16—*Chicago* 12, *All-America* 6
> Birmingham, Monday, March 18—*Chicago* 4, *All-America* 4
> Sheffield, Tuesday, March 19—*All-America* 10, *Chicago* 0
> Bradford, Wednesday, March 20—*Chicago* 6, *All-America* 3

SCOTLAND
> Glasgow, Thursday, March 21—*All-America* 8, *Chicago* 4

ENGLAND
> Manchester, Friday, March 22—*All-America* 7, *Chicago* 6
> Liverpool, Saturday, March 23—*All-America* 2, *Chicago* 2

IRELAND
> Belfast, Sunday, March 24—*All-America* 9, *Chicago* 8
> Dublin, Wednesday, March 27—*All-America* 4, *Chicago* 3

William "Buffalo Bill" Cody's show toured Europe several times in the 1880s, bringing Indians, cowboys, and livestock to England, Italy, France, Austria, and Germany. On one trip, Native Americans met the pope; on another, at Queen Victoria's Fiftieth Jubilee in June 1887,

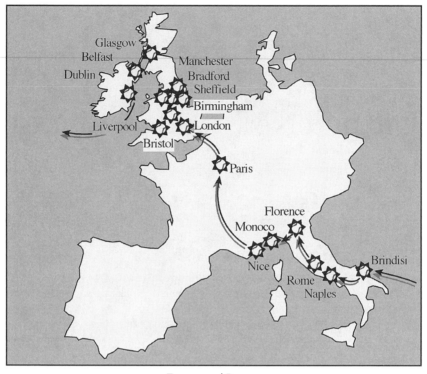

*Tour around Europe.*
(David Underwood, Graphic Design, CU-Boulder)

Sioux, Cheyenne, and other tribes stood in front of the monarch herself. Victoria shook hands with each one, who noted she was "little but fat and we liked her, because she was good to us." The queen then expressed her disappointment about the degradation of the natives of America.[1]

Reception by royalty, the chance to show off American culture, and lure of solid profits—hallmarks of Buffalo Bill's Wild West Exhibition—could not help but grab the attention of another entrepreneur. Cody trafficked in America's pioneering spirit of the past; Albert Spalding marketed America's modern love of baseball. Europe had embraced Buffalo Bill, but would it applaud the national pastime, too? In baseball's version of the Grand Tour, Spalding entered Europe through the imperial outpost of the Suez Canal and exited from Britain, the core of empire. Along the way, as the process of globalization integrated the Anglo-Saxon world, he offered up the New World to the old imperialists in an attempt at what, a century later, would be labeled "Americanization."

Spalding's tourists had certain advantages in this mission. British entrepreneur Thomas Cook had developed European tourism by capitalizing on technology. Beginning with local excursions by train in England in the 1840s, Cook envisioned a virtual tourism empire by 1876, with the advent of the steamship. His tourists meandered into Italy, then gazed on the dramatic Alps of Switzerland by the 1860s, and strolled on the boulevards of Paris and the English country lanes, all reached by train. He also opened up the Holy Land and Egypt to travelers a decade later, at around the same time that he sent tours to the United States. By the 1880s, Cook Tours packaged trips by railway, steamship, and hotels worldwide. By the time of Cook's death in 1891, a plaque on his house read, "He made world travel easier."[2] And he had. Only thirty-five thousand American travelers had crossed the Atlantic in 1870. Fifteen years later, this number nearly tripled, aided by technology's lowering of transportation costs and growing per capita prosperity. Constantly improving ocean liners sped up travel time and reduced its cost. A ten-week, first-class tour of the European continent now cost three hundred dollars, a drop of several hundred dollars from two decades before. Europe opened up to Americans, as did Mecca for the first time in 1889, the year of the Spalding trip. Periodicals such as *A Pointer for the Tourist, Outing,* and *Travel,* and guidebooks, whose publication augmented with rapidity due to the development of machine-set type, popularized tourism for U.S. citizens.

Travel writers served as unwitting promoters for Cook's entrepreneurialism. In the mid-nineteenth century, visitors to picturesque Italy ranged from social critic Charles Dickens and the champion of female perspectives, Frances Trollope, to the historical and romantic musings of Henry James, James Lowell, and Nathaniel Hawthorne. Western author Bret Harte left for Europe in 1878, never to return. Mark Twain delighted in his Americanism while criticizing "old world fraud." He wrote a guidebook of sorts with *The Innocents Abroad* in 1869, selling thirty thousand copies in six months after returning from a trip across the Atlantic into Europe and the Holy Land, in the reverse direction of the Spalding tour. The oftentimes mocking Twain pinpointed the value of tourism with his cutting wit. Near the end of the book, he commented that "travel is fatal to prejudice, bigotry, and narrow-mindedness"—although his travelogue documented his ill will toward beggars and other foreign irritants in rather racy language. Henry Adams, the son of a former U.S. minister in London, roamed Europe and the Pacific for twenty years after his wife's suicide. Writers tended to comment on European traditions and differences with the United States. Along with speeches, guidebooks, and Cook's tours, they also enhanced the attractiveness of tourism for the rising middle class and professionals—including sportsmen—who had previously thought of travel as an extravagance.[3]

Prominent American travelers only added to the prestige of journeying abroad. Budding leaders among the well-to-do class visited Europe—in Theodore Roosevelt's case, on his honeymoon in 1883. The Astors and Vanderbilts became pivotal members of the international wedded set, and Andrew Carnegie and J. P. Morgan were also as active in society abroad as they were at home. Furthermore, they helped generate U.S. interest in visiting foreign attractions, especially European sites, for educational purposes. Artists lived on Paris's Left Bank; Winslow Homer, John Singer Sargent, James Whistler, and Mary Cassatt had acquaintances among the French masters and the new Impressionists. Rich collectors followed them in the 1880s to bring Europe's culture home. Late in the decade, millionairess Mrs. John Gardner of Boston befriended Cassatt, who introduced her to the world of Impressionism. Mrs. Potter Palmer traveled from her castle in Chicago, replete with a Louis XVI salon and the first private elevator, to fill out her seventy-foot picture gallery with paintings from the Barbizon school, as well as four Renoirs that she purchased for a mere five thousand dollars. While U.S. students comprised the largest group of Americans in Europe, famous figures enhanced the reputation of travel for a fellow entrepreneur and self-promoter like Albert Spalding.[4]

Yet it is questionable whether Twain's statement, however tongue-in-cheek, that tourism reaped a liberal and expansive worldview was entirely valid. Hailing as they did from a dynamic country did not necessarily make the baseball tourists less stuck in their ways and stereotypes. Like the typical tourist whose imagery of the world was grounded in myths and fantasy rather than reality, the baseball entourage was also not immune to the fascinations that international tourism promised. No doubt they were told that old Europe contained an outmoded sense of privilege and stodgy aristocracy, classiness in the arts but also military belligerency that seemed to compel a life at the point of a gun rather than coexistence through civilized diplomacy. Meanwhile, to these proud Americans, the United States represented democracy, freedom, and opportunity; unacknowledged was its materialism, rowdiness, racism, and ignorance of world affairs.[5]

In essence, the Spalding party embarked on this last part of its global mission by simultaneously respecting Europe while trying to avoid deference to these nations. When it came to tourism in Europe, in other words, Spalding's ambition was far from unassuming. Baseball, he believed, would become the universal athletic sport of the world, including in venerable Europe. His entourage took pleasure from the grand tour of the Continent and Britain. Yet Spalding also set himself up for a fall, because Europeans might prove more resistant to the New World than his wide-eyed aspirations allowed. It turned out, however, that Europeans—who cultivated the core of Western culture—could look on with amusement, disdain, or ignore altogether American forays abroad. The Old World might teach the Americans a thing or two about culture, customs, and humility, and ultimately reveal the United States to be an empire in waiting rather than a nation that had already come of age in the world arena.[6]

## ITALIAN PROPRIETY

Tutoring for the baseball tourists began immediately the night that they boarded their small ship and steamed through the Suez Canal. This great waterway, constructed by France and opened in 1869, was one of the great European feats that made travel around the Horn of Africa obsolete, boosted commerce, and consolidated the French and British empires in the Near East, the rim of the Indian Ocean, and Africa. A tool of imperialism, the canal was also a marvel of European engineering genius. With a mean depth of 27 feet, it stretched to 350 feet across and 87 miles long as it connected two large natural lakes. As the tourists went through it, hundreds of men and animals were busy widening the canal to make it ever more accessible. In the moonlight, dozens of ships passed by them, taking advantage of the fruits of European technology, labor, and finance, as they made their way to Port Said at the northern end of the Suez Canal.

The entourage boarded the steamer *Stettin*, a luxury liner run by North German Lloyd, and sailed on rough, cold seas for the next three days across the Mediterranean. The vessel slipped past the snowcapped mountains of Crete and other Greek isles and into the harbor of Brindisi, a port at the mouth of the Adriatic Sea midway up the back of the heel of the Italian boot. Mail and American newspapers arrived at the dock, a much-welcomed first contact with the United States since the Spalding party had left the country two months before. Included was a letter to Spalding from Secretary of State Thomas Bayard requesting all U.S. consuls and ministers in Europe to extend courtesies to the entourage baseball travelers.[7] Government officials perceived the tourists as worthy representatives of American culture and enterprise.

The next few days in Italy gave them a taste of European ways, however. Because the choppy crossing had delayed the *Stettin* by half a day, the tourists stayed in the charming but "queer" town of Brindisi for the night. The next day, Cap Anson felt more like he was confronting an umpire at home plate than a welcoming audience in Italy. The tourists entered the Brindisi station to board the train for a trip across the peninsula to Naples. They had four trunks in tow and hand baggage, the bulk of their belongings going on to Southampton, England, on the *Stettin*. Anson took a bag of bats as a carry-on, but because it seemed too heavy to be a handbag, a fastidious railway official demanded Pop pay an extra tax on it. The ballplayer protested, but the gold-laced old man snapped his fingers in insistence. Anson paid the extra fee; as well, his wife paid a duty on a two-pound box of candy. He had experienced "the power of the Italian Government," that is, European rules and customs that did not bend to American wishes.[8]

It would not be the last run-in with Old World ways. The train ran through groves of olive and orange trees that encircled white-walled villages and historic castles and wended its way into snow-covered mountains until descending along the Bay of Naples. A group of players on the right side of the train exclaimed in astonishment as Mount Vesuvius loomed up gray in the distance, the red-haloed volcano belching flame and lava every few seconds. Arriving in Naples, ten Italian gendarmes in military cloaks and three-cornered hats surrounded the tourists, taking player Marty Sullivan into custody for stealing the horn of a train guard in Brindisi. Spalding and three interpreters negotiated their way out of the prank, and the party proceeded to the Hotel Vesuve, past the Royal Palace, the Via Roma, and the Church of St. Francis. Tired from the trip and legal hassles, the tourists retired to their rooms to gaze at Mount Vesuvius from their windows.

By their standards, Naples was mired in poverty, and Italy as a whole seemed backward. The region lacked natural resources and thus trailed behind the northern part of the country and the rest of Europe in development. A system of patronage, combined with the lack of a middle class and a democratic tradition, had brought a series of near-dictatorial strongmen into power in Italy, including the current prime minister, the rather unbalanced Francesco Crispi. His diplomatic intrigues led to tensions with France, a close trading partner, while Italy lagged in the imperial game. Not surprisingly, many southern Italians had fled abroad. The U.S. State Department had its hands full processing requests by Italians or their government for marriage certificates, extradition, and other legal matters.[9] Yet the country's cultural riches attracted tourists from all over the world; the pomp of empire, the papal presence, and its ancient and Renaissance art, architecture, and music drew tens of thousands of tourists a year. Americans were easily awed.

The baseball tourists looked forward to the sights, but they also noted the lack of enthusiastic greetings they received in Italy. Unlike the receptions outside of Europe, there were no parades from train depots or hotels in store for the tourists. The Spalding party was just one more group of travelers to visit the Continent. This was not disdain as much as Old World ambivalence toward tourists, bred from centuries of encounters. Also, because this leg of the tour was freshly planned, it lacked the steady stream of marketing, as had been the case in Hawaii, New Zealand, and Australia, where the baseball tour was major news. Europeans might not care or, with all of the distractions in their cities, simply be unaware of the tourists altogether.

Baseball also seemed to be second on the agenda for the tourists themselves, as they combed over Naples and its environs. They did not play a game until the fourth day after their February 15 arrival, so they had plenty of time to sightsee and attend the ballet at Bellini's and an opera at the San Carlos Theater. All accounts of the tour spend pages on descriptions of Pompeii, the ascent of the trembling Vesuvius, and the elegance of the people. The well-attired crowds and sumptuous shop-window displays impressed them as much as the magnificent cathedrals. Distinct from their earlier stops, they also visited museums; imperial Europe displayed its splendor in glass cases rather than in everyday buildings.[10] The tourists got the feeling that Europe offered its culture as a standard by which other nations were judged.

They did play baseball. During the afternoon of Tuesday, February 19, the tourists entered carriages and, "without any special demonstration," rolled out to the Campo di Marte for an exhibition. About three thousand spectators awaited, diplomats and high society brought out by invitation of the U.S. consul in Naples. The fashionable ladies and gentlemen pressed in on the field, which was not enclosed, and thus disrupted play. Neither the police nor the players nor Spalding, who spoke halting Italian, could wave them back, and ground balls continually scattered people as the fielders chased them down. The predictable then occurred when Fred Carroll hit a big Italian above the eye with a line drive, although the crowd spiritedly took this as an accident. The game was knotted until the fifth inning, when John Ward's triple began a flood of All-America scoring. After his side scored seven runs in the inning, the crowd evidently thought the contest was over and rushed over the terrain despite wild gesticulations and shouts from the players. Ward mustered his team back on the field and then asked for a forfeit by the fleeing White Stockings. Umpire Tener called the game, an 8–2 victory for Ward's nine.[11]

The fashionable crowds did not abate that night, but they took little interest in the tourists. At the grand venue of the San Carlos Theater, the U.S. minister procured two gilded boxes for a dozen Spalding tourists. The great tenor Gayorra sang *Lucretia Borgia* amid a cast of six hundred people on stage, most of the royal and wealthy audience familiar with every note. They paid little attention to the foreigners; there was no special applause for the tourists on their farewell night in Naples. The next day, after visiting more museums and the monastery of San Martino and reveling in the description of the history behind these antiquities, the entourage took an uneventful six-hour train ride north to Rome. With no fanfare, and lucky to find accommodations because of the many other tourists in the city, the White Stockings went to the Hotel Alamagne and the All-Americas and reporters to the Hotel di Capitol at an end of the Corso.[12]

At first, the stay in Rome was marred by the U.S. minister. Subjected to their first discourteous treatment of the trip, the tourists learned that he disdained athletics and would certainly not lend his office for Spalding's supposed "mercenary purposes." Big Al reportedly offered five thousand dollars and a donation of profits to charity if the Colosseum were made available for a game. Because the city lacked enclosed grounds to facilitate the charging of spectators at the gate, Spalding faced a serious problem. But the minister rejected such a financing scheme, and took further umbrage when Spalding asked for an audience with the pope. The most the tourists got was Mass at St. Peter's. Fortunately, Charles Dougherty, the secretary of the U.S. Legation, organized the game so that Spalding broke even. Yet the reception came with a message; Americans should not expect Europeans to throw themselves at any Yankee who paid a visit. To be sure, the Italians did not want their crumbling ruins desecrated by sportsmen. But the attempt to play in the Colosseum revealed substantial ignorance about Rome's cultural sites, for the ruin's floor was no bigger than a softball field and its "floor" had collapsed into a debris-filled basement.[13] The American minister had made a point on behalf of the Europeans.

The tourists enjoyed a much more pleasant time taking in Rome's splendors, and they even found a welcome for their sport. They entered St. Peter's Cathedral and the Vatican, realizing why so many literary figures had attempted such detailed portrayals of the galleries and chapels. Players, "silent and open-eyed" or enthusiastically inquisitive, gazed at the towering arches and dome of the church. A drive down the Appian Way to the tomb of Cecilia Metella and the Catacombs, as well as visits to the Forum, the Colosseum, and a bridge across the Tiber River showed them Rome's past glory, while the lighted promenade of the Corso convinced them of the city's continued cultural prominence. The flow of people surpassed Chicago's State Street, but their varied backgrounds proved even more extraordinary. The Prince of Naples rode by, followed by a California millionairess wintering in the city and some English dandies. Rome certainly defied expectations as a city in ruins. When the students of the American College crowded around the famous ballplayers in the gardens of their school, moreover, the tourists encountered baseball enthusiasts to top off the sightseeing. The rector of the college had informed Spalding that the number of Catholics waiting for an audience with the aged pontiff prevented a visit by the players. Nonetheless, the American priests-in-training made up for this disappointing news. After speeches by various bishops, and a popular performance by Clarence Duval, the college boys pledged to attend the game the next afternoon.[14]

They came out on Saturday, along with 3,500 other spectators (a large number of them Americans) to a public park on the grounds of the elegant Villa Borghese. Terraces, supporting the royalty and wealth of Italy, arose above the playing field of the smooth Piazza di Siena. King Umberto entered the exhibition in its later innings with the queen, while the host, Prince Borghese, watched with princesses, counts, and the wife and daughter of the prime minister. This was the first professional baseball contest in the Eternal City, and the teams lived up to their billing amidst the marble columns, arbored terraces, and the regal men and women. Carroll's rare home run off Tener tallied two runs for All-America, but Fred Pfeffer's double, a poor throw, and a wild pitch allowed Anson's crew to tie it. For the next four innings, brilliant double plays and outfield catches kept the bases clear until Tom Burns tripled and scored on a passed ball to give the White Stockings a 3–2, seven-inning win. This was "the most remarkable game of the trip," wrote Palmer, and "a success socially and artistically," as was fitting for the great city of Rome, whose journalists wondered at how the American "devils" slid into bases.[15]

Art and baseball mixed again in Florence on Monday, February 25. The sunny and soft Tuscan city was a gem of refinement, home to artistic grand masters. The party scattered after an early breakfast to the Duomo, the Pitti and Uffizi galleries, the palace of the Medicis, and the studio of Michelangelo before going to the *cascine*, or the racetrack grounds, to play a game, once again in front of Italy's blue bloods. A wealthy American, Leroy de Koven, had arranged this social event. Contessas and marquisas, and the Florence Jockey Club, were among a group of two thousand, the most fashionable assemblage to watch a game on the tour. Again, as in Rome, and later in France, the bulk of the fans were American expats, but the Italian press noted the play of the "atleti-gentlemen." The on-field artistry did Michelangelo proud, for both sides competed intensely, and All-America won, 7–4, due to its own skilled base-running as well as Chicago pitcher Mark Baldwin's inability at times to find the plate.[16] There was little time for dallying, as the tourist's train left Florence at five o'clock the next morning for France.

En route to Nice, sightseeing continued, and so did the tense encounters with the law. The tourists entered Pisa and saw the Leaning Tower before going on to Genoa for lunch. At the Franco-Italian border, after a dramatic ride along the coast through dozens of tunnels, European justice again cost the Americans some out-of-pocket expenses. A train guard in the station of Vingt Mille, about twenty miles from Nice, stopped the party from reboarding for France until Ed Crane had paid fare for the pet monkey he had picked up during the Pacific crossing. This was revenge

*Tourists at the Colosseum in Rome.*

(Harry C. Palmer, *Athletic Sports in America, England, and Australia*. Philadelphia: Hubbard Brothers, Publishers, 1889, p. 367) taken on him, as well as on James Fogarty and Fred Carroll, by two irate Italian train compartment mates who believed the three ballplayers had ridiculed them during the trip from Florence. They had informed Italian officials of the monkey's presence in Crane's coat pocket. Crane stalled until giving in, paying the seventeen francs only to be told that he owed an additional nine. Refusing this demand, the tourists found themselves surrounded by soldiers. Crane forked over the balance, but Spalding scoffed at the interpreter who asked for twenty francs more for his services during the incident. Big Al was not about to be taken for a patsy. He had lost money on the Italian leg and he would lose no more. At long last, Italy disappeared into the distance as the train sped into France.[17]

## FRENCH SOCIETY

As the tourists checked into Nice's Hotel Interlachen and headed for the gaming halls of Monte Carlo, great crowds roamed about in anticipation of the Battle of Flowers the following day. The players were just as amazed by the grandeur of the betting palaces but stunned by the high prices for food and drink. John Ward paid an outrageous dollar for a cup of coffee and $7.50 for three orders of asparagus. He was furious, but unfairly so, for the casino was known as one of Europe's premier pleasure palaces for the rich. He should have removed his blinders and realized he was in Europe's leading resort city. Like his compatriots, however, Ward also goggled at the splendor of the grounds, the carpeted, high-ceilinged rooms hung with crystal chandeliers and decorated by paintings, and the royalty around him. The tourists returned the following night, most to lose at roulette once again, although a few walked away with winnings. Some had qualms about the morality of gambling, but in Europe, sentiment was different.

Europe's playground also proved ignorant of baseball. During the day, the entourage watched the flower festival along with thousands of other visitors, including the Prince of Wales, who was escorted by beautiful English and American women and threw bouquets to admirers along the Promenade des Anglais. Significant distress ensued when Spalding learned that Nice had no grounds for any field sport. Plans for an exhibition game, and the hopes of the few hundred Americans in the town as well as sailors from the close-by naval vessel, the *Lancaster*, were dashed. How could a resort not possess well-equipped athletic grounds, or even "the suspicion of a cricket oval," wondered the party? Perhaps the answer lay in the French love for other diversions, their instinct for the arts, or the casino at Monte Carlo, which, during that February alone, attracted more than twenty-one thousand people.[18] The new sport of baseball simply did not grab much attention from the old bon vivants of Europe.

The tourists hoped to have better luck in Paris. March 1, a Friday, saw the tourists leave Nice for snowy Lyon, where they spent the night before entering the City of Lights near midnight on Sunday. As usual for Europe, no grand reception waited at the station but they hardly cared as they made their way past Notre Dame and the Louvre and up the avenue de l'Opera to the rue Caumartin and the Hotel St. Petersbourg. "La Belle Paris" offered them five days of world-famous sights, and one—the Eiffel Tower—in the making. Paris, wrote Cap Anson, was "the Mecca of all Americans who have money to spend and who desire to spend it," and the tourists obliged. Opening their wallets, they spent days visiting the galleries and parks, wandering around the Bastille, Napoleon's tomb, and under the Arc de Triomphe; they devoted their nights to dancehalls, theaters, and ballrooms. A novel air race, in which four large gas balloons rose from the ground and then raced back to earth, was a curiosity. But Anson contrasted the sneaky residents with Americans, and thus the Old and New Worlds. "As a business man the Parisian is not a decided success when viewed from the American standpoint, but as a butterfly in pursuit of pleasure he cannot be beaten." Parisians were also wont to prey on American tourists, taking advantage of their honesty, claimed Pop, but in their defense, all European hoteliers and shopkeepers believed U.S. visitors of the mid-nineteenth century, traveling in luxury from a land of riches, could easily afford their swollen prices.[19]

One can hear the naiveté of the grand tourist in such generalities, of the somewhat overwhelmed American out of his depth in cultured Paris. The baseballists experienced Mardi Gras, or Shrove Tuesday, the closing day of the Carnival festival in which several costume balls took place around the city. Diarist Jimmy Ryan attended some but he was so unaware that they signaled the holiday's end that he complained that the streets were dead the next day. Others, like Ward and Palmer, were more in tune with the excitement. Masquers seemingly appeared out of doorways, carriages tooted and bells rang, people yelling in laughter. "Paris seemed to have gone crazy," wrote Palmer, who looked for calm among the bookstalls of the rue de Rivoli and the drama of the Comédie-Française. Yet he also entered a student masquerade ball with a group of players, there to be accosted by lines of fun-loving students in "shockingly short skirts!" One shapely girl kicked Ned Hanlon's silk hat off his head and into the chandeliers. Even the more sedate midnight ball at the Eden Theater, full of elegant French people, dissolved into a frenzy of can-can dancers. The tourists rolled out of the festivities and into the rue Montmartre before daylight chased them home to their hotels. Such revelry was uncommon for them, and the women's forthright attitudes a bit disconcerting, though definitely exciting.[20]

That some of the tourists who were unaccompanied by spouses chased skirts was implied in reports of the trip, and their behavior reflected the conceptualization of gender relations of the times. "Those who have visited Paris can doubtless imagine how much there would be for twenty-five able-bodied, fun-loving, much-traveled young Americans to see and to do, and we were seeing and doing through every available hour of our time," recalled Harry Palmer.[21] The number of references to pretty, coquettish women rose when the tourists visited France, yet Spalding had long stressed the "manly virtues" of baseball and the tour, so notions of gender were always present. Stressing manliness (and contrasting American manhood with the supposed femininity of French culture) also ensured that the attainment of empire through aggressive means remained a viable concept for males. By the 1880s, some women challenged traditional values of domesticity, to the consternation of the male-dominated society. Lacking the vote, concerned about alcohol abuse and other scourges that threatened their families, enjoying higher levels of employment in the decade than before, and increasingly pivotal to the well-being of the country, women moved into the public sphere by advocating reform and civil rights. Most were homebound, but a majority of middle-class wives of professional men had gained autonomy as consumers who shunned household labor. Divorce was on the rise; elites worried about the American social fabric. They attempted to balance their views, but the new clashed with the old, and hypocrisy was often the result. Men revered women, but not the women's causes that would strengthen womanhood.

Women's activism likely catalyzed the male impulse to tout imperial-minded masculinity, as Spalding and other sportsmen constantly did in their rhetoric. Whereas in mid-nineteenth-century America sports had been frowned upon as wasteful, now it was a character-building activity promoted by "apostles of muscular Christianity" seeking both order and morality in a rapidly changing and diverse society. In Britain, too, sportsmen had transformed their loutish behavior to chivalric manliness. Late nineteenth-century sport in France, for its part, affirmed the segregation of the sexes to the advantage of men. But bureaucratization the world over during the Second Industrial Revolution led to an identity crisis among middle-class males, who worked in a feminized environment of offices rather than factories and farms. The post–Civil War generation of American men also had not proved their masculinity in war, and they were uncomfortable, as well, with the overly civilized nature of life in the United States in which "hordes of fertile immigrants" might soon supplant the effete Anglo-Saxon male. They turned to sports as an outlet, and afterward to war and empire-building, to express their gender concerns.[22]

Baseball, among such other sports as boxing, football, and hunting, filled a need for exhibiting masculinity. It was a sport requiring strength, agility, quickness, and a sound mind, the traits of "true manhood" and the "man of nerve." Physical fitness, peppered with the rhetoric of vigorous maleness, became the mantra of the late Victorian period. A team sport encouraged pride and spirit and allowed individuals to flourish by contributing to the greater whole. Baseball had a martial side to it; games were competitions that oftentimes turned violent. Courage was at a premium, for it was dangerous to stand in a batter's box awaiting a speeding pitch or to break up a double play with a slide. Urban classes, then, redefined their masculinity by adopting and playing sports like baseball, all the while remaining within the bounds of a proper society that encouraged traditional values. It should be noted, moreover, that the British encouraged cricket and rugby for the same reasons: to promote manly imperial virtues. Meanwhile, the French and the Italians later stressed combativeness and patriotism as a means of centralizing their masculine pastimes of soccer, rugby, cycling, gymnastics, track and field, and boxing into national sports and enhancing global prestige.[23]

The era of the world tour was not one of militant feminism challenging the male preserve of sports, for that came much later, but it did reveal that change in gender relations was under way. Gilded Age America, like Victorian England, considered the "woman question." Physical fitness concerns emerged among women, as much a result of the notion that they were chronically weak as from the push for liberation. More middle-class women participated in recreational sports than ever before, as scientists debated whether physiology determined the destiny of a human being. In England, by the 1870s, it was acceptable for girls to play cricket at school; the first professional women's team in any sport was the Original English Lady Cricketers, formed a year after the Spalding tour. Men might enshrine women as pure and gentle or treat them as sexual objects, but women confronted quaint beliefs when it came to sports and society in general. This happened on a global level in many areas of daily life.[24]

As far as the Spalding tourists were concerned, the challenge would be met by men asserting themselves by the manly sport of baseball. Women had played baseball at Vassar College in 1866 and in exhibitions in Illinois in the following decade. Attempts at organizing a woman's club failed until 1890 and the creation of the Young Ladies Baseball Club in New York, which played games in various cities. A women's team or league did not gain acceptance until World War II, but it was short-lived.

More acceptable to the baseball tourists were female spectators. Baseball officialdom encouraged their attendance and so did active career women like John Ward's wife, actress Helen Dauvray. She insisted that American women cast off their enfeebled ways and take an interest in outdoor sports, especially baseball, just as their vigorous English sisters did with cricket. Furthermore, women at the ballparks meant not only higher revenues, but, as the magnates hoped, their presence might make baseball a more respectable, and thus a more profitable, game by drawing ever more fans. Indeed, women "patronized all manly pastimes in which gentleman can participate," wrote Henry Chadwick, and they watched baseball in greater numbers than ever before. Curiosity, the acceptability of physical fitness, and outdoor activities as a form of healthy living and socializing brought them to the Spalding world tour exhibitions in large numbers.[25]

Women's fitness was far from the minds of the revelers in nighttime Paris, but cultivating manliness was foremost in Spalding's in his vision of the world tour. He linked sports to social purpose and the U.S. presence in the world, and he designed his global project to exhibit American manliness. Just as British soccer had been feminized by colonialists in Ireland, so Spalding characterized baseball and cricket in gendered terms. He claimed that cricket was effete and would "not satisfy the red-hot blood of Young or Old America." It was a "genteel game" played by men who donned a "negligee shirt" and "gorgeous hosiery" to "sally forth to the field of sport, with his sweetheart on one arm and his cricket bat under the other" in the hopes of not "soiling his linen or neglecting his lady." On the other hand, a baseballer said "goodbye to society," caring little about sliding in deep mud or for his sweetheart, who was "not for him while the game lasts." An exponent of "American Courage, Confidence, Combativeness; American Dash, Discipline, Determination; American Energy, Eagerness, Enthusiasm; American Pluck, Persistency, Performance, American Spirit, Sagacity, Success; American Vim, Vigor, Virility," the sport of baseball was, simply, manly. "Baseball is War!" Spalding proclaimed, and it was not for the feminized people of Old Europe, who supposedly preferred a more peaceful and "gentle pastime."[26]

The tourists finally got to show off their manly game but that event was most significant for its setting. A wet morning cleared to sunshine at the Parc Aerostatique on the banks of the Seine River, situated opposite the World Exposition of 1889, which had recently convened. Shadowing the playing field was the yet uncompleted Eiffel Tower. This iron structure, the tallest structure in the world, had been built to the height of 790 feet when the tourists saw it, and workers busied themselves to raise it to its full 1,000 feet for the Exposition Universelle. Many observers condemned it as an expensive eyesore, a dangerous lightning rod, or a useless observatory that would dishonor the Third Republic. Yet others believed it might be helpful as a military observation post or for meteorologists and astronomers to watch the skies. In reality, the Exposition Universelle also commemorated drivers of globalization, particularly technological innovation; the Eiffel Tower (along with Thomas Edison's phonograph) was the marvel of the age. The structure certainly symbolized the grandeur of France, then celebrating the one hundredth anniversary of its famous revolution, and pointed to other endeavors by the country, such as building an Isthmian Canal in Central America. Indeed, Gustave Eiffel had designed the sluice locks of the Panama Canal, as well as the interior framework for Bartholdi's Statue of Liberty, which had arisen in New York Harbor just three years before. The tourists could not help but be inspired by the Eiffel Tower's message of progress, prowess, and power emanating from the colossal edifice, decked out with the tricolor flag at its summit.[27]

Underneath the Eiffel Tower, in the presence of three thousand people on the afternoon of Friday, March 8, French and American spectators milled about, awaiting the baseball match. Military leaders represented

*Playing near the half-built Eiffel Tower.*
(Harry C. Palmer, *Athletic Sports in America, England, and Australia.*
Philadelphia: Hubbard Brothers, Publishers, 1889, p. 395)

President Sadi Carnot, who sent Spalding his regrets that other responsibilities pulled him away from his "interest to the development of physical exercise in the education of our youths." The latter were a particular concern for French leaders, who believed that their drubbing at the hands of Germany in 1871 rested, in part, on a lack of fitness among the young. Recently, French youth had looked to the English for guidance and advocated the development of muscular and manly "Bicepmen." For his part, Carnot focused on holding together his moderate government under France's Third Republic in the face of pressure from the radical Left and conservatives. In any case, Spalding was just as busy with preparations for his target audience in Britain (he had already written off France as a hopeless case for baseball), and had already departed for London with the English agent and railway representative S. S. Parry.[28]

Spalding might later have wished he had hung around in order to monitor the injury of Ed Williamson. American foreign service officers and their families, cheering Parisians evincing little understanding of the game, and skeptical journalists who regarded the game as a copy of English rounders, cricket, or the French *la longue thèque*, witnessed a seven-inning 6–2 win for All-America. Feeble Chicago hitting weakened when Williamson fell on a sharp stone while trying to steal second and tore his knee cap. His wife hurried him back to the hotel, but his injury would end his time at shortstop. In fact, he was confined to his room for the remainder of the tour and he did not return to the White Stockings' "stonewall infield" until the latter part of the 1889 season. By then, labor activists accused Spalding of having dumped the Williamsons on their own in Paris. Big Al might have better accounted for his player's welfare, considering the impending player's revolt that lay in store against the magnates.[29] Yet lacking faith in the prospects of baseball emerging anywhere else on the Continent, Spalding had abandoned Paris's high living and welcomed the party's imminent arrival in England.

## A ROYAL YAWN

Unlike the 1874 trip, Spalding this time came armed with two superb teams and significant advance planning that promised large turnouts at the games. In the last fifteen years, Spalding's country had grown even stronger in its world presence, compelling the British, he believed, to take note of American power and its favored sport. With Great Britain as his target, the White Stockings owner understood enough about international power to know that, even if John Bull was the diplomatic leader, Uncle Sam was a worthy rival and the true economic strength behind the throne.

Between the Civil War and World War I, globalization had a distinctly Anglicized bent, even though Americanization was fast approaching. During that period, the United States grew twice as fast as Britain, yet the sun still shone high in the sky over the British Empire. The same month that the Spalding tour had departed from Chicago, for instance, imperialist Cecil Rhodes had begun to organize financial backing for the myriad diamond mines in southern Africa. Queen Victoria's global domain was expanding. Thus, America found a secure economic competitor in Britain at the same time that a powerful combination of American goods and culture streamed across the Atlantic. Britain controlled the flow of information and consequently led this era of globalization, having produced and laid the cables that whisked news around the globe at a progressively cheaper rate and faster than ever before. Cable communications left either side of the Atlantic just a few minutes apart, while telephones, tested by Alexander Graham Bell in 1876, promised even faster messages in the future.[30]

These elements of Anglo-American globalization helped overcome a century of bad blood between the two nations. During much of the nineteenth century, Americans blamed Britain for their problems, seeing the British as an enemy who reveled in Yankee misfortune and meddled in its internal affairs. In the quarter-century since the Civil War, the United States had boxed with Britain over influence in the Western Hemisphere, especially regarding control of an Isthmian canal. Deep distrust remained in many quarters. Just months before, President Benjamin Harrison had won election thanks to publicity surrounding the indiscrete endorsement of Democrat Grover Cleveland by a British minister. Still, in general, from the 1870s onward, the two powers stood on the brink of a "great rapprochement," in which Americans transformed their views of Britain from antagonist to friend.[31] British travelers in America during the mid-1880s were surprised to find celebrations of Queen Victoria's birthday and the national anthem of their country sung heartily in such former revolutionary hotspots as Boston.[32]

Indeed, despite periodic flare-ups of Anglophobia, American commentators noted an "Anglo-mania" in the United States. Many appreciated the worth of associating with a globe-girdling empire. Calculations of the number of Anglo-American marriages, as well as friendly receptions by British social clubs for U.S. visitors, revealed that the English actually liked their American cousins. For their part, the British recognized the need to cultivate relations, for America's booming industrial power promised to transform global relationships to the extent that the Uncle Sam would succeed John Bull as beneficiary of the world economy. Furthermore, the tens of thousands of British expatriates living in the United

States engendered an appreciation for customs, laws, and practices of the former colony.[33]

Placed in this context, the Spalding tour can be viewed as both offering a fig leaf of friendship and as serving notice of a competitive thrust. It seemed natural to offer baseball to the British, owing to the mutual interest in outdoor sports. Yet Spalding's campaign faced formidable odds for one key reason: the tradition of cricket. As British historians have noted, the "games ethic" developed within British public schools was designed to build such qualities of character as courage, leadership, team spirit, and fairness in men who would then carry these values abroad. Imperialists deemed athletics critical to the dissemination of Anglo-Saxonism in the international arena. British sports proselytizing had already educated people at home and had greatly shaped native cultures throughout the empire. Thus, the British might resist U.S. sports imperialism because they had their own, well-tried version, in the form of cricket.[34]

Rising to the challenge, the tourists arrived in Dieppe just after midnight on Friday, March 8, and boarded the side-wheeled steamer *Normande* for the English Channel crossing in stormy weather. This tempest turned out to be the worst of their trip, as waves engulfed the vessel, carrying away one end of the bridge in what the captain confessed was the most violent weather he had encountered in his thirty-five years of plying the Channel. Huddled and seasick in the first-class cabin, the tourists finally arrived in the tiny seaport of New Haven at seven o'clock the next morning in bright sunshine. Passing through customs looking the worse for wear, they took a train to London's Victoria Station. Spalding and the secretary of the Surrey County Cricket Club, C. W. Alcock, escorted the miserable company to the First Avenue Hotel in Holborn, where they dove into the baggage that had been shipped from Port Said to Liverpool. Alcock, also the editor of the influential journal *Cricket*, was an appreciative friend of the Americans, knowing how well they had treated the many English cricketers who had toured the United States over the past decade. He maneuvered several English aristocrats and dignitaries into feting the tourists.[35] Under this cricket magnate's supervision, the tourists began their nearly three-week stay in the British Isles by sleeping off the effects of the Channel crossing and spending two days sightseeing in London.

Likely because they could converse in their own language, the Spalding tour members immediately loved London. The city, familiar in its buttoned-up ways, had been much in the popular press because of the thrilling violence of the recent Jack the Ripper murders, from August to November 1888. The terror still gripped London in mystery. The tourists found the city to be "greater, grander, more interesting and more impressive than all other cities of the world combined." The air was, expectedly, cold and damp, which curtailed their walks down the nearby Strand into Trafalgar Square. The big double-decked buses and the total absence of streetcars were strikingly pleasant, but less so was the "miserable failure" of London tailors, whose suits were ill-fitting. The evening of their first day included a performance of *Good Old Times* at the Princess's Theater. Wilson Barrett, a famous, resonant-voiced actor who had recently toured the United States with his huge hit, *The Sign of the Cross*, presided over musical selections and toasts for the baseball party.[36] The next night, March 12, theater patrons gave them box seats at the Lyceum and then invited them backstage for wine.

Celebrated sights occupied the tourists. They got a special escort by the secretary to the chairman of the House of Commons and the American chargé d'affaires, Henry White, who also booked them entry into Westminster Abbey for a special Sunday service (though they had time only to glimpse the interior) and a visit to Buckingham Palace. They did not linger to witness the arrival of Prime Minister William Gladstone in Parliament, although Harry Palmer did note Arthur Balfour's "ambitious and intellectual" but "somewhat kind and cruel" face, and all also heard Sir William Harcourse speak to the House of Commons about "the treatment of political prisoners in Ireland," which must have interested some descendants of that country in the party. Noted by Anson were paintings in the corridors worth "thousands of pounds."[37]

A typical mid-March downpour of rain awakened the tourists the next day, as they readied for their first exhibition match. Newspapers advertised the match by welcoming "our American cousins" and covering their round-the-world "pilgrimage," which British sportsmen appreciated for its "wearisomeness" and its "romance."[38] By lunch, the dreary fog had lifted enough to attempt the game, and the party made its way to the clubhouse of the Surrey County Cricket Club at Kennington Oval, London's popular cricket grounds owned by the Prince of Wales. They ate lunch and toasted the queen, the president of the United States, and several dukes, earls, and lords. Present also were the lord mayor, U.S. consul-general T. M. Waller, and chargé d'affaires White, as well as Britain's top cricketer, W. G. Grace. Under the gloomy circumstances, in which fog and rain shrouded the field and made shoe spikes stick in the muck, the game was a good one. Encircled by thick hedges, the Oval was a pretty setting for the eight thousand spectators to watch the exhibition, which Chicago won, 7–4. The ball could barely be seen when hit fifty feet above the ground, as runners slipped around the bases, yet the crowd appreciated their effort. They also liked their distinctive uniforms—All-America in white caps, white shirts with blue cuffs and collars, and blue stockings; the White Stockings sporting gray and black with their names inscribed on their shirts.

The game included the most famous encounter of the tour. In the third inning, the Prince of Wales appeared in a window behind the catcher's box, prompting the players to walk to home plate and cheer His Highness. At his request, after the fifth inning, the Spalding party was introduced to the future King Edward VII. He shook the mud-stained hands of every player, calling them by their first names, and then released them back to their game to the applause of the crowd. Spalding remained behind with him. At this point, Spalding revealed an innocent lack of knowledge of protocol. The prince suffered from a swelling on his neck, having trouble turning his head to look up at the much taller Big Al. Spalding placed a chair between the Prince of Wales and his brother-in-law, Prince Christian, which allowed him to continue to talk without having to bend over. Thousands of spectators, by some reports, held their breath when Spalding sat down next to the Prince in a breach of court etiquette.

The future monarch fired questions as he watched the game. When Anson whacked out a long hit, he slapped Spalding on the leg and exclaimed, "That was a hard clip!" A moment later, as a White Stocking slid into a base, Spalding returned the favor by tapping His Highness on the shoulder and asking, "What do you think of that?" Nearby British newsmen were aghast. But the Chicago magnate was unfazed, later explaining that he was not at court but at a baseball game, and if he "sat in the presence of Royalty, it is certain that Royalty sat in mine." Besides, the tap on the shoulder "was nothing more offensive than a game of tag" in which the Prince had slapped Spalding's leg first.[39] The event was harmless, but the faux pas was another example of American ignorance at best, and crassness at worst, toward European ways.

Like most observers of the eleven matches played in England, Scotland, and Ireland, the Prince of Wales enjoyed them because of their novelty, unconvinced that the game rivaled cricket. The *New York Herald* passed out a survey to spectators, asking whether they thought baseball was more scientific than cricket and if the sport would catch on in England. When asked what he thought of baseball, the prince graciously expressed interest but considered "cricket as superior." This loyalty to the British game was taken in part as jest; along these lines, one reporter decided to attend the game not so much to see baseball but to observe if the Prince of Wales was any the worse for wear after his losing streak at the horse races. But it was also a reminder that Europeans did not bend easily to American ideas and practices, no matter how vigorously marketed by the Spalding promotional machine. Like the 1874 tour, the 1889 trip so far seemed to have made no converts; baseball was said to be in its "caterpillar stage" in British public opinion and all spectators professed an unawareness of baseball. Audiences saw skilled play, yet, based on the lukewarm reception, it was doubtful that the game had a future in Great

*The Prince of Wales.*

(Harry C. Palmer, *Athletic Sports in America, England, and Australia.*
Philadelphia: Hubbard Brothers, Publishers, 1889, p. 417)

Britain. Cricket, that most English of sports, was just too popular for baseball to become "a standard game with us," wrote a newsman.[40]

Baseball did earn some positive appraisals, but it ultimately failed for the British. Press reports revealed it to be a fine display of athletic skills. The Americans were, moreover, "an exceedingly fine lot of fellows" who compared favorably to English and Australian cricketers. Spectators particularly enjoyed the three cheers and the "tiger" given for the Prince of Wales that interrupted play. Also, the outfield catching, base-running, and throwing was "wonderful." Yet the game had certain problems. First off, there was Nature; Britain lacked enough room for many diamonds, while some held that the sport could only be played under blue skies and, for that reason, would never succeed in overcast England. Then there was the style of play. Stealing seemed more "amusing" than skillful, and the outfielders' long throws did not compare to those of cricketers. Furthermore, baseball was too complex, too burdened with rules. For British observers, who schooled themselves in the finer points of the game with the help of newspaper explanations and illustrations, the batting and scoring were insufficient. The pitching was so fast and the curves so "tremendous" that the throw "seems to bring with it either permanent injury or sudden death." Meanwhile a hitter might get on base, but then never reach home, and thus fail to score. This "absolute failure of batting," combined with the pitcher having too much power, would prove fatal to the game in England, pundits predicted. Learning of this latter criticism, Spalding was rumored to have asked his pitchers to moderate their speed so that the scoring would increase.

The American pastime also suffered from its seemingly obvious origins in the child's game of rounders, as well as from the influence of American-style capitalism. With too much defense, baseball ended up being "nothing more nor less than scientific rounders," which many believed had fathered baseball and was so much in vogue in British schools. Journalists described the game to their readers as the "good old English game of rounders" that, they argued, had been carted across the Atlantic on the *Mayflower* and developed in America into baseball. British spectators wrote in to the newspapers with such views as, "Oh, it is familiar. I believe I have played it myself."[41]

English comment ran, on the whole, against baseball, the more moderate saying it was dull, and many others voting with their feet when they exited the game before it ended. Journalists took note of the advertising and circus atmosphere that brought out the crowds, declaring that the tourists were in Britain only because they had been floated by "their rich backer," Albert Spalding. Some felt suckered into watching baseball by the Americans' vigorous promotional efforts. Repeated commentary alluded to the expense of mounting a game or building a team; in

America, "baseball is a professional institution" (as if cricket were not). In sum, the exhibition appeared to be part showy advertising and part an adult version of rounders. Such views "were by no means encouraging to our baseball missionaries," confessed Harry Palmer, and they confirmed for Cap Anson "that baseball would never become a popular English sport, an opinion that since then has proved to be correct."[42]

The New World would not redress the Old on this score. That became clear early on in a diagram of the game in *The Sporting Times*, on March 16, with a caption that described the game as "exceedingly simple." The explanation made Spalding's head swim. The object of the "Shifter and the Pitcher," whoever they were, was to run around the bases without encountering the fielders, that is, the "Writters and Catcher." But should they indeed meet up in a "mishap," the Shifter and Pitcher "are promptly put out of play by being driven to the "Prisoner's Base," which was a mysterious box, probably some sort of early dugout. The six bases drawn along the "thoroughfare," or base paths, were also unidentifiable to the tourists; among their labels were the "court's base," "roman's base," and "abbot's base."[43] Clearly, the journalists mocked the American game in their likening it to "rounders, with a difference." The British did not take baseball very seriously. Worse, they certainly did not view baseball as a threat to cricket or even a help to cricketers who might practice hitting in the off-season, for that matter.[44]

## CONTESTING JOHN BULL

The next day, March 13, the tourists encountered the same responses when they played on the velvety green turf of Lord's cricket ground of the Marylebone Cricket Club in St. John's Wood. Fully seven thousand people flocked to this back-and-forth Wednesday contest, at which they applauded at the good base-running and fielding. Timely hitting allowed Chicago to overcome a three-run deficit in the eighth inning, but errors by Mark Baldwin and Cap Anson let All-America sneak back on top with a one-run victory, 7–6. The head of the Marylebone Cricket Club, the Duke of Buccleuch, showed an understanding of the game but the critics were in the majority. That this game of modified rounders "will become popular with our countrymen is very doubtful," wrote journalists, due to its costliness to manage and seemingly sole reliance on pitching and fielding cleverness. Spalding hoped that the tourists would find more favor once they traveled northward from the sophisticated metropolis into the hinterlands.[45]

The next day, at the Crystal Palace Cricket Grounds in the residential area of Sydenham, Spalding lost John Ward along with the argument over

*The clubhouse at Lord's cricket grounds.*
(Harry C. Palmer, *Athletic Sports in America, England, and Australia.*
Philadelphia: Hubbard Brothers, Publishers, 1889, p. 414)

baseball versus cricket. A majestic glass-and-iron structure, a memorial to Queen Victoria, and a popular destination of touring Americans, the Crystal Palace was the backdrop to another well-played victory for All-America, who won without their captain. Citing personal reasons, Ward departed England for home that morning. Anson and some of the others were likely glad to be rid of his bad moods, which he exhibited by surliness on the ball field, and Ward was happy to be leaving, too, although he promised to rejoin the tour in New York. He left, some said, in an attempt to save his crumbling marriage, yet most believed he wanted to return home to take up the mantle of the Brotherhood union in its efforts to reform baseball's reserve clause before the upcoming 1889 season. This drama awaited Spalding upon his return. In the meantime, the American party took heart that the dry but cloudy day brought out six thousand spectators who manifested the most enthusiasm for the sport thus far in England. Jostling spectators cheered some brilliant plays, including catches of "high flyers," the pitching that "dismissed" batters, and the rapid runners who were rewarded "for their daring" by putouts at home plate. In general, they were excited by the close score, 5–3, in favor of All-America, now guided by Ned Hanlon.[46]

An early Friday morning departure in a big saloon train car took the tourists west to the coastal shipping town of Bristol. They had intended to play their first match on English soil there to honor the nation's greatest cricketer, W. G. Grace, had not the storm in the Channel soaked the field and diverted them to London. That was the public reason; kept on the quiet was a deal between Spalding and Grace to play at the brand new Gloucester County Cricket Club, with its green sward and gray stone walls. These grounds in the suburb of Ashley Hill had cost nearly nine thousand pounds, and Grace saw a chance at some pre–cricket season marketing to get out the spectators and earn money. For his part, Spalding welcomed the endorsement of the imposing "W. G.," a forty-year-old physician and cricketer best remembered for his record-setting 344 score in the "eight days" of August 1876, the first "triple century" in first-class cricket. Grace was still the best batsman in the game and a hero of the era, an exceptional player in a sport just entering its golden era of popularity.[47]

At the depot, Club officials, led by Grace, as well as members of the board of trade and the Duke of Beaufort, met the Spalding party and held an audience with them at the Grand Hotel. The sporting duke raised racehorses at his nearby Badminten estate. After a convivial banquet of toasts and an admonishment from Spalding for the cricketers not to prejudge his game of baseball, a bright day greeted the tourists. A sterling double play by Ryan and Baldwin, complemented by solid base-running, could not overcome a listlessness on the part of the players. Still, the three thousand spectators were appreciative, as was the duke, who sat near home plate and listened to Spalding's coaching. The reporters were not so kind, some of the sharpest believing that the All-America players were journeymen rather than true all-stars, and the more patronizing issuing the well-worn complaints that pitching overwhelmed batting, that the players should be given a larger bat, and that baseball was a good game—for Americans.

The crowd might have been more interested in their cricketers attempting to play baseball after Chicago's 10–3 victory. The White Stockings took the field while Grace and other cricketers took turns trying to hit. When Ryan and Crane bore down with speedy pitches, the British came up empty. Slowing down their throws over the next fifteen minutes allowed the cricketers to make contact with the ball, but only E. M. Grace, W. G.'s brother who was known mysteriously as "the Coroner," made a safe hit. Hometown rooters believed he had done quite well, though. To the dismay of Spalding, the "exhibition pleased the crowd even more than the game had done." The party received a hearty farewell applause before they left the field and returned to London that evening.[48] Cricket had trumped baseball once again.

Back in London, the tourists played a match on a gloomy Saturday afternoon at the Essex County Cricket Club in Leyton, before a large crowd of eight thousand people who actually grew more excited by the action after the game. There were hopes for more hitting; the Leyton grounds, noted reporters, were a half-acre larger than the Kennington

Oval and thus "there should be ample space for even the hardest hitters on both teams."[49] The pitchers seemed to ease up, and the British spectators, including two members of Parliament, got their wish for more scoring. Chicago won a sloppy offensive battle, 12–6, but the Londoners approved because of the numerous hits. Again, a sideshow enthused the spectators more than the national pastime. "Cannonball" Crane was scheduled to compete in a throwing contest with an Australian cricketer, G. J. Bonner, who backed out at the last minute. The American displayed his strength, anyway, by launching a cricket ball more than 110 yards with little apparent exertion and followed by tossing a baseball an even longer distance. The thousands who poured onto the field to watch the exhibition were duly impressed, and Crane might have thrown the balls further had they not crowded him by swarming around the turf.[50]

## INTO THE LION'S HEARTLAND

The tourists now embarked on a grand tour of Britain, although most of the trip involved quick one-day visits to towns and cities. They arrived, played ball, and departed for the next city, leaving little time for sightseeing. Negotiations between Stamford Parry, the Burlington and Quincy London agent who had arranged the British leg of the tour, and C. W. Alcock of the London and Northwestern Railway (and Surrey Country Club) had fitted out the entourage with a nine-car luxury train with a twenty-seven-ton engine waiting at Euston Station. Two dining saloons, joined by a vestibule, were connected to two smokers and five sleeping cars that each accommodated eight passengers in comfort. The food served for lunches and dinners included oyster soup, lamb, tongue, and fancy pastries. The exterior in white enamel, trimmed in gold and brown, with gold and scarlet Royal Arms on the carriage doors, was highlighted by banners on each car that announced "The American Baseball Clubs." Tired from the celebrations over the past few nights, the entourage nonetheless expressed its delight at the banners and the luxuriousness of the train. The train made up for the disappointment of departing from beloved London. Five hundred people saw them off, and they then chugged two and a half hours northwest to Birmingham, past fleeting glances of trimmed hedges and rolling green fields.[51]

After meeting a delegation from the Warwickshire County Cricket Club at the station, their hosts whisked the tourists to a wine reception, lunch, and then out to the cricket grounds where three thousand incredulous fans greeted them. Threatening weather did not detract from superb pitching by Baldwin and Healy after the latter allowed four first-inning runs. Only darkness called the tied game in the tenth inning, to the disappointment

*Traveling in the special train.*
(Harry C. Palmer, *Athletic Sports in America, England, and Australia.*
Philadelphia: Hubbard Brothers, Publishers, 1889, p. 422)

of the crowd, yet it appeared their enthusiasm had waned by the game's end. A reporter doubted that "a single visitor went away with a very exalted opinion of the American national game." It brought back childhood memories of rounders, although this version was just a bit more intricate and played by grown professionals. Base-running generated a bit of excitement, but the lack of scoring led one Birminghamian to quip, "Fancy having lost an afternoon's work for this, and wasted two pints into the bargain." Journalists concluded that "cricket and football are not likely to suffer on account of the introduction of baseball amongst us— not much!" At least the spectators, if not enamored with baseball, were struck by the gilded train that stood in New Street Station.[52]

A visit to the Prince of Wales Theater that evening topped off the day, and then the tourists departed north for the great cutlery manufacturing center of Sheffield the next morning. The trip aroused considerable interest, for the rural landscape gave way to industrial scenes of which they had read. Amidst fuming smokestacks, ironworks, and collieries of the "Black Country," locals greeted them at short stops throughout York. Met by members of the Yorkshire County Cricket Club, an influential organization that prided itself on representing North England values of populist determination and toughness (in contrast to London's supposed effete snobbery), the tourists were feted over lunch at the Royal Victoria Hotel. They were then spirited in two big coaches to the Bramall Lane grounds, a famous and ancient athletic field.

A crowd of four thousand opened umbrellas as the rain poured down until the game was called in the fourth inning with All-America ahead, 10–0. The audience had been interested, but not nearly to an extent that they normally focused on soccer. Sheffield remained for years a capital of British football; twenty-four thousand people had poured out to see a game the previous Saturday. Spalding wanted to tap these numbers, so ironically, in light of his disdain for rounders and single-minded focus on baseball, he bit the bullet and arranged some exhibitions of the child's game with the secretary of the National Rounders Association when the tour visited Liverpool. Such was his apparent desperation to make the tour a success. If the tourists could not attract the British by baseball, at least they would appear for another sport, even if it meant associating the dreaded rounders with the American national pastime.[53]

The entourage traveled an hour north to Bradford. The weather started off nice at the Bradford Cricket, Football, and Athletic Club, but a snowstorm that had moved through the day before had left the field in bad shape and returned in the form of a chill wind and rain by game time. With an English stiff upper lip, spectators, four thousand strong, entered the grounds in midafternoon wearing mackintoshes and carrying umbrellas. Prodded by club officials to play three innings in the deplorable conditions, the tourists performed brilliantly. They also proved to be game competitors. James Fogarty tore the sole of a shoe in a slide and played the rest of the way with his foot wrapped in towel. Stopping with Chicago in the lead, 6–3, the tourists gladly retired to the cozy smoking cars as the train sped through the raw evening to Scotland.[54]

Sports fans in sports-crazy Scotland were plainly interested in the tourists. At breakfast on Thursday, March 21, they entered Glasgow, which gave them a warm welcome in decidedly cold weather. Hundreds of people had braved the snow to see them off from Bradford, dozens more appeared at intervening stations during a night in which gales blew down telegraph wires, and hundreds bustled around the train as it stood in the Glasgow depot. Women drove up in carriages to take a peek, people as curious as if the "Shah of Iran himself" had just arrived, wrote Palmer. Wearing heavy coats over their uniforms, the players walked to the shipyards on the Clyde and then lunched at the train company hotel at the station while the crowd grew larger. They then set out in a double-decked four-horse carriage, driving past the Exposition and University buildings en route, for the West of Scotland Cricket Club grounds where timely batting and wild throws by Chicago handed All-America the victory, 8–4, before four thousand spectators. The applause was constant.

Returning to the train, the party donned suits for the Grand Theater performance of *King Lear*, with champagne backstage afterward at the invitation of American Osmond Tearle, who was a crowd favorite. As in their other stops since London, they had virtually no time for sightseeing in Glasgow. That evening, the train headed back south for the birthplace of the industrial revolution, Manchester.[55]

Arriving at Central Station in "Cottonopolis," they enjoyed time to look around during that Friday, although the highlight was, once again, an exhibition game. Because wealthy, industrial Manchester encountered palatial dining cars all the time, the tourists' "special" train did not evince much curiosity. After lunch, the tourists went to the Old Trafford cricket grounds to play one of the tour's best games before 3,500 appreciative fans, many of them distinguished businessmen. In the bracing cold, Hanlon's squad tied the game at five runs, and took the lead in the eighth inning, only to have Chicago knot the score in their bottom half. Hanlon scored the game-winner for All-America in the bottom of the ninth with a single and a daring steal of second base, after which Fogarty doubled him home. Hanlon was so cold that after he scurried home, he kept on running into the clubhouse. The rest of the players followed as the crowd applauded loudly.

They warmed up at an evening banquet of salmon, veal, and truffled capon chaired by the U.S. consul, Major Hale, as guests at the Anglo-French Club of Raymond Eddy, European representative of a Chicago investment house. After the reception ended, the tourists went to the Comedy Theatre to see Miss Annie Vivian perform in *Aladdin*, as well dance to "Yankee Doodle Dandy" in a costume of silken American flags. They went to bed late for an early morning departure for Liverpool, just an hour away.[56]

Another crowd of staring patrons awaited the teams at the depot in overcast Liverpool, their last stop on English soil, where they felt at home until rounders intruded once again. To many, it had "an unmistakable American air to it." Liverpool's familiarity likely arose because the mass of 6,500 at the Police Athletic Club grounds seemed like a National League crowd awaiting a championship game. The nines played to a 2–2 tie in five innings, Baldwin and Crane both pitching superbly. Even though the teams wished to continue, the locals called the shots—and indicated the futility of the mission of baseball in Britain. A rounders game ensued, with eleven American players confronting a side from the Rounders' Association of Liverpool.

In rounders, the fielders are stationed like baseball players, except for one who backstops the catcher and another who plays behind the third baseman. Hitting a ball with a tiny paddle, the runner runs clockwise to iron stakes, instead of bags, and is called out only if touched or hit with the ball. The British defeated the Americans 16–14 in two innings and then the teams switched to two innings of baseball, with the Yanks rolling 18–0. The tourists noted that only Frank Sugg, a champion cricketer, seemed able to catch a fly ball, and even he was no match as a "bowler" for the American hitters. The crowd enjoyed both contests, standing in the drenching rain, as did the players, who felt the matches were "a good deal of sport." But the Spalding tourists also hoped they never encountered rounders again; it seemed so childish and primitive, and a "fine game for the girls."[57]

Yet criticism, even ridicule, continued regarding their own sport of baseball. A cartoon, entitled "One Offer," ran in the British *Sporting Life*, picturing two English boys who hailed from a "United Grand Boys Rounders Club" approaching some big American ballplayers, one of them wearing a catcher's mask. The caption read, "Baseball. The American game about which so much has been said, is simply 'rounders.'"[58] The British flocked to the games, but either because of the spectacle of the American tourists or seemingly due to the fact that it reminded them of their happy childhoods.

In any case, after brief appearances at the theater, the party boarded the *Princess of Wales* that evening and went up the coast to Fleetwood before crossing the Irish Channel to Belfast to promote the game in Ireland. To their relief, unlike their arrival in England, the weather was pleasant as they entered Belfast Loch. The Irish had a sporting tradition as manly as the American and English, although it was enmeshed in the politics of independence. Thus, many Irish viewed soccer as a foreign, effeminized sport that was inimical to native culture. A Gaelic Athletic Association had been formed in 1884 to break from British cultural domination in sports, although it was largely ignored by the revolutionary Charles Parnell. The Irish saw baseball as an outlandish import, too, although one to view with benevolence because of their immigrant ties to America.

After carriages transported the tourists to the Imperial Hotel that quiet Sunday morning, each player received an Irish translation of the British national anthem from dignitaries and then the tourists looked around Belfast's famous linen warehouses. Bad weather cleared by the next afternoon's game at the North of Ireland Cricket Club that straddled the Lagan River. The teams thrilled the more than 2,500 people who watched a great game on the damp turf. The fans were rapturous over the 9–8 victory for All-America when Wood and Healy both singled and Earle tripled them home in the ninth inning. Another banquet followed that evening, with the mayor of Belfast presiding at the cricket grounds, and then the evening closed with shows at the Theatre Royal and Ginett's Circus.[59]

Another early morning train trip took them to Dublin, about five hours south, where the U.S. consul greeted them at the station. They stayed at Morrison's Hotel, famous as the spot where Charles Parnell had been arrested. Parnell had visited America and Canada in 1880 to obtain sympathy for the Irish against England, and even addressed Congress, so some of the tourists likely knew of him. In the green of Dublin, most of the entourage went sightseeing and then attended the Gaiety Theater performance of *The Arabian Nights*. Three players took off to visit friends and relatives in the vicinity. Jim Manning's uncle in Kilkenny boasted pictures of the ballplayer but he confessed to be stumped as to how a man could earn a salary playing ball. Tom Daly headed down to Kildare and saw uncles who expressed befuddlement at the sport of baseball. And John Tener's family in Londonderry was thrilled to catch up; many had not seen him or their American family for two decades and none understood the national pastime. That the families naturally asked about relatives abroad was no surprise, for Ireland's population had been nearly cut in half by the late 1880s due to the years of famine. Parnell was ever in the news, but it was likely that local sports—horseracing and the Yankee pastime of baseball—grabbed the attention of the Americans' transatlantic relatives at the moment.[60]

The final game on foreign territory took place the next afternoon, March 27, after the tourists scooped up souvenirs from Ireland, including sod for Irish-Americans back home. At the Mansion House, the lord mayor welcomed them before they sat down to lunch and then proceeded to the Landsowne Road Grounds through the beautiful old city. The grounds were better suited for tennis or football, but the teams made do. At least the weather was bright and clear. The crowd of four thousand watched a gem of a game. All-America came from two runs down in the ninth inning, on a triple, walk, error, and game-winning double, for a 4–3 triumph. The problem was that the spectators expected a high, cricket-like score, and they did not understand why these large men did not hit more. Pfeffer's sacrifice fly that brought in an early run met with sarcasm; at last, a score had squeaked across. Still, the players were honored by the appearance of the lord lieutenant-governor of Ireland and Prince Albert of Saxe-Weimar, who commanded English forces in Dublin, as well as the lord mayor and U.S. officials.[61]

That evening, the Southern Railway Company brought in three elegant coaches, each decorated with a U.S. flag, that spirited the celebrating All-America squad, and the more subdued White Stockings, away to Cork. To date, All-America had won fifteen and tied three of the thirty matches on foreign soil. Their good play prompted some American observers to talk about importing them all to a U.S. city. But only Anson seemed to care that Chicago had come up short, miffed that his team had fared so badly. The rest of the party determined to kiss the Blarney Stone. A dancing, whiskered old elf with a peaked hat tickled them near Blarney Castle, although he sustained the stereotype of Ireland as a fairyland despite their knowledge of the harsh side of the Irish experience. After the encounter, the carriages started for Queenstown, eleven miles away, where the White Star steamer *Adriatic* waited at the docks.

Purchasing their last blackthorn canes, *shillelaghs*, and sprays of shamrocks, they bantered with locals about their relatives across the ocean. Except for Williamson and his wife, who remained in London tending to his injuries, the Spalding party boarded the ship, along with nearly 1,200 other passengers, 900 of them in steerage. The *Adriatic* pulled off the dock into the river, past Cork Harbour, and headed west for the Atlantic Ocean and New York City.[62]

## MADE IN EUROPE

That Friday, March 29, the tourists were homeward bound, and Spalding assessed the trip's results. He had championed baseball and received a hefty sum of money from the British leg. The same could not be said of

*Entertainment outside of Blarney Castle.*

(Harry C. Palmer, *Athletic Sports in America, England, and Australia.*
Philadelphia: Hubbard Brothers, Publishers, 1889, p. 438)

any other foreign stop except the Australian cities. Netting 75 percent of the British gate receipts, with the cricket clubs keeping the rest, Spalding surely realized that while a profit had been turned, there would be scant rewards from future proceeds of European baseball, at least in the short term. Although the following year, the British organized a four-team league that drew a respectable number of spectators, roughly equivalent to the U.S. minor leagues, cricket and rounders still prevailed.[63]

Spalding's promotional efforts had brought the tourists plenty of pleasure but his marketing skills fell flat in the ancient cities and towns of the British Isles and continental Europe. Baseball interest either flagged after a few years or locals adapted the game to their own styles. For instance, in Wales, both men and women played a brand of baseball as an expression of Welsh autonomy. Asked by curious reporters in Belfast about the impact of baseball, Big Al replied that the sport had emerged as a serious contender to all outdoor activities in the fifteen years since he had last visited England. A cricketer might find the game difficult, but the British and their imperial subjects would also welcome it because it took just two hours to finish. "It fits American character," he concluded, for "there's a go about it with exercise and danger enough to lend spice."[64] But cricketers were not American, and they rejected baseball, despite Spalding's bold marketing. He was deluded if he believed the national pastime would rival Britain's wickets.[65]

Spalding erroneously believed that the tour had spurred the acceptance of the national pastime abroad, although he noted the difficulties in some places. He wrote about the creation of a half-dozen new clubs in Hawaii. In New Zealand, full of sports-loving people, he believed that the game would "become a fixture there." He had high hopes for Australia, but Egypt was a tough sell, "for in a country where they use a stick for a plow, and hitch a donkey and a camel together to draw it, and do many other things as they did twenty years ago, it is hardly reasonable to expect that the modern game of base-ball will become one of its sports." The "small stature" of the Italians and French meant an uphill battle, although the latter might adapt. Unfortunately, the British seemed stuck in their cricketing ways, never looking "with much favor on any new thing."[66]

In a broader sense, the American tourists had more to learn from their forebears across the Atlantic than Europeans cared to learn from them. Alexis de Tocqueville, a French visitor to the United States in the early 1830s, had commented that "an American leaves his country with a heart swollen with pride; on arriving in Europe, he at once finds that we are not as engrossed by the United States and the great people who inhabit them as he had supposed; and this begins to annoy him." The frustrated American often turned to "invidious comparisons and lofty boasts" as a result.[67] Over a half-century after this observation, the tourists bore out de

Tocqueville's view. Spalding's mission, however determined to make its mark, had seemingly passed through Europe with just a flutter of interest. Royalty and affluence had appeared at the games, and statesmen had welcomed the tour. Yet Europe had remained nonchalant, even indifferent, toward this cultural icon of the United States, no matter how hard Albert Spalding campaigned. In this case, Americanization had failed, as the Old World had graciously resisted the penetration of the New. Despite nascent U.S. international influence across the Earth, when it came to the process of Anglo-American globalization and cultural integration, the case of baseball revealed that the "Anglo," rather than the "American," side of the equation remained in favor.

## NOTES

1. Dulles, *Americans Abroad*, 96–97. See also Carter, *Buffalo Bill Cody*; Wilson, *Buffalo Bill's Wild West*.

2. Sigaux, *History of Tourism*, 79. See also Feifer, *Tourism in History*, 183; Tissot, "How Did the British Conquer Switzerland?"; Bradley, "Around the World"; Simmons, "Railways, Hotels, and Tourism"; Salomone, "Nineteenth-Century Discovery."

3. Twain, *Innocents Abroad*, 427–28; Dulles, *Americans Abroad*, 109–11. See also Steinbrink, "Why the Innocents Went Abroad"; Drabble, *Oxford Companion to English Literature*, 1007–8; quoted in Plesur, *America's Outward Thrust*, 62; Sigaux, *History of Tourism*, 74–78; Feifer, *Tourism in History*, 188, 192–200; Buzard, *Beaten Track*, 47–79, 155–216.

4. Plesur, *America's Outward Thrust*, 104–10; Dulles, *Americans Abroad*, 123–27, 134–38; Endy, "Travel and World Power," 567. President William McKinley tapped Mrs. Palmer to help manage the great Chicago Exposition of 1893; in this capacity, she helped procure loans of paintings from European galleries. Gardner actually exhibited one of her paintings at the Exposition, but two years before, she became a major figure in collecting art when her father, upon his death, left her $2.75 million. See also Borocz, "Travel-Capitalism," 709–19; Rannella and Walter, "Planned Serendipity."

5. Plesur, *America's Outward Thrust*, 126–28.

6. Carlson, "Universal Athletic Sport."

7. Dulles, *Americans Abroad*, 49; James Ryan, *Tour of the Spalding B.B.C. around the World* [diary] (hereafter cited as Ryan Diary), James Edward Ryan Biographical File, National Baseball Hall of Fame, Cooperstown, New York, entries for February 11–15, 1889, pp. 63–64; Palmer, *Athletic Sports*, 343–44; Anson, *A Ball Player's Career*, 242–43.

8. Palmer, *Athletic Sports*, 345–46. See also "The American Baseball Teams," newspaper clipping, *Albert Spalding Scrapbook*, vol. 10, Albert Spalding Collection, Society of American Baseball Researchers Lending Library, Cleveland, Ohio (hereafter cited as Spalding Scrapbooks).

9. Albrecht-Carrié, *Europe after 1815*, 95–97; "Italy in 1888–89", *Littell's Living Age* (April–June 1889): 707–17; "Italian Emigration," *Nation* 48 (May 30, 1889): 440; Thomas Bayard to Fava, February 1, 9, and 12, 1889, M99, "Notes to Foreign Legations in the United States from the Department of State," roll 63, RG 59, Records of the Department of State, National Archives and Records Administration of the United States, College Park, Maryland (hereafter cited as RG 59, NARA).

10. Palmer, *Athletic Sports*, 346–56.

11. Anson, *A Ball Player's Career*, 245.

12. Palmer, *Athletic Sports*, 357–63.

13. Palmer, *Athletic Sports*, 364; Stevens, *Baseball's Radical*, 76; Newton MacMillian, "The Boys Disappointed," *New York Herald*, February 17, 1889; Di Salvatore, *A Clever Base-Ballist*, 242.

14. Palmer, *Athletic Sports*, 364, also 370; Anson, *A Ball Player's Career*, 247–48; Rector O'Connel to Spalding, February 22, 1889, Spalding Scrapbooks, vol. 10.

15. Palmer, *Athletic Sports*, 262, 375, 376. "Devils" cited by Tener in Lane, "Greatest President," 262.

16. "Baseball, a Villa Borghese," newspaper clipping, Spalding Scrapbooks, vol. 10. See also Palmer, *Athletic Sports*, 378–79; Heard, "Florence the Beautiful"; "The Continent," newspaper clipping, Spalding Scrapbooks, vol. 10.

17. "The Baseball Teams," newspaper clipping, Spalding Scrapbooks, vol. 10; Ryan Diary, February 26, 1889, p. 70; Palmer, *Athletic Sports*, 382–83.

18. Palmer, *Athletic Sports*, 384, also 385–91. See also Di Salvatore, *A Clever Base-Ballist*, 242; Brownell, "French Traits," 241; Anson, *A Ball Player's Career*, 254; Ryan Diary, February 27, 1889, p. 70.

19. Anson, *A Ball Player's Career*, 255, 256. See also Dulles, *Americans Abroad*, 109. For the balloon race, see Ryan Diary, March 3, 1889, p. 72.

20. Palmer, *Athletic Sports*, 396, also 397–99. See also Ryan Diary, March 6, 1889, p. 73; Dulles, *Americans Abroad*, 74–75.

21. Palmer, *Athletic Sports*, 400.

22. See, for instance, Faithfull, *Three Visits to America*, 14–29, 299–333; Johnson, "One Reason"; Phelps, "Divorce in the United States"; Allen, "Woman's Intuition." See also Brownell, "French Traits," 74–82. For gender and foreign policy, see Bederman, *Manliness and Civilization*; Hoganson, *Fighting for American Manhood*.

23. Riess, "Sport and the Redefinition," 10, 15, 16, also 17. See also Kimmel, "Baseball and the Reconstitution," 47–61; Mangan, "Muscular, Militaristic and Manly"; Dalisson, "Asserting Male Values"; Holt, "Contrasting Nationalisms"; Holt, "Women, Men, and Sport."

24. Park, "Physiology and Anatomy"; McCrone, "Class, Gender, and English Women's Sport"; Parratt, "Athletic 'Womanhood,'" 142; Park, "Sport, Gender, and Society." For Britain's manly empire, see Adair, Phillips, and Nauright, "Sporting Manhood." For the global theme, see Hoganson, "Cosmopolitan Domesticity."

25. Chadwick notes, K 27, undated, Henry Chadwick Scrapbooks, Society of American Baseball Researchers Lending Library, Cleveland, Ohio (hereafter cited as Chadwick Scrapbooks), vol. 26, reel 4. See also Light, *Cultural Encyclopedia of Baseball*, 792. Dauvray in "Baseball and the Ladies," *New York Herald*, April 7, 1889, p. 10.

26. Spalding, *Baseball*, 4–7. See also Levine, *A. G. Spalding*, 98–99. For feminization, see McDevitt, "May the Best Man Win."

27. "Paris," *New York Herald-Paris*, March 5, 1889, p. 2. See also Levenstein, *Seductive Journey*; Lane to Bayard, November 1, 1888, "Despatches from U.S. Ministers to France," roll 105, M34, RG 59, NARA; "The Eiffel Tower," *Littell's Living Age* 66 (April–June 1889): 378–80; Hervé and Bergdoll, *The Eiffel Tower*; Flammarion, "Of What Use"; Lautreppe, "Preliminary Walk"; Hodeir, "En route pour le pavillon americain!"; "Exposition Universelle," *Le Monde Illustré* 33 (March 2, 1889): 135; Bishop, "Paris Exposition"; Hall, "Images of the French Revolution"; Navailles, "Eiffel's Tower"; Lemoine, "L'Entreprise Eiffel"; Barry, "Eiffel." Eiffel built the Bordeaux bridge before setting up his own firm in 1868 and engineering the Maria Pia bridge over the Douro River, the Budapest railway station, the Garabit viaduct, and the Nice equatorial observation cupola among his designs for factories, churches, and breakwaters. Designer of the world's first wind tunnel, Eiffel secured commissions because he began the technique of standardizing and prefabricating parts, which eased and lowered costs of construction. He had an early presence in Indochina, but withdrew from public view when he was implicated in the corruption scandal that ruined the Panama Canal Company. See also Trocmé, "Les Etats-Unis et L'Exposition."

28. "Athletics in France," *Nation* 47 (September 27, 1888): 245–46; "Paris," *New York Herald-Paris*, March 5, 1889, p. 2; "The Political Situation in France," *Littell's Living Age* 66 (April–June, 1889): 259–67.

29. Palmer, *Athletic Sports*, 401–2; Rene De Gas, "Au Jour Le Jour" and "Les Sports Athletiques," newspaper clippings, Spalding Scrapbooks, vol. 8; "World of Sport," *New York Herald-Paris*, March 9, 1889, p. 3; Spalding, *Baseball*, 259.

30. Levine, "Business, Missionary Motives," 62; Eckes and Zeiler, *Globalization and the American Century*, 11, 23; Ferguson, *Empire*, 223.

31. Perkins, *The Great Rapprochement*, 4–5; Beisner, *From the Old Diplomacy to the New*, 38–71.

32. Brierly, *Ab-O'Th-Yate*, 222–23.

33. Collier, "Better Side of Anglo-Mania"; Vambery, "Is the Power"; Wilder, "Our English Cousins"; Lambert, "Americanized Englishmen."

34. See Mangan, *Athleticism*; Mangan, *Games Ethic*; Mangan and Hickey, "Globalization."

35. "England Astir," *Sporting Life*, February 27, 1889, p. 1.

36. Curtis, *Jack the Ripper*. For Barrett, see Hartnoll, *Oxford Companion to the Theatre*, 83; Thomas, "Wilson Barrett's New School 'Othello'"; Banham, *Cambridge Guide to World Theatre*, 77. With a flair for melodrama, the handsome Barrett had restored the text of Shakespeare's *Othello* and then turned to managing the Princess Theater in 1881. He met with great success, and even more when he formed the Wilson Barrett Company and toured the United States and Britain with *The Sign of the Cross*, a play about a Roman patrician who was converted to Christianity by a beautiful girl as both entered the lion's arena to meet their deaths by mauling.

37. White to Spalding, March 10, 1889, Spalding Scrapbooks, vol. 10; Palmer, *Athletic Sports*, 402, 406, 412–13, 415; Ryan Diary, March 9, 1889, 75–77; Anson, *A Ball Player's Career*, 259. See also Wilson, *The Victorians*, 525.

38. "Current Events and Croydon Anticipations," *Sporting Life*, March 12, 1889, p. 2.

39. Spalding, *Baseball*, 263. See also Palmer, *Athletic Sports*, 408.

40. Palmer, *Athletic Sports*, 412; "Baseball," *Sporting Life*, March 12, 1889, p. 3; "American Baseball: What Is It?" *Sport and Play*, March 12, 1889, p. 95. See also "Royalty at the Ball Match," *New York Herald*, March 13, 1889, p. 5, and Simons, "'Englishness' of English Cricket." See also Spalding, *Baseball*, 263–64; "Croydon Notes and Anticipations," *Sporting Life*, March 13, 1889, p. 4.

41. "The Base Ball Team," *Athletic Journal*, March 19, 1889, p. 10; March Hare to the editor, *Sporting Times*, March 16, 1889, p. 2. See also "American Baseballers at Kennington Oval," *Sporting Life*, March 13, 1889, p. 6, and "The American Baseball Teams," *Illustrated Sporting and Dramatic News*, March 16, 1889, p. 6.

42. Palmer, *Athletic Sports*, 412; Anson, *A Ball Player's Career*, 262, also 42. See also "The Base Ball Team," *Athletic Journal*, March 19, 1889, p. 11; "American Baseballers at Kennington Oval," *Sporting Life*, March 13, 1889, p. 6; and "Sporting Notions," *Referee*, March 17, 1889, p. 1.

43. "Base Ball," diagram, *The Sporting Times* (March 16, 1889): 2.

44. "American Baseball," *Sporting Clipper*, March 16, 1889, p. 2. See also Lane, "Greatest President," 307, for Tener, who heard a spectator laugh that the game was nothing but rounders and then watched approvingly as a red hot foul ball sizzled at the man. The ball nearly took his leg off. Tener dubiously believed that the English had a different view of baseball after the incident.

45. "American Baseballers at Lord's Cricket Ground," *Sporting Life*, March 14, 1889, p. 4.

46. "The American Baseballers at the Crystal Palace," *Sporting Life*, March 15, 1889, p. 1. See also "Ward's Return," *Sporting Life*, March 20, 1889, p. 1, and Dulles, *Americans Abroad*, 70.

47. Carroll, "Baseball in Graceland," 5; Howat, *The Great Cricketer*, 3–4; Toghill, "Dr. W. G. Grace"; Mandle, "W. G. Grace."

48. Palmer, *Athletic Sports*, 420. See also Carroll, "Baseball at Graceland," 7; Anson, *A Ball Player's Career*, 264–65; and "The American Baseball Team at Bristol," *Sporting Life*, March 16, 1889, p. 3.

49. "The American Baseball Players," *Sporting Life*, March 16, 1889, p. 3.

50. "The American Baseballers at Leyton," *Sporting Life*, March 18, 1889, p. 4; Palmer, *Athletic Sports*, 420–21; "The Cricket-Ball Throwing Record," *Sporting Life*. March 18, 1889, p. 4; "In Epping's Shade," *New York Herald*, March 17, 1889, p. 15.

51. London and North Western Railway, American Base Ball Clubs First-Class Saloon and menus, Spalding Scrapbooks, vol. 10; Palmer, *Athletic Sports*, 421; "The American Baseball Teams at Birmingham," *Sporting Life*, March 19, 1889, p. 4.

52. Leather Stocking, "The Game of Baseball," *Sport and Play*, March 26, 1889, p. 126. See also "At 'Orchid Joe's' Home," *New York Herald*, March 19, 1889, p. 5, and Palmer, *Athletic Sports*, 422. The British reporter ridiculed the Chicago record in the game. The line score read 4 runs for the White Stockings in the first inning, and 0 for the next eight, which led the reporter to joke, "four hundred million duck-eggs!"

53. Palmer, *Athletic Sports*, 424.

54. "The American Baseball Teams at Sheffield," *Sporting Life*, March 20, 1889, p. 3; Russell, "Sport and Identity"; "En Passant," *Athletic News and Cyclists' Journal*, March 18, 1889, p. 2; Harvey, "Epoch in the Annals"; London and North Western Railway, brochure of "Tour in England and Scotland," Chadwick Scrapbooks, vol. 1, reel 1.

55. Palmer, *Athletic Sports*, 424–25. See also "The American Baseball Teams at Glasgow," *Sporting Life*, March 22, 1889, p. 4; Anson, *A Ball Player's Career*, 268; and "Letters and Sports in Scotland," *Nation* 51 (November 6, 1890): 358.

56. "Baseball at Cottonopolis," *New York Herald*, March 23, 1889, p. 9; "The American Baseball Teams at Manchester," *Sporting Life*, March 23, 1889, p. 3; Palmer, *Athletic Sports*, 425–26; Anglo-French Club, Manchester, dinner menu, March 22, 1889, Spalding Scrapbooks, vol. 10.

57. Ryan Diary, March 23, 1889, p. 81; "Fine Game for the Girls," newspaper clipping, Chadwick Scrapbooks, vol. 1, reel 1. See also "The American Baseball Teams at Liverpool," *Sporting Life*, March 25, 1889, p. 4; Palmer, *Athletic Sports*, 427–28.

58. Cartoon, Spalding Scrapbooks, vol. 9.

59. Garnham, "Football and National Identity"; Bradley, "Unrecognized Middle-Class Revolutionary?"; Cronin, *Sport and Nationalism*; Mandle, "Parnell and Sport"; Post, "Charles Stewart Parnell"; "The American Baseball Teams at Belfast," *Sporting Life*, March 26, 1889, p. 4.

60. "The Condition of Ireland as Exhibited by Official Statistics," *Nation* 47 (December 27, 1888): 1226; "Irish Affairs," *Nation* 47 (August 30, 1888): 167–68; MacRaild, "Parnell and Home Rule"; "Mr. Balfour on the Improvement in Ireland," *Saturday Review* 67 (May 4, 1889): 523–24; Wilson, *The Victorians*, 449–60; Blackwell, "Reminiscences of Irish Sport"; Palmer, *Athletic Sports*, 432–36.

61. "The American Baseball Players in Dublin," *Sporting Life*, March 28, 1889, p. 4; "The Last Game of the Great Trip," *New York Herald*, March 28, 1889, p. 10.

62. Palmer, *Athletic Sports*, 436–41; Anson, *A Ball Player's Career*, 271–72; Ryan Diary, March 28, 1889, 84; "Chicago Neatly Whipped at the Crystal Palace," *New York Herald* (March 15, 1889): 3, reported that President Howe of Cleveland said he would offer $30,000 for the All-Americas and take them home, for they exhibited the best base running and hitting he had ever seen. See also Pamela J. Kincheloe, "Two Visions of Fairyland: Ireland and the Monumental Discourse of the Nineteenth-Century American Tourist," *Irish Studies Review* 7 (1999): 41–51.

63. "The American Baseball Players," *Sporting Life*, March 29, 1889, p. 4. The figure on the gate receipts was provided by L. A. Spring of the Surrey History Centre, letter to author, April 10, 2002, who notes the finances from the game at Kennington Oval; it is assumed that the tourists received similar deals elsewhere in Britain. See also Patrick Morley, "A Brief History of UK Baseball," http://www.sabruk.org/history/uk.html, and Johnes, "Poor Man's Cricket." Backed by industrialist Francis Ley of Derby, who had become interested in baseball during business trips to the United States, the National Baseball League of Great Britain formed in 1890 with four teams: Ley's Derby County squad, and sides from Preston North End, Aston Villa, and Stoke City. Spalding gave his encouragement, but the first season ended with Derby well ahead in the standings but withdrawing

from the league when others protested the number of American veterans on the team. The game spread afterward, especially in England's northeastern area, with clubs in Middlesbrough, Darlington, Stockton, and Thornaby, and *Spalding's Official Base Ball Guide* opined in 1899 that the future of British baseball looked bright. World tourist Ed Hengle moved to England after the world tour and, in 1906, reported on London's first completed season under the newly organized British Base Ball Association. Yet interest flagged by the end of the first decade of the twentieth century, and it would not be until the 1930s that another league formed. U.S. servicemen stationed in Britain during World War II revived the game after that.

64. "The Visit of the American Base-Ball Players," *Belfast Evening Telegraph*, March 29, 1889, p. 2.

65. Bloyce, "Just Not Cricket."

66. Spalding, "Field Papers."

67. Quoted in Dulles, *Americans Abroad*, 5.

# 5

# National Identity

## Return to America

NEW YORK
  Brooklyn, Monday, April 8—*All-America* 7, *Chicago* 6
  Brooklyn, Tuesday, April 9—*Chicago* 9, *All-America* 6
MARYLAND
  Baltimore, Wednesday, April 10—*Chicago* 5, *All-America* 2
PENNSYLVANIA
  Philadelphia, Friday, April 12—*All-America* 6, *Chicago* 4
MASSACHUSETTS
  Boston, Saturday, April 13—*All-America* 10, *Chicago* 3
DISTRICT OF COLUMBIA
  Washington, Monday, April 15—*Chicago* 18, *All-America* 6
PENNSYLVANIA
  Pittsburgh, Tuesday, April 16—*All-America* 3, *Chicago* 3
OHIO
  Cleveland, Wednesday, April 17—*Chicago* 7, *All-America* 4
INDIANA
  Indianapolis, Thursday, April 18—*All-America* 9, *Chicago* 5
ILLINOIS
  Chicago, Saturday, April 20—*All-America* 22, *Chicago* 9

Totals: *All-America*, 30 wins; *Chicago*, 20 wins; 4 ties

Four years after the world tour ended, Brig. Gen. Abner Doubleday died in Mendham, New Jersey. An 1842 West Point graduate who had served in the Mexican-American War, Doubleday was stationed at Fort Sumter in 1861, where some believe he ordered Union troops to fire on attacking Confederate soldiers and, thus, begin the Civil War. Eventually gaining safe passage to the North, he saw action at the second battle of Bull Run, Gettysburg, and Antietam. Doubleday kept sixty-seven diaries and wrote several books and letters. He never once mentioned the game

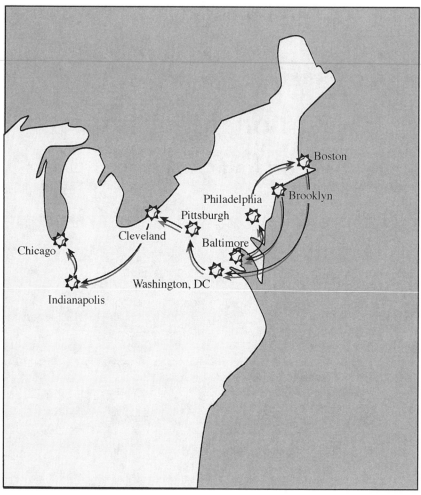

*Tour around the Eastern and Midwestern United States.*
(David Underwood, Graphic Design, CU-Boulder)

of baseball, nor did his obituary in the *New York Times*. Yet in 1907, fourteen years after Doubleday passed away, Major League Baseball proclaimed him the "Father of Baseball." Albert Spalding was the instigator of this, having urged the creation of a special investigative commission to determine that baseball had evolved from entirely American roots, rather than from British cricket and rounders. The seven-member panel, which included three National League presidents, two sitting U.S. senators, former players, and the head of the Amateur Athletic Union (AAU), proclaimed that baseball had no "traceable connection whatever with 'Rounders' or any other foreign game." Furthermore, the panel concluded that in June 1839, Doubleday had invented the national pastime at Cooperstown, New York.[1]

This was pure fantasy. Doubleday was a twenty-year-old West Point cadet in 1839, but Spalding's "Mills Commission" seized on the dubious evidence written in a letter by a mining engineer in Denver, who claimed to be present in Cooperstown that historic day. He turned out to be demented, later dying in an asylum. The venerable sage of baseball, Henry Chadwick, moreover, thought the report was nonsense; in a way, he had actually inspired the report a few years before through a light-hearted bet with Big Al regarding baseball's roots. Indeed, Spalding's reply to Chadwick jokingly referred to the notable journalist as having been "rocked in a 'Rounders' cradle" because of his English birth. Nonetheless, the commission stood by its ruling even though the report was so suspect, even ridiculed. Chairman Abraham Mills, who served in Doubleday's military unit, later admitted to the tenuous nature of its findings. In addition, the powerful secretary of the commission and head of the AAU, James Sullivan, an Irishman who naturally despised the British, claimed that he would never admit the link of baseball to English sports. But it was Spalding, above all, who perpetuated the notion that baseball was a wholly American sport and even a national civil religion. The town of Cooperstown became so heavily invested in the legend that it lobbied for a Hall of Fame to be built for baseball's make-believe centennial celebration in 1939.[2]

Spalding's zeal for the Mills report showed how nationalism energized baseball during the Gilded Age. He packaged the Americanism of the pastime as the sole domain of a country trying to stake a claim to greatness in the global arena. Like other imperial-minded leaders, he constructed a distinctive nationalism in a relatively disunited country of ethnically diverse, economically stratified people whose political institutions had been nearly destroyed during the Civil War. Unable, as Europeans could, to claim nationhood based on cultural likeness, Americans imagined themselves part of a national community and an emerging empire. However artificial, leaders alleged a shared mind-set and a common foundation of ideology; their core values were similar. One way to define and pass on these ideals involved glorifying the accomplishments of their forefathers as well as by conjuring legends of an America as a distinct place in the world.[3]

This exceptionalism, an outgrowth of the "city on a hill" metaphor, guided the builders of baseball. In his valedictory *Baseball: America's National Game*, Spalding held that the sport was integral to the very identity of the United States. He believed it reflected values of manliness and fairness that had actually converted into reality the imagined national community. The Doubleday creation myth, therefore, played a role in the nation's story, of which imperial status was a natural result. Spalding supplemented the fable with other ingredients pivotal to success, such as clean competition, the rule of owners over the players (and gamblers with whom they consorted), and the sacred nature of the country and its pastime. Thus, both the United States and baseball supposedly represented the democratic process and also served as beacons to the world of America's rise to prominence. Just as baseball was a dynamic sport that would sweep the planet, so America, too, would ascend to the pinnacle of global power. The country's political system, culture, "and even its forms of recreation" would prove superior to those of empires, monarchies, colonies, and parliamentary government, exclaimed Spalding.[4]

The baseball tourists were part of this massive propaganda campaign to celebrate American virtues. Spalding, of course, sought to market his own business, but to do so, he cleverly linked the sport to values of Americanism to render it an irresistible national product. In that sense, the tour's nationalist crusade, in a small but perceptible way, girded the country for its even greater pursuit of leading the global economy and engaging the era of globalization itself. With fervent backing of fans, journalists, team owners, and National League officials, baseball had already become a national game by the end of the 1880s. Now Spalding and fellow magnates took the next step: "to equate the game's origins with the ethos of America's national destiny."[5]

That was the reasoning behind the Mills Commission, yet Spalding had launched the campaign for American exceptionalism well before, in 1888–1889. Nationalism now resounded anew as the tourists returned home. The mission abroad had fallen rather flat, but it found an eager audience back in the United States. As Spalding told a reporter the day of arrival in New York, he had traveled the world, dined with royalty, gazed at ruins and into the eyes of beautiful Parisian women, shaken hands with heirs to thrones, and despaired over Irish poverty. Yet "I never fully appreciated anything nor experienced such keen delight in all my travels as that which swelled through my breast this morning when I stepped ashore. I am Proud to be called an American."[6]

## SAFE AT HOME

Long after the entourage crossed the Atlantic, held exhibitions along the East Coast, and then played across the Midwest back to Chicago, Spalding put a gloss on the trip. Upon returning to U.S. shores, he expected numerous greetings, banquets, and speeches to laud the very "Pluck, Persistence, [and] Performance" of "American Spirit." He also announced that not only had the receipts more than paid for his fifty-thousand-dollar outlay—which was not true; he had lost about five thousand dollars on the tour—but it had also "created interest in the game in countries where it had never been seen before, and where from that day to this the sport has been growing in popular favor." That was falsehood, too, yet in his eyes, the tour's more important contribution hinged on its promotion of the *national* pastime. The trip "gave to the masses everywhere an opportunity to witness a pastime peculiarly American," while it also showed Americans themselves in the best light as professionals and gentlemen. For the rest of his life, Spalding alluded to baseball as an exemplar of American manliness, democracy, and power.[7]

He also got his applause once near New York Harbor. Eight days on a rough sea on board the *Adriatic* made the crossing difficult. Poker games, storytelling, roulette, Clarence Duval's dancing, and dining in the first-class section of this ship of the White Star Line (which would become infamous as the owner of the doomed *Titanic*) eased the tourist's discomfort. But, like all Atlantic travelers at this time of year, they had to endure the gale winds and high waves that pitched the ship and sickened its passengers. They were thrilled to see Fire Island on April 5, and the next day, a Saturday, they arrived at the quarantine station. As the sun peeked over Brooklyn and a gun on Governor's Island boomed its customary "good morning," two boats carrying acquaintances and excited followers slipped alongside the steamer. These well-wishers, who included journalists, relatives, baseball officials, and actor DeWolf Hopper, awakened the entourage. Some players had tears of joy in their eyes as they reciprocated with whistles and tossed caps. Cap Anson's father hugged his son as the players boarded one of the small vessels, the *Starin*, for the ride to the Twenty-First Street dock. They were back in "God's country," remembered the big captain of the White Stockings.[8]

Once at the elegant Fifth Avenue Hotel overlooking Madison Square, and having overcome their disappointment that neither the president of the United States, the mayor of New York, nor any aldermen had bid them welcome, the tourists began their final two weeks of travels in which they were the toast of the town. Their first night included a performance of *The May Queen*, starring Hopper and Digby Bell at Palmer's Theatre, which was festooned with American flags. A gilt eagle and a shield of crossed bats, gloves, and a catcher's mask topped the archway to the theater. Bell and Hopper made joking allusions to the players. The deep-voiced Hopper recited a poem that explained how the tourists had "shown effete Europe the noblest of sports / They've shown the old foreigners how to have fun / With the mystical curve and the lively home run."[9] Calls followed for special bows by Anson and then John Ward, who had come to New York City as promised to rejoin the tour, before Hopper brought the house down by reciting "Casey at the Bat."

The great "noncapital," as a British visitor called it, was the national cultural and commercial hub, and thus a fitting place to welcome globe-trotting marketers of sports and nation. An elegant city of long avenues, including fashionable Fifth Avenue, New York's graceful Union Square hosted the celebrated Tiffany's jewelry store. Stately brownstone mansions, majestic buildings and churches, and palatial hotels extended alongside the green swath of Central Park that gave New York a unique pastoral contrast amid the clutter of old Wall Street and the din of traffic. Cosmopolitan in hosting nationalities speaking every tongue of the world, residents related to Spalding's grandiose scheme. Here robber barons—Cooke, Gould, Vanderbilt, and Morgan—dictated to government. Technological marvels of skyscrapers with elevators and the Brooklyn Bridge dazzled all, while the Statue of Liberty generated patriotism. Artistic success brought fame, while journalistic enterprise, most notably by the *New York Herald*, which Harry Palmer had represented on the baseball tour, garnered influence. The tens of thousands of immigrants who resided in the city or trooped through on their way west made New York a melting pot as well as scene to numerous labor and ethnic struggles. A truly international metropolis, New York City thrived, as a British observer claimed, as the "great monetary, scientific, artistic, and intellectual centre of the Western world."[10] In essence, it perfected the business, technology, popular and refined culture, and ethnic diversity so evident on the world tour and which comprised this age of globalization and imperial longing.

Into this commotion entered Spalding's players, all of whom had signed contracts to play exhibitions until mid-April, when they would return, to the relief of grumbling magnates, to their home teams. Ward, rumored to have been sold to the Washington club (although he resigned with the Giants), worked his magic again for All-America as the matches began in Brooklyn on this last leg of the tour. On Monday, April 8, the teams played the first of two games in cold weather before 2,800 fans shelling out twenty-five cents apiece for admission. Baseball was king in the nation's third most populous city, which was intimately tied to Manhattan by commerce. Businessmen lived in Brooklyn and commuted to Manhattan for work while they cheered for Brooklyn teams, which dominated amateur play in the 1860s and later participated in all the professional baseball associations. The city sponsored a National League franchise, the (Trolley) Dodgers, in 1890, but a team of the same name had played in the American Association from 1884 to 1889. Local resident and eventual Hall of Fame pitcher Candy Cummings had a claim on inventing the curveball by launching clam shells from Brooklyn beaches as a boy in 1864; he introduced the breaking pitch to baseball four years later. Now the "City of Churches," with its superb playing grounds, hosted the famous tourists.[11]

On this day, Ward's side won by a run in their first game on American soil since the past November. Anson's team failed to score until the seventh inning, but seven costly All-America errors got Chicago back into the game. Still, Ward's squad eked out a run in the ninth that proved the difference, 7–6. There was no time to celebrate. The most famous reception of the tour, scheduled for that evening at the opulent Delmonico's restaurant, compelled the teams to flee the Brooklyn grounds and return to Manhattan, where they traded in their uniforms for dress clothes.[12]

## AMERICAN EXCEPTIONALISM

This banquet was the centerpiece of New York's three months of planning to fete the tourists. John Day, a local figure in the Democrats' Tammany Hall machine and the original owner of the New York Giants in 1883, consulted with Giants' manager Jim Mutrie over preparations. They headed two committees, with members drawn from the national sports associations and executives of athletic clubs in Manhattan, Staten Island, and surrounding areas, that oversaw the local arrangements. Given carte blanche by Day, Mutrie focused on the large banquet at Delmonico's. Besieged by hundreds for tickets to the dinner, he sold a limited number at a ten-dollar premium. These lucky few joined metropolitan notables and world-famous figures to greet the entourage that had taken part in "an event unprecedented in the annals of sports."[13] Mutrie and company awaited the tourists to give them "a reception so hearty and warm and enthusiastic that all the fetes of their tour will pale into insignificance," wrote Henry Chadwick in the *Brooklyn Eagle*.[14]

Delmonico's was the premier institution in New York City, and perhaps the entire country, for hosting such banquets. Opened in 1827 (closing in 1923), the restaurant became the dining place for celebrities. Close by the tourists' stylish Fifth Avenue Hotel, it had ample space for a large number of guests, room now in demand as the reception numbered 253 people spread out among eight tables. Around the large dining room on the second floor of Delmonico's hung large photographs of the two teams in Rome and Egypt. Perched on a balcony, a band played popular American tunes. The menu card, decorated with baseballs and bats, announced a dinner in nine innings, labeled with dishes from the places the tourists had visited. A souvenir book of the trip, patriotically bound in red-white-and-blue ribbons, lay open for viewing. Waiters were prepared to be liberal with the wine and champagne.[15]

A who's who of society joined the entire entourage of tourists and its organizers. National League officials and figures from the sporting world, as well as dozens of politicians, civil servants, newsmen and newspaper owners, theater stars (Hopper and Bell among them), and businessmen flocked to the banquet. Consul General G. W. Griffin, several judges, three New York mayors, and a U.S. senator (Gorman, who later joined the Mills Commission) were present. Sitting among fellow New Yorkers was former state legislator Theodore Roosevelt, soon to become a member of the U.S. Civil Service Commission in May, and his amiable brother Elliott; both related to the tourists because of their own travels in Europe and the American West. The most illustrious diner of them all, however, was Mark Twain, who was seated near one end of the head table occupied by the senators, mayors, Abraham Mills, and Spalding.[16]

Mills called the banquet to order at ten o'clock by linking sport and country. He read testimonials from several absent dignitaries. The Hawaiian minister, H. A. P. Carter, sent his regrets in a letter stating that "Mr. Spalding and party could justly claim to represent the nation" because there were so many baseball players and fans in America. Although the King of Hawaii had not seen one of their "manly" exhibitions, he prized the qualities of obedience, self-command, and skill of the tourists.[17] Mills then paid tribute to sport and country. "It was truly the national game, and Mr. Spalding and his men had given it world wide reputation," said Mills, who then provoked catcalls of "No rounders!" by proclaiming that "patriotism and research" had revealed that baseball "was American in its origins." He applauded Spalding and his players, "in every sense, rep-

*A banquet at Delmonico's.*

(Library of Congress, Prints and Photographs Division, Digital ID: pan 6a24866)

resentatives of American manhood and citizenship." After local mayors acclaimed baseball and Spalding, who was regaled by the playing of "Hail to the Chief," Big Al thanked Leigh Lynch for running the business end of the tour and the correspondents for filing stories on it. He vacated the floor to team captains Anson and Ward, who expressed gratitude to their players for participating, Spalding for his sponsorship, and then told of the delights of "first-class" travel and the hospitality of their foreign hosts.[18]

Then arose the star of the evening: Mark Twain, as Samuel Clemens demanded to be called in public. His speech was vintage tongue-in-cheek Twain, but it is important to note that he used baseball as a metaphor for American drive and achievement, namely by contrasting it to the supposed laxity of Hawaiians and the impurity of Europe. After Mills introduced him as a native of the Sandwich Islands, Twain noted that he had visited that idyllic place more than twenty years before, in 1866, and baseball seemed out of place. Drawing on the first speech he ever made in London, in 1873, when he had labeled the natives as "savages," he claimed that Hawaiians did everything "wronger," from mounting a horse on the wrong side to tracing descent through the female line. A hilarious account of "the soft airs of those Isles of the Blest" followed, and then Twain wound up with humor peppered by nationalistic rhetoric. He envied the tourists "the glories they have achieved in their illustrious march about the mighty circumference of the earth, if it were fair; but no, it was an earned run, and envy would be out of place." Still, Spalding's players had "carried the American name to the uttermost parts of the earth—and covered it with glory every time."[19]

Like the tourists, Twain found fault with European customs while he promoted the superiority of the low-brow, innocent Yankee principles and practices. By debunking Europe, he boosted the prestige of the United States. In fact, he went farther down the exceptionalist road by reprimanding foreign critics of the United States, a country that, he wryly noted, had invented liberty and democracy. Still, irony did not disguise this reminder that Europe's democratic institutions sprang from the American Revolution. To be sure, by the end of the next decade, Twain would criticize U.S. imperial ventures, yet in his speech at Delmonico's, he alluded to future American greatness.[20]

The jammed banquet continued with paeans to the national archetype of baseball. Businessmen Chauncey Depew, a one-time presidential hopeful, gave a speech entitled "The Invasion of the Old World by the American Ball Players." Nations of culture engaged in sports and the arts, he said. To be sure, the Founding Fathers had not seen a baseball game, and Depew himself had never played the sport. Yet civilization was marked by participation in the "manly arts," best represented by the "National Game."[21]

The Honorable Daniel Dougherty, another public servant, followed with even more jingoistic statements. The tourists hailed from a generation with an "athletic spirit" that effectively prepared American men "for the future defense of the country against foreign foes." Outdoor sports like baseball "ignite the fires of emulation, create thirst for distinction, the longing to desire to win a name that will mark them among their fellows," he proclaimed, and these qualities "rear a race fit for peace and war"—an American race.[22] The exceptionalist rhetoric had reached a fever pitch.

Comedians DeWitt Hopper and Digby Bell entered the hall directly from the stage. Hopper offered verses about the Giants' troubles renting out the Polo Grounds (Spalding announced to cheers at night's end that their lease had been renewed) before he brought the crowd to its feet with "Casey at the Bat." Bell then recited a new poem, "Spalding's Ride," a worthy successor to Paul Revere's gallop. It told of his efforts to sail out and meet the tourists when they were just "twenty miles away" off the coast. As the distance closed to a matter of feet, hurrahs rose up for Spalding. On the magnate's "statue of bronze" would be inscribed the words: "From the baseball cranks / Who in manner befitting express their thanks / To Spalding, who, freighted with ardor sublime / Played our national game in every clime. / From 'Frisco, globe-circling, to New York Bay / In lands ten thousand miles away."[23]

It appeared as if baseball had linked people of all classes and culture in one big American pageant. So ended the festivities at Delmonico's, which had witnessed a joyous mixing of millionaires and athletes, fans and players, who roamed among tables shaking hands, drinking, and enjoying the camaraderie. At close to two in the morning, the large salon emptied. Surely, as an early April morning approached, "the baseball season has begun," announced the *New York Times* in its coverage of the banquet.[24]

"The Wine Was Very, Very Red," headlined the *New York Herald*, "and perhaps that was why the globe-trotters played such a poor game" the next day at Washington Park, an American Associations grounds in Brooklyn. John Tener held a big lead from the start, and All-America's error-prone fielding victimized their pitcher, Ed Crane. More than three thousand fans watched Chicago pile up runs, but both teams seemed understandably sluggish after their late Monday night. Hopper took delight when Anson, the "mighty Casey," came to bat in the fourth inning with the bases loaded and promptly struck out. The gangly comedian, a favorite of the White Stockings, waved his hat and cane in a spirited defense of poetic justice. Ward's squad could not overcome the big Chicago lead, however, and the spectators filed out of a 9–6 White Stockings ball game.[25]

That evening, the teams left for Baltimore. The most important commercial and manufacturing city of the American South was situated upriver from the Chesapeake Bay. Overlooked by Fort McHenry, its harbor served as passage for a vigorous and enriching trade. Colonnaded merchant and government buildings abounded, as did such new structures as the Johns Hopkins Hospital. Baltimore, known for its free educational institutions and its art collections, was also famous for its monuments. A colossal statue of George Washington stood thirty-five feet high, while a memorial to those who fell in the gallant defense of their city in the War of 1812 rose from the ground at the intersection of Calvert and Fayette Streets. Former resident Edgar Allan Poe had a shrine, and so did orphans.[26]

Locals watched the tourists ride in carriages from the Carrollton Hotel in the early afternoon of Wednesday, April 10, behind a marching band, past a waving mayor at flag-bedecked City Hall and thousands of people, and into a big omnibus that took them to the playing grounds. By game time, nearly six thousand people filled the park, with hundreds more sitting on surrounding risers. Clarence Duval, "as black as midnight," marched in at the head of the teams. The circus atmosphere excited the fans, which included the police commissioner and government officials. Their enthusiasm did not wane even though All-America was bereft of a sick John Ward, who remained behind in New York. His replacement, Billy Shindle of the American Association's Baltimore Orioles, could not help his teammates. Chicago bunched up hits and right fielder Bob Pettit prevented All-America from getting closer than 5–2 with some brilliant catches. His ninth-inning shoestring grab, a gem that he caught just before the ball hit the turf, robbed Ned Hanlon of a three-run, inside-the-park homer, and his quick throw to the infield caught John Healy, who had not tagged up, at second base for the final out. The crowd went wild in its applause. A night of attending a performance of *John Cristo* at Ford's Opera House ended the day.[27]

## HURRAH FOR THE NATIONAL GAME

The next morning found the tourists in Philadelphia. A reception committee of journalists, including Henry Chadwick and reporters from the Spalding-friendly *Sporting Life* (published in the city by Frank Richter), local officials, and owners A. J. Reach and John Rogers, as well as others from the National League Phillies and the American Association Athletics, waited at the Baltimore and Ohio Station. Philadelphia had lost its second major league franchise, the Athletics, in 1877 after only a year of play, branded by rumors of gambling and failure to complete its schedule. The Athletics were reborn in 1882 as a charter member of the American Association before that league dissolved in 1891, then were born again in the American League in 1901. Reach, a local sporting goods manufacturer, had bought the Phillies from small-market Worcester in 1883 and eventually sold the team to Rogers in 1899. The club remained in the National League. Reach and Rogers had business to do with Spalding, discussing a trade (which was never consummated) of their star, John Fogarty, for Chicago's Jimmy Ryan.[28]

Meanwhile, the remainder of the day was festive for the tourists. In Gloucester, upriver from Philadelphia, one hundred people dined on shad, fresh vegetables, and a dessert of hot waffles and then heard and gave toasts over champagne and cigars. Two long tables stood in a big pavilion in the Thompson Hotel, where the party gazed at the Delaware River. Spalding gave his standard toast, declaring that wherever English was spoken, baseball would take root. Britain and its colonies favored the pastime, he prevaricated, because of "their love of athletic sports." A return to the boat got the party back to Philadelphia, where they were conveyed to the athletic grounds to watch the Phillies play Boston. As the ball players arrived, a band struck up "Home Again" and the crowd gave them a standing ovation as they marched to the diamond in front of a line of Phillies and Red Stockings players. Sitting in a reserved section, they recognized Mike "King" Kelly, recently traded by Spalding, who came in for a particular roasting by the Chicago team.

Frank Richter and his *Sporting Life* newspaper hosted a banquet that evening which rivaled Delmonico's. He had spared no expense on the second-floor dining room of the Hotel Bellevue, which was packed by a throng of admirers. Ivy, evergreen, and roses, interspersed with folded copies of the *Sporting Life*, twisted around the chandeliers, and from the sidelights hung blazers with team names. Roses encircled the iron support pillar in the middle of the room; a catcher's mask, bat, uniform shirt, cap, and a base appeared from the flowers. Belts of red and white roses were strung along the walls and trails of vines ran down the center of the room. Four tables were arranged in a horseshoe to seat 140 guests, among them club presidents, owners, and managers; journalists and editors from across the country; state and city politicians; railway agents, stock brokers, and bankers; and theater personages, retired players, and a physical culture professor, Dr. Leuf, from the University of Pennsylvania. An elaborate four-page menu faced each guest. The first page was a miniature cover of *Sporting Life*, the second contained the guest-list, and the fourth the toasts to be given. The third page, headed "Score," laid out a nine-inning meal, with the first played between the diners and Little Neck clams, then followed by soup, fish, veal, salad, ices, cognac, and cigars. Wine flowed in abundance, while Harry Wannemacher's orchestra sat among plants and flowers, playing the baseball tunes of the day.[29]

This was appropriate, for music, like baseball, reflected the powerful impulses of Gilded Age nationalism. Collectors have discovered at least fifty thousand baseball songs, of which more than three hundred were published. Many were comedies and almost all were lighthearted pieces that offered spirited tunes and lyrics about the game. There were several dance songs, including a few versions of "Home Run Polka," the "Three Strike Two-Step," and the "Base Ball Waltz," and others about the styles of play, teams, and athletes. They alluded to the disease of "Base Ball Fever" that struck the country after the Civil War; the last stanza of this mindless ditty ended with "We've got clubs no end, and players sharp / But I will bet my Beaver / That I can catch, as well as they / For I have kotcht the fever."[30] Team songs in the late nineteenth century were popular. "Steal! Slide! Anyway!" of 1889 mentioned that "Johnny Ward's our short-stop" in its dedication to the New York Giants. There was a tribute to the Chicago Atlantics in 1867, the "Home Run Galop," in honor of "the Boys Who Make 'Em," as well as music about individual players, such as "Slide, Kelly, Slide," recorded in 1893. Songs spread across the country to honor local teams, such as the Una Base Ball Club of Charlestown, outside of Boston, in the early 1870s, and a St. Louis publication dedicated to the Union Base Ball Club, the champions of Missouri in 1867. The sport's most famous song, "Take Me Out to the Ballgame," was not written until 1908, but at the time of the Spalding tour, audiences certainly recognized music about baseball. "Catch It on the Fly," published in 1867 for Spalding's old Forest City Club and the Chicago Excelsior Club, crowed that "Throughout the East, throughout the West / The game is all the rage."[31] Indeed, jockeys, gamblers, and cricketers might take pleasure in their sporting activities, but Americans should shout "Harrah for Our National Game," urged songwriter Walter Neville. The national pastime taught honor and obedience to authority. And American followers of baseball could take "A thrill of delight in its very name / A joy in its simplest sound / It lends new strength to our hardy race / And its pleasures are never tame."[32] Baseball music struck a chord of nationalism.

One imagines that the orchestra in Philadelphia played some of these tunes as it serenaded the banqueters, beginning with "The Day I Played Baseball" and continuing with other hits until interrupted by a rising tide of nationalistic speeches. Chairman Richter rose from his seat at 10:30 P.M., holding a bat with a red band as a gavel, and introduced the president of *Sporting Life*, Thomas Dando. Dando acclaimed the globe-trotting tourists as "heroes who so successfully carried this gigantic enterprise which adds not only immeasurably to the grandeur of our national game" but which "also in a measure appeals directly to every American heart, insofar as its inception and execution is entirely typical of the essentially American characteristics, originality, pluck, liberality, unwavering steadfastness, unyielding courage, sagacious management, and brilliant execution." Such jingoism preceded statements, comic and serious, which rendered the sport as a foundation of the country.

William Smith, the president of Philadelphia's Common Council, sunk baseball's roots in the pages of Greek mythology; he earned applause by describing how the God of Discord threw an apple into a room of assembled guests and contention ensued. Of course, the apple was a metaphor for a baseball and thus the sport "had its origins as far back as the gods and goddesses." Even Shakespeare "knew all about baseball," Smith continued, for Hamlet was a ballplayer who, once reaching first base, had to decide not whether "To be, or not to be," but whether "To go, or not to go." This silliness provoked cackles of laughter, but, saying that he had read of the "glories" of the world tour, Smith concluded, "As far as the honor and credit of the United States of America can be carried by anyone abroad they have done it."[33]

They uttered similar lighthearted remarks but they also stressed the exceptionalism of the global endeavor. John Rogers, a city official and a Phillies executive, proclaimed that Chicago and All-America had carried the game "where even our flag has not been, as a great American institution." The game would be established so firmly that no American tourist would again suffer a brush-off like that delivered by the nasty consul in Rome. Added the publisher of the *Philadelphia Times*, journalists needed to inject the "integrity and honest merit" of baseball into the nation's "social life—into the churches" as well as into politics. Extended to the global level, baseball would "teach the world from the American standpoint" of "integrity, physical development." Transferred from the noble United States to the international arena, the sport would "be doing missionary work every day of its existence," and it would "make the whole world better for its presence." In the same vein, the journalist Henry Chadwick recalled how the tourists of 1874 had failed to show the British "how we had Americanized—that is, improved—their old boy's game of 'rounders.'" But this was not the place to contest cricket, because the 1888–1889 tour ultimately had a larger "national significance" of promoting closer relations with the "English-speaking people of the world" and aiding "the cause of 'peace and good will toward men' to an extent they little dream of. . . ."[34] By such chauvinism, Chadwick spoke to the power of imperial imagination.

Well after midnight, after old-timers like A. J. Reach, Harry Wright, and Boston's Tim Murnane had given toasts, the tourists had spoken of the pleasantries of the trip, and Spalding had thanked Richter and his newspaper for their rousing welcome, the banquet ended. The night belonged to everyone connected with the enterprise of baseball, the comments avowing muscular nationalism as well as the message that such American institutions as baseball undergirded progress toward the greatness of the country. The Delmonico's banquet became known for the notable figures in attendance; the Philadelphia dinner clarified baseball's place in the national project of organizing society and Americanizing the world through a U.S. empire of sport. Thus, the next afternoon, jingoism continued.

The Weccacoe Band serenaded the tourists at their hotel before a thousand people and then escorted them to City Hall, a magnificent building covering four and a half blocks with a stately tower topped by the huge statue of William Penn, where Mayor Edwin Fitler received the teams. He called the tourists "a credit to the country." His six grandchildren constantly held bats and balls because they idolized the men who played the sport; Fitler pledged to encourage the game as long as he remained mayor of the city. Spalding responded in kind, noting that foreign potentates had welcomed the tourists, too, "because we were American citizens." Now standing a few blocks from Independence Hall, where the Declaration of Independence was first read, in Philadelphia, "the cradle of liberty and the mother of base ball," Spalding's tourists basked in the glory of Americanism.[35]

The ceremonies concluded, the players filed into carriages that conveyed them to the Phillies' playing grounds. Amid the banners of the Philadelphia Ball Park and the tunes of the Weccacoe Band, less than four thousand spectators greeted them because of threatening skies. Among the select crowd were leading businessmen, politicians, forty uniformed cadets from the Chester Military Academy, and elegant ladies in private boxes, brilliantly attired against the somber, cloudy skies. They cheered each player, who performed well to repay the Philadelphians for their generous treatment. Chicago scored in several innings, All-America tallying only in the fourth, and the White Stockings won a pretty game, 6–4. It was Anson's third straight victory; his side seemed to play better on domestic soil than abroad.

This ended the stay in Philadelphia for all the tourists except Billy Earle, who was inadvertently left behind on the platform talking to admirers as the train sped to Boston, and Healy, who intentionally stayed behind. Pettit also did not accompany the teams, as he headed home to Meriden, Connecticut, to care for his wife. Arriving in Boston on Saturday, April 13, Spalding made up for the losses with two replacement players.[36]

## OF NATIONAL IMPORTANCE

The tourists had few comments about their brief stay in Boston, but they made a splash with the locals. They spent several hours visiting Beacon Street, the Old State House, the public gardens, Faneuil Hall, and Commonwealth Avenue after they dropped their baggage at the Quincy Hotel. In a chilly rain, All-America won a one-sided game, 10–3, at the South End Grounds. One of the new acquisitions, Hugh Duffy, turned a brilliant triple play with John Tener and Cap Anson. With Hanlon on third, Ward broke from first on a sharp liner to shortstop Duffy, convinced the ball would get through. But Duffy caught it for the out, and whipped it to Tener at first base for the tag-out of Ward. When Ned Hanlon saw this, he ran home, only to be caught by Anson. Of more interest than the contest were the players. Locals Tom Brown and Ed Crane got receptions, the latter accepting a basket of flowers at home plate with the inscription "Welcome Home." That evening, another hometown favorite, George Wright, enjoyed a banquet at the Vendome Hotel attended by cultural, business, and baseball figures who presented him with a gold locket. Meanwhile, talk persisted about Spalding's criticism of King Kelly, the "old man" Pop Anson (who stepped in at third base to replace an injured player), and the possibilities of Tener joining the Boston club.[37]

Continuing their yo-yo trip up and down the East Coast, the tourists arrived in Washington, D.C., a perfect place for a display of pride in America and its pastime. The capital's numerous statues commemorating military heroes, its stately buildings, and its broad avenues conjured up visions of exceptionalism. The visit was less than satisfactory, however. On Monday morning, April 15, the Spalding train appeared in the station before a committee of just three National League officials. Registering at the Arlington Hotel, Spalding received the exciting news that newly inaugurated President Benjamin Harrison would greet the tourists at the White House. The teams expected a rousing welcome from the nation's chief executive. Proceeding to the president's White House after parading through the streets, the entourage entered the dignified mansion, with its grand porticoes supported by columns dating from 1826, through the north doorway into a spacious, frescoed vestibule. The president's private secretary and Harrison's son, Russell, greeted them before escorting them to the Blue Room.[38]

In this oval-shaped parlor finished in blue and gilt, the president of the United States waited for the tourists, but the white-haired and bearded Benjamin Harrison did not share his predecessor's animation. He possessed a glacial demeanor, although his keen eyes and stern face lit up with a kind smile. Some observers likened him to Abraham Lincoln, although Harrison was even taller. A former military commander and ineffectual senator from Indiana, he had served Republican Party king-makers; one had employed his son Russell. Losing the popular vote but tallying the highest count in the electoral college, Harrison won the presidency the past November by appealing for protective tariffs, smearing the Cleveland administration with a pro-British taint and charges that its foreign policy as lacking firmness, buying votes by promising Republican Party leaders rewards, and running a mistake-free campaign. At his rainy inauguration a month before, he spoke of limiting immigration and excluding "men of all races, even the best," who might burden the national treasury or threaten the "social order"; preserving friendly relations with Europe but avoiding domination by the Old World; and the necessity to "exalt patriotism and moderate our party contentions."[39] These were issues to which the baseball tourists, with their experiences in meeting other cultures, could surely relate.

Perhaps because Harrison had busied himself for most of his first six months in office by spreading patronage around, an effort that consumed four to six hours a day, he was a bit distracted when he met the baseball tourists. Before smiling, his rather severe first impression could also be off-putting, and indeed, he appeared to be depressingly remote to the entourage. When the tourists entered the Blue Room, Harrison shook each of their hands, although some reports said he remained seated at his desk without raising his head. Whatever the case, silence ensued after the formalities until Spalding extended an invitation to watch the game that afternoon. The president queried, "What game?" and then begged off because of his full schedule. "I used to go to the games once in a while at Indianapolis, and also at Chicago," he said. "I enjoy seeing a good game, but I do not see how I can spare the time to go to-day." Harrison added that it would be unbecoming for the president of the United States to be seen at a ball game, an opinion that stunned these big-headed tourists who had carried with them the national pastime with such fanfare. He tried to make amends by asking his private secretary to represent the administration before bidding the party good day and walking from the room. The tourists, stammering at such abrupt treatment, exited the White House for carriages that whisked them back to their hotel, where they dressed for the game. Cap Anson later wrote that Harrison "was about as warm as an icicle."[40]

Their reception at the hands of Washingtonians did not thaw at the ballpark. When the Marine Band led the tourists into Capitol Park, fans hissed at John Ward, who had refused a trade from the Giants to the Hewitt brothers' Senators, formerly the Statesmen when the team entered the National League in 1886. But Ward's problems off the field paled when compared to the three errors he made in a game that ranked as one of the worst exhibitions of the entire tour. Chicago won, 18–6, with All-America pitcher Ed Crane giving up seventeen hits, many of them in a first inning that yielded eight White Stocking runs. Still, the White Stockings also played indifferently. Actually, Ward had a nice hit at his first at-bat, but after each of his errors, the cynical crowd of less than three thousand roundly applauded him. In summing up the exhibition, the *Washington Post* concluded, "No wonder the English regarded baseball no better than 'rounders' if that's the kind of game they played."[41]

## PATRIOTIC FINISH

Disappointed in the nationalism in the nation's capital, the teams left that evening for Pittsburgh on the B&O Railroad, arriving the next morning, April 16. Meeting fans and a brass band at the depot, they drove to the Anderson Hotel then paraded to Recreation Park. Pittsburghers Tener, Mark Baldwin, Fred Carroll, and Tom Burns were welcomed warmly by friends and relatives, including Tener's six-year-old grandniece who, as an old woman in 1964, recalled that her first baseball game was this exhibition match on the "Round the World" tour. The day was chilly but sunny, and the cold seemed to dampen the playing skills as well as the meager enthusiasm of the three thousand in attendance. Things looked dim from the outset for Anson's squad when Hanlon chugged out an inside-the-park home run after Sullivan and Baldwin collided in the outfield and the ball scooted past them. Both Burns and Carroll had three hits, but the game ended in a 3–3 knot after nine innings. After the contest, the players assembled for praises in the Bijou Theater, the hall decorated with American flags, before departing the Steel City for Cleveland.[42]

The next day, in this rapidly developing city named for Gen. Moses Cleveland on the banks of the Cuyahoga River, Chicago struck back. Fans were ready for baseball, for this was opening day for the American Association, with the National League following close behind. A transport center, Cleveland had emerged in manufacturing; it was headquarters of John D. Rockefeller's massive monopoly, the Standard Oil Company, and also housed lumberyards, breweries, flour mills, nail works, and other industries—and thousands of baseball fans.

After taking up residence at the Weddell Hotel, the Spalding group met some local ballplayers who took them down Superior Street, the main thoroughfare, to the league grounds. The ballpark overflowed with people in the stands and down the foul lines. Journalists noted that the players doffed their hats "with the grace of French dancing masters" as they marched in behind the "irrepressible and grotesque youngster of African descent," Clarence Duval, to the music of "Home Again." The game was another listless affair, yet the spectators fixated on their favorite stars. All-

America hit well and held the lead through much of the game, but the White Stockings ran better, including Pop Anson, who had a memorable slide into second in the fifth inning. Crane's pitching disintegrated, and so did Ward's squad, as Chicago rolled, 7–4. Spalding left Cleveland's ballpark, his pockets bulging with gate receipts, and Ned Hanlon left the tour for Detroit to negotiate his release to Pittsburgh that year.[43]

The tourist's train traveled overnight to Indianapolis, a city of 125,000 people situated in the Indiana heartland amidst rich agricultural land and a hub to fifteen railroad spokes. Nicknamed "Park City" due to its shaded streets and lush spaces, the capital did an enormous business in farm goods, stockyards, and manufacturing, which in turn attracted banks, insurance companies, and so forth. It seemed a good place to stop, for its prosperous residents viewed their emerging city with pride and as a dynamic urban area with a bright future.[44]

Hoosiers were dedicated to baseball. Their own team was about to play its third and final year in the National League before dropping out, so the locals knew and loved baseball. They were aware of Anson's boast in Pittsburgh that Chicago would win the championship that year, and thus they reveled in seeing this larger-than-life sporting hero. He told journalists that their team would be decent that season, his White Stockings better, and that so successful had been the world tour that Australians had pledged to send a team to the United States within three years. Locals also heard accounts of the trip from John "Egyptian" Healy, who was originally from Egypt, Illinois, but now had visited the real thing. Tom Burns, formerly of the Indianapolis club, told listeners that he saw a great many sights and had "lots of fun, but America suits me pretty well." A buoyant street parade with a brass band led the tourists from the Denison House, but that was the high point of the baseball day. Just 1,200 spectators witnessed a dull game that sunny afternoon, the low numbers reflecting interest in their own team's play, most likely. The tourists displayed little enthusiasm except for daring base-running by Manning, Burns, and Fogarty, and the fans showed even less passion. Pop Anson was atrocious once again at catcher. The game, won by All-America 9–5, had few merits.[45]

The Spalding tourists seemed to care little about the impression they left because the end of their grand circuit was near. A special train car took them on the Monon Route to Chicago, where they arrived on Friday evening, April 19. Along the way, they donned dress suits and twenty-six miles out, in Hammond, Indiana, a party of Chicago fans and newsmen boarded the train and fired off questions until they rolled into Union Station. Spalding had been forewarned that a celebration awaited, and, indeed, the city made the final festivities memorable. A howling mob pushed against police and train guards as the players stepped onto the platform and entered eleven carriages, bearing "themselves with the dignity becoming the men who had shown the nobility of the effete monarchies that they could take the flies off anything, especially a bat," in the words of one reporter.[46]

The procession wound to Peck Court and down Wabash Avenue, then across to Michigan Avenue amidst bursting rockets and lights to the Palmer House. Scottish bagpipers joined a zouave company, a drill team dressed in exotic military uniforms made popular by French soldiers stationed in Algeria in the 1830s and by units in the American Civil War. Roughly 150,000 people of all classes—"business-men" as well as "toughs and sports" and many "ladies"—circulated in the streets. Amateur associations were represented—the Commercial, Garden City, Market Street, Mercantile, Grocers, and Northwestern Sub Leagues—with players in uniform. Spalding presented each one of the amateur athletes with a souvenir bat commemorating the tour. Members of the Hay Market, M&G, McNeil, Higgins & Co., Palace, U.S. Rolling Stock Co., and Royal teams volunteered their services to guide the parade. Fully 130 sporting organizations cheered, representing gymnastics, cycling, boating, cricket, lacrosse, and other athletic pursuits. Reception planners divided them into four "divisions" and stationed them along the route from the station to watch the special honor guard of Spalding Bros. employees march with the tourists. The throng was just as dense when a reception committee of Chicago dignitaries shook hands with the tourists at the Palmer House. The hotel itself was also packed with people, as was the banquet hall, which the entourage reached half an hour later. This tremendous reception for the returning global warriors was all-American in its grandeur.

In the banquet room, huge baskets of garlands and wreaths decorated the walls and ceilings; designs of baseball symbols in flowers and confection lay on the twenty-four tables, each with twelve settings for leaders in Chicago's business, baseball, and journalism world. A cornetist played throughout the dinner. Two hundred tickets, at ten dollars each, had been sold days before. Menu cards contained pages with different stops on the world tour. At the speaker's table at one end of the room sat the current and former mayors of the city, the head of the Chicago Press Club, a minister to give the opening benediction, Spalding, and a few other White Stockings officials. The *Sporting News* gushingly called the event "unquestionably the most elaborate, elegant and costly affair ever given at a public banquet in the West, if not in the country."[47]

The feast lasted until ten o'clock, when Mayor DeWitt C. Cregier opened the speech-making with the now oft-heard rounds of nationalist oratory. He welcomed the men not as players but as "representatives of a free America" as well as of the city of Chicago. Spalding thanked his hosts and the fans who had mobbed the tourists from the train station to the hotel, and he described the pleasures of the tour. Anson rose to toast the Prince of Wales, claiming that such royal recognition had raised "the social standard of the national game to the highest point it had yet attained." Ward and others followed with stirring talks about the greatness of Chicago and the members of the entourage, and the merits of athletic sports to the national well-being. The jingoism got even more hyperbolic. Maj. Henry Turner urged the assemblage to help "God in building up a country of men all powerful in protecting a country such as this. Long life to baseball and athletics. Long life to the National Guard. Long life to America, the freest land on earth." Other solemn proclamations erupted before the banquet adjourned.[48]

The final game of the Spalding world mission occurred the next afternoon, six months to the day after the tourists had left Chicago for the west. Two marshals had led Ward's team into the park, with a brass band tooting "When Johnny Comes Marching Home." The White Stockings arrived to greater acclaim, and then the scoring against Baldwin began. The White Stockings thanked fortune that this was the last contest, because All-America crushed them 22–9 before 3,700 fans at West Side Park. Never throwing "so wretchedly in his life," Baldwin gave up twenty-one base hits and nine bases on balls, a record that "will stand at the bottom for many a day." All-America hitters continued to bash Tener after he replaced the forlorn Baldwin in the fifth. "The banquet might have had something do to" with Chicago's performance. In any event, the grand tour was over, soon to be overshadowed in baseball by a much different expression of national purpose, but one nonetheless as American as Spalding's promotion of business, manliness, and exceptionalism: the first concerted labor fight for the rights of players.

## AMERICAN REBELLION

As a magnate focused on profit, Albert Spalding desired to keep labor costs low. Having just traveled the world, he also recognized that America's potential as a current and future powerhouse lay largely in marketing and selling competitively priced goods abroad; his world tour, in essence, aimed to disseminate the baseball "product" on the global market. One of the drivers of globalization that advanced the U.S. economy and, eventually, its imperial presence abroad was low-wage labor. A workforce paid at a negligible cost, and having (at this point in history) no mandated health or retirement compensation, fueled productivity (and, thus, manufacturing competitiveness) for many industries. Of course, workers slowly gained more leverage through unionization. Yet the dictates of private enterprise ruled the country because of a capitalist culture, nominal government regulation of the economy, and the law of supply and demand—that is, masses of immigrants were willing to work at minimal pay.

The baseball industry was well versed in this process, with magnates controlling the rules and governance of the sport and the reserve clause chaining players to one team under contract terms formulated at their whim. And except for a handful of stars, the pool of eligible players ran deep. Like the U.S. economy, baseball enjoyed a boom in profitability in part because of the strictures on labor, but as the Spalding tour ended, the budding union movement in the sport—led by All-America's John Ward—intended to change that system to assist the "workers," that is, the players. Thus, the world tour concluded on an anxious, if not sour, note due to impending management–labor struggles, and it is appropriate to consider the trip's end in light of the impending Brotherhood union strike and the creation of the Player's League of 1890. Union organizers, like owners, waved the flag in their interests—in their case, on behalf of the masses. They justified the fair treatment of players as the American way, as well as a crucial element in the rise of U.S. power overseas by providing economic stability, equality, and satisfaction at home.

There were, therefore, plenty of other unresolved issues that grabbed the attention of the tourists, as the Chicago residents among them unpacked their bags while All-America players bade their farewells to their fellow travelers. As far as the exhibitions had gone, the last game left Anson's team with twenty victories in fifty-four games. All-America carried the entire series, winning thirty games, while the teams tied four times. Yet All-America teammates did not dally over their overall series triumph; nearly all departed that evening to join their respective teams. Hanlon went to Pittsburgh and Ward to New York; others awaited the fruition of trade rumors. Confirmation came that the Ryan-Fogarty deal was off, and Ryan remained in Chicago, having sensibly agreed to abide by club rules of discipline. Reportedly never having touched liquor in his life until his world travels, Ed Crane had acquired his first taste of hard drinking in Paris, and from there, he experienced a tragic downward spiral to alcoholism and premature death in 1896, at the age of thirty-two. Returning to Pittsburgh, Fred Carroll still pined for the elegance of London hotels, while "Egyptian" Healy arrived in his small hometown in Illinois, where the mayor honored him with a special ceremony and a pin. Back in Kansas City, Jim Manning soon retired. Decades afterward, he was struck blind when hit with an iron beam while working in a Newark steel factory, only to have his sight miraculously restored four years later.[49]

Most significantly, many players also leaned toward labor organizing after the tour. Pitcher John Tener actually became better known as a labor organizer and politician than as a player. His résumé developed impressively once he abandoned the diamond. Tener pitched during the 1889 season, but the following year, he joined a Pittsburgh club that took part in the Brotherhood union rebellion against the National League. After the revolt aborted, he became a banker, represented Pittsburgh in the U.S. Congress from 1909 to 1911, and then became governor of Pennsylvania until 1915. Baseball authorities then appointed him president of the National League until 1918.

Foxy Ned Hanlon also jumped to Pittsburgh to the mutinous Player's League in 1890 before his stellar career as a manager of the Baltimore Orioles, a team that perfected "inside" or "scientific" baseball—advancing runners through singles, sacrifices, and bunting and otherwise winning games by scoring a run here or there rather than relying on the sensational power game of the home run so common from Babe Ruth onward. Jim Fogarty left the National League, too, conspiring in 1890 with Ward and Hanlon in the Brotherhood rebellion before dying suddenly of consumption the next year.[50]

Unhappy times awaited Tom Daly, Mark Baldwin, and Bob Pettit of the White Stockings, who were all released a few days after the tour ended. The *Sporting News*, a Spalding mouthpiece, claimed that these players owed Spalding for expenses incurred on the world tour and that they would not play again until they had redeemed their debt. This was further indication of the tensions between players and management that now plagued baseball. Daly went to Washington, Baldwin to Columbus of the American Association before joining the insurgent Player's League in 1890, and Pettit, who was taking care of his wife's medical problems, did not play again until 1891, the final year of his career, for Milwaukee of the American Association.[51]

The fates of these three players, and reference to the Player's League, pointed to a fundamental problem in baseball's labor structure and also represented a bump in the road of globalization. The tour had muffled these problems, but with the trip concluded, Spalding could no longer hide from them. That is, he could not disguise the players' dissatisfaction toward National League rules that governed salaries and contracts. These issues erupted in a revolt against Spalding and the National League; clearly, like other sectors of the American workforce, baseball was not immune to national trends of labor discord. The national pastime—the chauvinistic rhetoric and patriotic fetes of the world tour notwithstanding—was in jeopardy.

All was not well in the American baseball kingdom. John Ward had left the world tour in London, in part, to huddle with members of the Brotherhood union that he had formed in 1885. The organization now tried to redress some of the wrongs that players endured at the hands of league officials and the owners, chief among them being Albert Spalding. There were specific grievances, among them Spalding's ill-treatment of injured tourist Ed Williamson, a key link in Chicago's stonewall infield. Spalding claimed that reports of his abandoning Williamson to his own devices in London were groundless; he gave the player "ample funds," sent him more from Chicago, and "cared for [Williamson] liberally." Yet the knee injury suffered in Paris by the charming White Stocking third baseman, whom Anson considered the game's best all-around player, had left him bedridden with blood poisoning. Williamson finally took the field, in August 1889, but by that time, his speed had diminished. In the meantime, Spalding had deducted close to two-thirds of his 1889 salary for not playing during much of the season and charged his wife $500 for expenses on the world tour. The couple also footed Ned's medical expenses alone. Williamson retired in 1890 and bought a saloon, but died at four years later from kidney or liver disease at the age of thirty-six. That calamity aside, Spalding claimed he made a profit on the world tour, so why not help out his third baseman?[52]

There were other, more general complaints. The players detested the fines levied for "abuses" like dishonorable conduct—gambling, drinking, and the like—and bad play. In 1889, Louisville's owner, John Davidson, charged six players for their "lack of zeal" and threatened additional penalties for continued poor play. The team went on strike until the league rescinded the fine and bailed out Davidson from his financial hardship. Ward's Brotherhood had had enough, however.

The union was especially against the so-called Brush Plan, which instituted a system of five salary categories from which a player could not escape. In essence, the owners created a salary cap that rewarded a handful of stars. New players earned less money; in the lowest "E" class, they had to sweep the ballparks. How a player was classified also depended on his behavior as well as his playing abilities. This opened the way for arbitrary rulings, as owners might lower a salary for a player deemed a bad teammate or for one who dropped a fly ball at a key moment. Most galling, in 1889, the Brush Plan undermined a deal on the reserve clause between National League officials and the Brotherhood union. Both had agreed to insert the reserve clause into every contract on the condition that if an owner cut a player's salary, he could then test the market as a free agent and thus not automatically suffer a pay cut. The Brush Plan dashed that compromise by capping salaries at $2,000. No longer were the stars bought off and placated. No longer did the magnates follow precedent and confer with the union. Not all the owners were blind to the implications of their actions; Spalding thought many of his fellow proprietors foolish and selfish. Yet the classification scheme and reserve clause connivance left all players vulnerable to the capriciousness of management.[53]

Such injustices energized John Ward. The Giants star had capped off the world tour by writing a book, *Base-Ball: How to Become a Player*, which included acceptance of the reserve clause. His assessment did not represent appeasement, however, for he welcomed the Brotherhood as a counterbalance to the greedy magnates. He orchestrated the revolt against the Brush Plan because it compressed even the stars' paychecks, while relegating others to pick up the scraps. As well, Ward criticized the owners' disciplinary harshness and disregard for the well-being of their charges, the Williamson case being a main point for grievance. Thus, Ward departed from Chicago and the world tour to meet with Brotherhood members in New York just days before the 1889 season, resolved to give players their rights as Americans: more freedom and a larger share of the financial pie. Some talked of a strike. A meeting a few weeks later resulted in the establishment of a grievance committee that formally asked the National League to terminate the Brush Plan. In June, Ward met with Spalding, who recommended tabling the issue until the November 1889 annual league meeting. Spalding also devised a compromise, retaining the Brush classification scheme but exempting players with three years of service and "exemplary" behavior from the categories. Yet neither the greedy owners nor Ward's hot-headed players changed course.[54] Baseball headed into its first major conflict on the contested terrain of national labor rights. Ward hoped the sport would stand for fair dealing and labor justice, the antithesis of globalization's usual free-market crassness.

Peace in baseball ended as the selling of players as if they were slaves on the trading block caused the eruption of the Player's Revolt of 1890. Ward led dozens of union members into the Player's League, an association bereft of the reserve clause that competed with the National League and American Association on their own turf. Yet this experiment, which attracted 80 percent of the National League's players and several magnates disgruntled with the status quo, lasted only a year. National League owners and officials, backed by such influential newsmen as Henry Chadwick, colluded to destroy the association. They underpriced tickets for National League games and thus ruined the Player's League at the gate, branded it as destructive of the national pastime, and bribed some players to return to their National League teams. Cleverly, Spalding drove a wedge between the new owners and the players by offering the former a place at the National League and American Association tables. Some balky Brotherhood members prematurely compromised with Spalding, who saw the revolt as unnecessary but also as a "war to the death."

By 1891, the Player's League had disbanded, some of its teams absorbed into the National League. Along with the Brotherhood union itself, the American Association also went out of business. The National League now held a monopoly on Major League Baseball, and the magnates' lock endured for a decade until the acceptance of the American League as a legitimate organization in the majors in 1901.[55] Ultimately, Spalding the spider had lured the Brotherhood into his web and killed the union.

Surprisingly, organized baseball's most famous player, Cap Anson, a man who kept order on the tour and ruled over the White Stockings, also ended up on the wrong side of the magnates. He concluded his account of the global trip with an edgy statement claiming that Spalding's sporting goods business had "greatly benefited from the tour," while it had cost him about $1,500. Spalding later "repaid" Anson, the ballplayer claimed in 1900 in one of the first baseball autobiographies ever published, by reneging on his promise to give Anson a controlling interest in the Chicago club once Spalding stepped down as chief. This drove Anson into retirement in 1897. Such bitterness placed Anson alongside many other players who were tired of the robber barons, although he had refused to join the Player's League. At that time, he believed that the owners had treated him honestly while he thought many of the players in the Brotherhood were driven by simple greed rather than by the higher motivation of fraternity. In the end, however, his view of forbearance toward the magnates certainly changed.[56]

The player's revolt, a nightmare come true for capitalists, reflected national values of the pursuit of fairness, a curbing of Gilded Age greed, and nascent reform of exploitative practices toward workers. Its moneyed advocates trumpeted baseball's representation of American virtues, but the players more equitably addressed the national trends of progressive and populist reform that soon reshaped the country's political, social, and economic landscape. Yet despite the coming reforms, like the world tour on the global scale, the player's revolt at the national level ultimately exemplified the sport's importance in the marketplace. In baseball, workers would often be pitted against the capitalists. While John Ward and Albert Spalding might claim mutual admiration at receptions throughout the world, the players were no match for the skilled organization and the shrewd business dealings of Spalding, a paramount capitalist in the U.S. free enterprise system that bludgeoned aside weaklings and competitors alike. And in marketplace capitalism lay the future of American success, at home as well as in the empire abroad that lurked just a decade off. The applause for the tour confirmed this. Admirers of Spalding vigorously proclaimed his projection of American virtues abroad as they looked forward to the day when those exceptional traits would, finally, guide the world.

## NOTES

1. James E. Sullivan, "The Origin of Base Ball," in Sullivan, *Early Innings*, 288. The National League presidents on the commission included its first one, Morgan Bulkeley (in 1907, a senator from Connecticut), as well as A. G. Mills and Nick Young. Arthur Gorman, senator from Maryland and former president of the National Base Ball Club of Washington, D.C., joined former players Alfred Reach and George Wright, and James Sullivan, elected president of the AAU in 1906.

2. "A. G. Spalding Requests Formation of a Special Committee to Investigate the Origins of Baseball (1905)," in Sullivan, *Early Innings*, 281. See also Light, *Cultural Encyclopedia of Baseball*, 215, 529–31; Salvatore, "Man Who Didn't Invent Baseball."

3. Parish, "What Made American Nationalism," 194–98; Iriye, "Culture," 101; Heiss, "Evolution of the Imperial Idea," 513; Shaffer, *See America First*.

4. Evans, "Baseball as Civil Religion," 32, also 27–30; Voigt, "Reflections on Diamonds."

5. Evans, "Baseball as Civil Religion," 21. On exceptionalism, see Madsen, *American Exceptionalism*, and Lipset, *American Exceptionalism*.

6. Quoted in Levine, *A. G. Spalding*, 106.

7. Spalding, *Baseball*, 265. On tour finances, see Levine, *A. G. Spalding*, 109.

8. Anson, *A Ball Player's Career*, 272. See also Brierly, *Ab-O'Th-Yate*, 179–86; White Star Line steamers, *Albert Spalding Scrapbook*, vol. 10, Albert Spalding Collection, Society of American Baseball Researchers Lending Library, Cleveland, Ohio; "The Teams Still at Sea," *New York Herald*, April 6, 1889, p. 8; Palmer, *Athletic Sports*, 441–42.

9. Quoted in Sullivan, *Early Innings*, 175.

10. Aubertin, *A Fight with Distances*, 236, also 241, 259; Glazier, *Peculiarities of American Cities*, 317, also 287, 292, 297; Faithfull, *Three Visits to America*, 352–65.

11. Glazier, *Peculiarities of American Cities*, 72–74; Light, *Cultural Encyclopedia of Baseball*, 119, 195.

12. "No Trouble," *Sporting Life* (February 13, 1889): 1; Palmer, *Athletic Sports*, 442–43; "Arrival Home of the All-America and the Chicago Nine," *New York Times* (April 7, 1889): 8; "On Native Soil," *Brooklyn Eagle* (April 9, 1889): 1.

13. "The Grand Reception," *Sporting Life*, February 6, 1889, p. 1.

14. Henry Chadwick, "The Base Ball Tourists," *Brooklyn Eagle*, February 3, 1889, p. 7.

15. "Many Ovations," *Sporting Life*, April 17, 1889, p. 2; Andrews, "Delmonico's."

16. "Testimonial Banquet to Mr. A. G. Spalding and His Party of Representative American Ball Players, Delmonico's, April 8, 1889," Albert Spalding Biographical File, National Baseball Hall of Fame, Cooperstown, New York (hereafter cited as NBHOF); McCullough, *Mornings on Horseback*, 237–46, 316–50.

17. Carter to J. W. Curiss, April 2, 1889, Microfilm Edition of Mark Twain's Previously Unpublished Letters, Bancroft Library, University of California, Berkeley.

18. Sullivan, *Early Innings*, 176–77; "Many Ovations," *Sporting Life*, April 17, 1889, p. 3.

19. Fatout, *Mark Twain Speaking*, 244–47. See also Hayes, "Mark Twain's Earliest."

20. Putz, "Mark Twain."

21. Anson, *A Ball Player's Career*, 277. See also Parmet, "Presidential Fever."

22. Palmer, *Athletic Sports*, 446.

23. Palmer, *Athletic Sports*, 449.

24. "Baseball at Delmonico's," *New York Times*, April 7, 1889, p. 5. See also "Ball Players in Clover," *New York Herald*, April 9, 1889, p. 4.

25. "The Wine Was Very, Very Red," *New York Herald*, April 10, 1889, p. 10. See also "After Effects," *Brooklyn Eagle*, April 10, 1889, p. 2.

26. Glazier, *Peculiarities of American Cities*, 86–106.

27. "Base-Ball Notes," *Baltimore Morning Sun*, April 10, 1889, supplement; "Expert Ball Playing," *Baltimore Morning Sun*, April 11, 1889, supplement.

28. "Fogarty Traded for Ryan," *Philadelphia Inquirer*, April 12, 1889, p. 6.

29. "The Ball Men Dined," *Philadelphia Inquirer*, April 12, 1889, p. 1.

30. H. Angelo, "The Base Ball Fever" (Philadelphia, 1867), folder A, "Baseball— General Songs," box 1, series 7.1: Baseball (A–K), Sam DeVincent Collection of American Sheet Music, no. 300, National Museum of American History, Washington, D.C. (hereafter cited as NMAH); F. W. Root, "Home Run Galop" (Chicago, 1867), folder T, box 3, Series 7: Sports, NMAH. See also Light, *Cultural Encyclopedia of Baseball*, 676.

31. Virginia Duncan and James Mascotte, "Steal! Slide! Anyway!" (New York, 1889), and L. B. Starkweather, "Catch It on the Fly" (Chicago, 1867), both in folder A, box 1, Series 7.1: Baseball (A–K), NMAH. See also M. J. Messer, "Una Schottische" (Boston, 1874), and T. M. Brown, "Union Base Ball Club March" (St. Louis, 1867), both in folder W, box 3, Series 7: Sports, NMAH.

32. Walter Neville, "Hurrah for Our National Game" (New York, undated), folder W, Box 3, Series 7: Sports, NMAH. The song was written for the Olympic Base Ball Club of New York.

33. "Many Ovations," *Sporting Life*, April 17, 1889, p. 2.

34. "Many Ovations," *Sporting Life*, April 17, 1889, p. 2. See also "The Ball Men Dined," *Philadelphia Inquirer*, April 12, 1889, p. 1.

35. "Many Ovations," *Sporting Life*, April 17, 1889, p. 2. See also Hole, *Little Tour in America*, 324.

36. "The Rovers' Good-Bye," *Philadelphia Inquirer*, April 13, 1889, p. 6; Palmer, *Athletic Sports*, 455.

37. Faithfull, *Three Visits to America*, 97; O'Rell, *A Frenchman in America*, 160; Glazier, *Peculiarities of American Cities*, 47–55; "Anson Was Downed," *Boston Sunday Globe*, April 14, 1889, p. 4; Palmer, *Athletic Sports*, 455; "Tourists at the Hub," *Sunday Boston Globe*, April 14, 1889, p. 6; "All America vs. Chicago," *Boston Courier*, April 14, 1889, p. 1; "Sizing Up Tener," *Daily Boston Globe*, April 13, 1889, p. 5.

38. James Ryan, *Tour of the Spalding B.B.C. around the World* [diary] (hereafter cited as Ryan Diary), James Edward Ryan Biographical File, NBHOF, entry for April 14, 1889, p. 90; Aubertin, *A Fight with Distances*, 273–74; Glazier, *Peculiarities of American Cities*, 530, 532–35, 544, 558; Hole, *Little Tour in America*, 313; Palmer, *Athletic Sports*, 456.

39. Quoted in Knox, *The Republican Party*, 497, 501. See also O'Rell, *A Frenchman in America*, 337; Wallace, *Life of Gen. Ben Harrison*, 263; and Harney, *Lives of Benjamin Harrison*, 203–37. GOP wheeler-dealer Stephen Elkin had given Russell Harrison a job in 1886 when the family teetered on bankruptcy due to its overinvestment in a Montana cattle enterprise.

40. Anson, *A Ball Player's Career*, 283. See also Blaine, "Why Harrison Was Elected!"; "President Harrison's Inaugural," *Nation* 48 (March 7, 1889): 193–94; Marcus, *Grand Old Party*; Socolofsky and Spetter, *Presidency of Benjamin Harrison*; "Harrison Snubs the Tourists," *Indianapolis Sentinel*, April 18, 1889, p. 4; Palmer, *Athletic Sports*, 456.

41. "The Two Great Nines," *Washington Post*, April 15, 1889, p. 7; Light, *Cultural Encyclopedia of Baseball*, 782.

42. Roberta Tener Johus to Lee Allen, July 28, 1964, John K. Tener Biographical File, NBHOF. See also "The Great Trip," *Sporting Life*, April 24, 1889, p. 2; Ryan Diary, April 16, 1889, p. 90; "Welcome to the Boys," *Pittsburgh Post Gazette*, April 16, 1889, p. 8; "An Easy Game," *Pittsburgh Post Gazette*, April 17, 1889, p. 8.

43. "Well Inaugurated," *Cleveland Leader and Herald*, April 18, 1889, p. 3. See also Glazier, *Peculiarities of American Cities*, 144–56; "Captured by Chicago," *Cleveland Press*, April 18, 1889, p. 1.

44. "The Sporting World," *Cleveland Plain Dealer*, April 18, 1889, p. 5; Warner, "Great West: Three Capitals," 262–64.

45. "From Around the World," *Indianapolis News*, April 18, 1889, p. 1. See also "Good Ball Playing, *Indianapolis News*, April 17, 1889, p. 4; "Remarks from Capt. Anson," *Indianapolis Journal*, April 19, 1889, p. 3; "All-America Wins," *Indianapolis News*, April 19, 1889, p. 4; "A Puzzler to the Cranks," *Indianapolis Sentinel*, April 19, 1889, p. 4; "Not a Very Exciting Game," *Indianapolis Journal*, April 19, 1889, p. 3.

46. "Return of the Players," *Chicago Tribune*, April 20, 1889, p. 3.

47. "Return of the Players," *Chicago Tribune*, April 20, 1889, p. 3; "Warmly Welcomed," *Sporting News*, April 20, 1889, p. 1. See also "Will Give the Boys a Great Reception," *Chicago Tribune*, April 17, 1889, p. 3; Palmer, *Athletic Sports*, 456–58.

48. Palmer, *Athletic Sports*, 458–60; Turner quoted in Levine, *A. G. Spalding*, 108.

49. "Last Game of the Tour," *Chicago Tribune*, April 21, 1889, p. 10. See also "The First Game at the Ball Park," *Chicago Tribune*, April 17, 1889, p. 3; "Separation of the All Americas," *Chicago Tribune*, April 21, 1889, p. 10; "Ned Crane Is Dead," *Sporting Life*, September 26, 1896; "Blind 4 Years, Ex-Pitcher Cured by Miracle, He Says," newspaper clipping, James Manning Biographical File, NBHOF.

50. Lane, "Greatest President"; Breedy, "Play Ball!"; "Fogarty Dead," *Public Ledger-Philadelphia*, May 21, 1891.

51. "Echoes of the World's Tour," *Sporting Life*, May 15, 1889, p. 4; "In the Big Nine Hole," *Sporting News*, April 27, 1889, p. 1.

52. Spalding quoted in "Echoes of the World's Tour," *Sporting Life*, May 15, 1889, p. 4. See also Di Salvatore, *A Clever Base-Ballist*, 149–50.

53. Di Salvatore, *A Clever Base-Ballist*, 148–50; Stevens, *Baseball's Radical*, 77–79.

54. Di Salvatore, *A Clever Base-Ballist*, 257–65.

55. Spalding, *Baseball*, 293. See also Light, *Cultural Encyclopedia of Baseball*, 578–79, and Burk, *Never Just a Game*, 112–15.

56. Anson, *A Ball Player's Career*, 284–85, see also 287.

# Conclusion

## Imperial Imagination

There is much credence to outfielder Jimmy Ryan's labeling of the 1888–1889 world tour as "the greatest trip in the annals of sport."[1] To be sure, chronicler Harry Palmer erred in claiming that the project would never be duplicated, for it was largely repeated, and even extended geographically, in 1913–1914. But, he was correct that Spalding had become a visionary path-breaker to organizers of future globe-girdling trips. The great circuit of more than thirty-two thousand miles, summed up Palmer, "must ever remain a credit to its projector" for "the nerve, the enterprise, the managerial ability and the sound business judgment displayed by Albert Spalding."[2] The American pastime owed its high standards of reputation to him, and later baseball travelers took his example as a guide when planning their own trips.

Thus, the story of the world tour returns, most appropriately, to Albert Spalding. After the Player's League episode, Spalding revitalized the National League monolith that had brought him riches and fame. As his supporters at numerous receptions had proclaimed, his world tour put baseball on display around the planet; his war against the Brotherhood continued that exhibition of business supremacy in the industrial era.[3] That was the American way, and it paid big dividends for corporations at home as well as feeding into the globalization process. Behind the patriotic rhetoric of the Spalding tour ran business calculations that served the nation's power structure, on which later imperial-minded leaders based the nation's strength.

Beyond running headlong into a clash over labor rights, the world tour had other results, although they were decidedly mixed. If Spalding aimed to convert the British to the national pastime, he clearly failed. To be sure, the tour stimulated interest in the sport in England and Scotland, as well

187

as Australia. Tour manager Jim Hart quit his managerial post with the National League's Boston club at the end of 1889 to devote his time to Spalding's dubious hope of developing the British Base Ball League in England and Scotland. This association grew from the inspiration of the world tour, although baseball did not catch on at the magnitude of Spalding's dreams. Hart returned to America in 1891 when that scheme fizzled, although he made annual trips to Europe thereafter. Spalding himself arranged for minor leaguers to act as player-coaches in England and, in the midst of the Brotherhood war in 1889, he even went to Britain to lend a hand. The sport never dislodged cricket from its pedestal but at least Spalding made foreigners aware of how important baseball was to American identity. Thus, as a means of warming up audiences, British travelers in the United States might mention baseball. For example, in 1922, during an American visit, Sherlock Holmes's creator, Sir Arthur Conan Doyle, spoke lightheartedly of his days as a shortstop and lauded the sport as a necessity for England.[4]

Albert Spalding never ceased his promotional efforts in foreign lands. In the early 1900s, he welcomed progress toward adopting baseball in Britain, Australia, South Africa, Japan, Mexico, and Cuba, writing that the game was "advancing slowly but surely" abroad. Yet his correspondence also revealed an unease that these nations were "tinkering with the Playing Rules." As a result, he ensured that his *Spalding's Guides* laid down a code mandated by Major League Baseball in non-English languages. Spalding urged "a little encouragement, aid, and cooperation from" the baseball establishment in the United States so that "the time will come when Base Ball will become the established and recognized Field Sport of the world."[5] That it made great strides in many parts of the world testified to his pluck. Interestingly, however, baseball took hold in places that the tour had not reached, such as Japan and the Caribbean, and it was ironic that these were nations of color rather than the white imperial outposts so lauded by the tourists. In reality, baseball never grabbed the fancy of mass audiences in the so-called advanced nations of Europe and the British Commonwealth. This was Spalding's ultimate failure in promotion.

The tour, however, left a legacy that energized the sport over the next century. For starters, it remained a proud topic of industry chatter for years, always mentioned as a great success when teams embarked on overseas travel. It also inspired others. Just before Spalding's death, on the twenty-fifth anniversary of the world tour, New York Giants manager John McGraw and Charles Comiskey, the president of the Chicago White Sox, organized a six-month traveling extravaganza along the Spalding model. While it, too, stopped in Australia, Egypt, Italy, France, and the British Isles, this trip of 1913–1914 was more extensive that Spalding's, as the tourists also visited Japan, China, the Philippines, India, and Belgium.

There were other significant differences. The 1913–1914 tour had less of a carnival atmosphere, for McGraw and Comiskey did not bring along anyone like Clarence Duval or the ballooning Professor. Nor were they out for self-promotion; both had disliked the grand deity Albert Spalding and his marketing of his sporting goods concern.

Yet like their 1888–1889 counterparts, these twentieth-century tourists included the stars of the day, such as Hall of Fame pitcher Christy Matthewson and the Native American legend Jim Thorpe. Like Spalding's tourists, the McGraw-Comiskey teams meandered westward across the United States, got seasick in the Pacific Ocean, wowed the Australians, mucked in gloomy English weather, marveled at the famous sights of Asia, the Middle East, and Europe, and sat before a motion-picture camera (rather than a still-life machine of 1889) on the Sphinx. Covered closely by journalists, they had an audience with the pope and played before Britain's King George V. Just as the Spalding tour gave way to the Brotherhood revolt, so, too, did the 1913–1914 precede another period of strife in baseball—the aborted Federal League war against the National and American Leagues. And these tourists, like their nineteenth-century forerunners, aimed to transplant the great national pastime among sporting nations abroad.[6]

Other tours followed, most notably barnstorming trips to Japan in 1931 and 1934 (the latter included Babe Ruth), throughout the century and beyond, as American baseball players performed before ever-increasing numbers of foreign spectators. A myriad of other transnational baseball contacts, moreover, showed that globalization was in full swing. Japan–United States contacts served as one example. Five years before the world tour, Spalding gave copies of his *Spalding's Official Base Ball Guide*, as well as equipment, to Japanese students who returned to their country to boost their own version of the U.S. national pastime. Seven years after the Spalding tour, a team of Japanese college-level players won a series of games against American expats and sailors in Yokohama; this victory by the Ichiko squad inspired the country to adopt baseball as a national sport. By the early twentieth century, Japanese college teams launched tours of their own to the American West Coast, and in 1925 they formed their own Tokyo League, which still exists today. Ten years later, catalyzed by the Babe Ruth tour, a professional league began, which after the World War II interregnum grew in popularity and prosperity. Fueled by superb play, periodic visits by American clubs and all-star squads, and, most recently, by the engagement of the Japan League in the process of globalization through the export of players to the United States, baseball (rather than sumo) can be considered Japan's national pastime.[7] Global baseball networks spread into Latin America, too.

Into the international realm traveled the sport, and with it, American encounters abroad flourished. Baseball was not the sole beneficiary of globalization. Just seven years after the Spalding tour, the modern-day Olympics began a worldwide phenomenon of expanding summer—and later winter—amateur sports. From 1896 to the present, the Olympic format has flourished. Furthermore, tours by the famous Harlem Globetrotters and then professionalization in the Olympics prompted the world to take notice of basketball. Professional American football teams exhibited their sport in Europe, while British soccer clubs toured the United States. Of course, for its part, baseball grew in popularity, at home and abroad.[8] The United States had long envisioned an empire; it had one in baseball (and other sports), and substantial credit is due to Albert Spalding and his tourists for pointing the sport in that direction.

The tour introduced baseball to the world, but its true import lay not so much in where it went and the pleasures of travel or, for that matter, in the development of the sport itself and the fulfillment of Albert Spalding's ambitions. For his part, Spalding continued to gather the accoutrements of his own empire; upon his return from abroad, he shocked colleagues by buying A. J. Reach's sporting goods firm. From his monopolist perch, he presided over the chief sports equipment house in the world, while his organizational skills maintained the authority of the National League.[9] That the bottom line stayed in Spalding's sights was critical to baseball's continued consolidation as the national pastime, but the tour meant much more in the long run to history and international relations. No matter the importance of baseball to America (and it remained an influence in all aspects of life, including the economy, gender and race relations, municipal and regional development, and labor), the sport provided a window through which to look out on an even wider world of significance. In other words, the impact of the Spalding tour ultimately lay in the development of an American imperial identity, itself forged by U.S. overseas encounters through the process of globalization. While a bit player in this imperial process, the tour nonetheless signaled the impending age of American predominance and the inevitable transformation of global power relationships.

The world tour of 1888–1889 symbolized aspects of the early era of globalization. Among them was the triumph of big business in the U.S. economy. Spalding epitomized this trend as an entrepreneurial product of a rapidly growing Chicago, itself connected to the world through manufacturing, transport, trade, and investment. The integration of the country, and the world, by transportation and communication networks was another element of globalization that the tour revealed as it moved through a new, ambitiously capitalist American West, a region far removed from the romance of the dusty frontier by technological and economic innovation. Into the Pacific sailed the tourists, who blatantly ranked people in terms of color and ethnic background. By looking favorably on their pioneering "cousins" in the British Empire, while denigrating nonwhites (including blacks at home), they voiced a cultural superiority that facilitated white Anglo-American unity and thereby entrenched white imperial dominance and a system of inequality over the commercial and political apparatus of globalization. Cultural competition between the New World and Old Europe proved a bar to baseball abroad, and Europeans served notice that the young power across the Atlantic—no matter how dynamic—must wait its turn at the helm of global leadership. Still, Spalding demonstrated how the United States had no fear of stepping into European, and especially British, cultural domains in the hopes of Americanizing the world economy. Finally, the tourists returned home to the blaring of nationalism on a job well done. The European experience likely prompted a defensive outpouring of such American values as masculinity, democracy, and unconcealed commercialism. Such exceptionalist rhetoric emphasized the determination to seize the reins of globalization and shape the process into a tool with which to hammer the imaginary American empire into a real one. In sum, the world tour packaged business, technology, culture, and political representation into a weighty national identity that promised a future of imperial eminence.

In the globalized economic system that paved an imperial pathway for the United States, it turned out that baseball was an exemplar of American identity. Examples abound of how the game mirrored society. The Brotherhood War and unionization during the Progressive Era; Jackie Robinson and integration; and the advent of fantasy camps in the 1980s, in which aging baby-boomers could relive their youths by associating with major leaguers, reveal means in which the sport became a bellwether of U.S. values and circumstances. "Whoever wants to know the heart and mind of America had better learn baseball," wrote scholar Jacques Barzun, and while this may be as much hyperbole as Spalding's adage that the game reflected the national character, it is clear that baseball provided ways to view patterns in American history, and does so today.[10] The sport seized the imagination, yet the Spalding world tour fired a major initial shot in the promotional effort to inject dreams from the national to the international stage.

The conceptualization of empire occurred years before its advent, and baseball played a role. Empire arrived after the Spanish-American War of 1898, as the United States assumed formal control of (or exercised preponderant influence over) Hawaii, the Philippines, scattered islands in the Pacific, and Cuba and much of the Caribbean. Yet a decade before, Spalding's elite cohort of the sporting establishment, itself a pillar of society, was imbued with a sense of destiny, even intellectual insight. They had begun to think about national greatness on a world stage, and they began spreading the American dream of disseminating their culture and the doctrines of free enterprise. Thus, the baseball party's baggage amounted to more than their personal effects. Spalding glorified the nation, selling America to the world during a working vacation. By the new millennium, it was clear that these missionaries had succeeded in building an empire. Globalization brought baseball players to American shores to play the national pastime while sixteen nations took part in the first truly world series in March 2006. Unlike the fabled Casey, Albert Spalding did not strike out.

## NOTES

1. James Ryan, *Tour of the Spalding B.B.C. around the World* [diary], James Edward Ryan Biographical File, National Baseball Hall of Fame, Cooperstown, New York (hereafter cited as NBHOF), entry for April 20, 1889, p. 92.

2. Palmer, *Athletic Sports*, 460.

3. Levine, *A. G. Spalding*, 56–65; "Baseball's Nightmare," September 27, 1890, newspaper clipping in Leagues: Player's League File, NBHOF.

4. "Baseball: Across the Sea," newspaper clipping in Henry Chadwick Scrapbooks, Society of American Baseball Researchers Lending Library, Cleveland, Ohio, vol. 14, reel 2; "The English and Baseball," *Literary Digest* 74 (August 5, 1922): 62–63. See also Bartlett, *Baseball and Mr. Spalding*, 219, and Light, *Cultural Encyclopedia of Baseball*, 64. Hart became a fixture in Chicago as well as on the National League rules' committees. He pushed the pitcher back to a spot 60 feet, 6 inches away from home plate, while pitchers compensated by throwing from an elevated mound from which they bore down on batters, and he also fathered the provision that counted the batter's first two foul balls as strikes.

5. Spalding to August Herrmann, April 29, 1907, Albert Spalding Biographical File, NBHOF. See also Spalding to Nelson P. Cook, April 27, 1907, Albert Spalding Biographical File, NBHOF.

6. "The First Tour of World," *Sporting Life*, November 15, 1913, p. 1; Elfers, *Tour to End All Tours*, 5–6, 10–12.

7. See Guthrie-Shimizu, "Love of the Game."

8. See Lyberg, *Fabulous 100 Years*; Green, *Spinning the Globe.*

9. Voigt, *American Baseball*, 218–20.

10. Barzun in Tygiel, *Past Time*, ix. See also Thorn, "Our Game," 1.

# Bibliography

## PRIMARY SOURCES

### National Archives, College Park, Maryland— Record Group 59, Department of State

T-30, Dispatches from U.S. Ministers in Hawaii (microfilm).
M34, Dispatches from U.S. Ministers to France (microfilm).
M99, Notes to Foreign Legations in the United States from the Department of State (microfilm).
M173, Dispatches from U.S. Consuls in Sydney, Australia, 1836–1906 (microfilm).

### National Baseball Hall of Fame, Cooperstown, New York— Biographical File

Adrian C. Anson
Mark Baldwin
Thomas Everett Burns
Frederick Herbert Carroll
Edward Nicholas Crane
William Earle
James Fogarty
Edward Hugh Hanlon
James A. Hart
John J. Healy
Edward S. Hengle
Michael Joseph Kelly
Herman Long
James Manning
Robert Henry Pettit
Nathaniel Frederick Pfeffer
James Edward Ryan
Albert G. Spalding
John K. Tener

Michael Joseph Tiernan
George Edward Martin Van Haltren
John Montgomery Ward
Edward Nagle Williamson
George A. Wood
George Wright

## National Baseball Hall of Fame, Cooperstown, New York—Other Files

James Ryan Diary
Players League File
Newspaper Clippings File
*New York Herald* File
Tours File

## National Museum of American History, Washington, D.C.

Sam DeVincent Collection of American Sheet Music, #300: Series 7: Sports Series
7.1: Baseball (A–K).

## Society of American Baseball Researchers (SABR) Lending Library, Cleveland, Ohio

Henry Chadwick Scrapbooks (microfilm).
Albert Spalding Scrapbooks (microfilm).

## Bancroft Library, University of California, Berkeley, California

Mark Twain's Previously Unpublished Letters (microfilm edition).

## NEWSPAPERS AND PERIODICALS

*Adelaide Observer*
*All The Year Round*
*American Cricketer*
*Athletic Journal*
*The Athletic News and Cyclists' Journal*
*Atlantic Monthly*
*Baltimore Morning Sun*
*Belfast Evening Telegraph*
*Blackwood's Magazine*
*Boston Courier*
*Boston Sunday Globe*
*Brooklyn Eagle*

*Cedar Rapids Evening Gazette*
*The Century*
*Century Magazine*
*Ceylon Independent*
*Chicago Tribune*
*Cleveland Leader and Herald*
*Cleveland Plain Dealer*
*Cleveland Press*
*The Contemporary Review*
*The Cosmopolitan*
*Daily Boston Globe*
*Daily Pioneer Press*
*Denver Republican*
*Denver Times*
*Fortnightly Review*
*Forum*
*Frank Leslie's Illustrated Newsletter*
*Harper's New Monthly Magazine*
*Hawaiian Gazette*
*The Illustrated Sporting and Dramatic News*
*Indianapolis Journal*
*Indianapolis News*
*Indianapolis Sentinel*
*Juniata Herald*
*The Literary Digest*
*Lippincott's*
*Literary Digest*
*Littell's Living Age*
*Los Angeles Times*
*Macmillan's Magazine*
*Melbourne Age*
*Minneapolis Tribune*
*Le Monde Illustre*
*Nation*
*New York Herald*
*New York Times*
*New Zealand Herald*
*North American Review*
*Omaha Daily Bee*
*Omaha Republican*
*Outing*
*Overland Ceylon Observer*
*Pacific Commercial Advertiser*
*Philadelphia Inquirer*
*Pittsburgh Post*
*Pittsburgh Post Gazette*

*The Referee*
*Rocky Mountain News*
*Saint Paul and Minneapolis Pioneer Press*
*Salt Lake City Daily Tribune*
*San Francisco Chronicle*
*Scribner's Magazine*
*Sport and Play*
*The Sporting Clipper*
*Sporting Life*
*The Sporting Life (England)*
*Sporting News*
*The Sporting Times*
*Sunday Boston Herald*
*Sydney Morning Herald*
*Washington Post*
*Wellington Evening Post*

## BOOKS AND ARTICLES

Adair, Daryl, Murray Phillips, and John Nauright. "Sporting Manhood in Australia: Test Cricket, Rugby Football, and the Imperial Connection, 1878–1918." *Sport History Review* 28 (1997): 46–60.

Adler, Jacob. "The Oceanic Steamship Company: A Link in Claus Spreckels' Hawaiian Sugar Empire." *Pacific Historical Review* 29 (1960): 257–69.

Albrecht-Carrié, René. *Europe after 1815*. 5th ed. Totowa, N.J.: Littlefield, Adams & Co., 1972.

Allen, Grant. "Woman's Intuition." *Forum* 9 (May 1890): 333.

Anderson, Stuart. "'Pacific Destiny' and American Policy in Samoa, 1872–1899." *Hawaiian Journal of History* 12 (1978): 45–60.

Andrade, Ernest. "The Great Samoan Hurricane of 1889." *Naval War College Review* 34 (1981): 73–81.

Andrews, Peter. "Delmonico's: The Restaurant That Changed the Way We Dine." *American Heritage* 31 (1980): 96–101.

Anson, Adrian C. *A Ball Player's Career*. Chicago: Era Publishing, 1900.

Appel, Marty. *Slide, Kelly, Slide: The Wild Life and Times of Mike "King" Kelly, Baseball's First Superstar*. Lanham, Md.: Scarecrow Press, 1999.

Ardolino, Frank B. "Missionaries, Cartwright, and Spalding: The Development of Baseball in Nineteenth-Century Hawaii." *Nine* 10 (2002): 27–45.

Arnold, Matthew. *Civilization in the United States: First and Last Impressions*. Boston: Cupples and Hurd, 1888. Available at http://memory.loc.gov/cgi-bin/query/r?ammem/lhbtn:@field(DOCID + @lit(lhbtn01389)).

Aubertin, John James. *A Fight with Distances: The States, Hawaiian Islands, Canada, British Columbia, Cuba and the Bahamas*. London: K. Paul, Trench & Co., 1888. Available at http://memory.loc.gov/cgi-bin/query/r?ammem/lhbtn:@field (DOCID + @lit(lhbtn01389)).

Baltensperger, B. H. "Newspaper Images of the Central Great Plains in the Late Nineteenth Century." *Journal of the West* 19 (1980): 64–70.

Banham, Martin, ed. *The Cambridge Guide to World Theatre*. Cambridge: Cambridge University Press, 1988.

Barry, Joseph. "Eiffel, Versatile Engineer-Builder of Towering Talents." *Smithsonian* 1 (1972): 49–53.

Bartlett, Arthur. *Baseball and Mr. Spalding: The History and Romance of Baseball*. New York: Farrar, Straus and Young, 1951.

Bederman, Gail. *Manliness and Civilization: A Cultural History of Gender and Race in the United States, 1880–1917*. Chicago: University of Chicago Press, 1996.

Beisner, Robert L. *From the Old Diplomacy to the New, 1865–1900*. 2nd ed. Arlington Heights: Harlan Davidson, 1986.

Betts, Raymond F. "Immense Dimensions: The Impact of the American West on Late Nineteenth-Century European Thought about Expansion." *Western Historical Quarterly* 10 (1970): 149–66.

Bishop, William Henry. "A Paris Exposition in Dishabille." *Atlantic Monthly* 63 (May 1889): 623.

Blackwell, Thos. "Reminiscences of Irish Sport: A Country Race Meeting." *Outing* (July 1889): 265–69.

Blaine, Walker. "Why Harrison Was Elected!" *North American Review* 147 (November 1888): 689–95.

Blair, John G. "First Steps toward Globalization: Nineteenth-Century Exports of American Entertainment Forms." In *"Here, There, and Everywhere": The Foreign Politics of American Popular Culture*, ed. Reinhold Wagnleitner and Elaine Tyler May. Hanover, N.H.: University Press of New England, 2000.

Bloyce, Daniel. "'Just Not Cricket': Baseball in England, 1874–1900." *International Journal of the History of Sport* 14 (1997): 207–18.

Bogart, John. "Feats of Railway Engineering." *Scribner's Magazine* 4 (July 1888): 3–33.

Borocz, Jozsef. "Travel-Capitalism: The Structure of Europe and the Advent of Tourism." *Comparative Studies in Society and History* 34, no. 4 (October 1992): 708–41.

Bradley, Joseph. "Unrecognized Middle-Class Revolutionary? Michael Cusack, Sport, and Cultural Change in Nineteenth-Century Ireland." *European Sports History Review* 4 (2002): 58–72.

Bradley, W. H. "Around the World with Thomas Cook." *British Heritage* 9 (1988): 56–61.

Breedy, James H. "Play Ball! The Legacy of Nineteenth-Century Baltimore Baseball." *Maryland Historical Magazine* 87 (1992): 126–45.

Brierly, Ben. *Ab-O'Th-Yate in Yankeeland: The Results of Two Trips to America*. Manchester, England: A. Heywood & Son, 1885. Available at http://memory.loc .gov/cgi-bin/query/r?ammem/lhbtn:@field(DOCID + @lit(lhbtn01387)).

Brock, Darryl. "The Wright Way." *Sports Heritage* (May–April 1987): 35–40, 93–94.

Brownell, W. C. "French Traits—The Art Instinct." *Scribner's Magazine* 5 (February 1889): 74–82, 241.

Burk, Robert F. *Never Just a Game: Players, Owners, and American Baseball to 1920*. Chapel Hill: University of North Carolina Press, 1994.

Burrows, S. M. "A Modern Pilgrimage." *Macmillan's Magazine* 58 (1888?): 467.

Buzard, James. *The Beaten Track: European Tourism, Literature, and the Ways to Culture, 1800–1918*. Oxford: Clarendon Press, 1993.

Cameron, Roderick. "The Commonwealth of Australia." *Forum* 11 (1890?): 250–57.

Cappio, Alfred P. "Slide, Kelly, Slide: The Story of Michael J. Kelly, The 'King' of Baseball." Passaic, N.J.: Passaic County Historical Society, 1962.

Carlson, Lewis. "The Universal Athletic Sport of the World." *American History Illustrated* 19 (1984): 36–43.

Carnarvon. "Australia in 1888." *Littell's Living Age* 66 (April, May, June 1889): 195–209.

Carpenter, Frank. "Cairo under the Khedive." *Cosmopolitan* 6 (October 1889): 48, 580–82.

Carroll, Patrick. "Baseball in Graceland." *SABR UK Examiner* (May 2001): 5–7.

Carter, Robert A. *Buffalo Bill Cody: The Man behind the Legend*. New York: Wiley, 2000.

Cashman, Richard. "Symbols of Unity: Anglo-Australian Cricketers, 1877–1900." *International Journal of the History of Sport* 7 (1990): 97–110.

Chadwick, Henry. "Cricket in the Metropolis." *Outing* 18 (April 1889): 43–44.

Chandler, Alfred D., Jr. "Entrepreneurial Opportunity in Nineteenth-Century America." *Explorations in Entrepreneurial History* 1 (1963): 106–24.

Chang, Gordon H. "Whose 'Barbarism'? Whose 'Treachery'? Race and Civilization in the Unknown United States–Korea War of 1871." *Journal of American History* 89 (March 2003): 1331–65.

Chin, Carol C. "Beneficent Imperialists: American Women Missionaries in China at the Turn of the Twentieth Century." *Diplomatic History* 27 (June 2003): 327–52.

Clark, Joe. *A History of Australian Baseball: Time and Game*. Lincoln: University of Nebraska Press, 2003.

Collier, H. Price. "The Better Side of Anglo-Mania." *Forum* 7 (June 1889): 577–78.

Cox, James A. "When the Fans Roared 'Slide, Kelly, Slide!' at the Old Ball Game." *Smithsonian* (October 1983): 120–31.

Crapol, Edward P. "Coming to Terms with Empire: The Historiography of Late-Nineteenth-Century American Foreign Relations." *Diplomatic History* 16 (1992): 573–97.

Cronin, Mike. *Sport and Nationalism in Ireland: Gaelic Games, Soccer and Irish Identity since 1884*. Dublin: Four Courts Press, 1999.

Cronon, William. *Nature's Metropolis: Chicago and the Great West*. New York: W. W. Norton, 1991.

Curtis, L. Perry, Jr. *Jack the Ripper and the London Press*. New Haven, Conn.: Yale University Press, 2002.

Dale, Elizabeth. "'Social Equality Does Not Exist among Themselves, nor among Us': *Baylies v. Curry* and Civil Rights in Chicago, 1888." *American Historical Review* 102 (April 1997): 311–39.

Dale, R. W. "Impressions of Australia." *Contemporary Review* 54 (July–December 1888): 821–33.

Dalisson, Remi. "Asserting Male Values: Nineteenth-Century Fêtes, Games and Masculinity—A French Case Study." *European Sports History Review* 2 (2000): 40–61.

Daniels, Roger. "Asian Americans: The Transformation of a Pariah Minority." *Amerikastudien/American Studies* 40 (1995): 469–83.

Davis, Lance E., and Robert E. Gallman. *Evolving Financial Markets and International Capital Flows: Britain, the Americas, and Australia, 1865–1914.* New York: Cambridge University Press, 2001.

D'Eramo, Marco. *The Pig and the Skyscraper: Chicago, a History of Our Future.* London: Verso, 2002.

DeConde, Alexander. *Ethnicity, Race, and American Foreign Policy: A History.* Boston: Northeastern University Press, 1992.

Di Salvatore, Bryan. *A Clever Base-Ballist: The Life and Times of John Montgomery Ward.* Baltimore: Johns Hopkins University Press, 1999.

Drabble, Margaret, ed. *The Oxford Companion to English Literature.* 5th ed. Oxford: Oxford University Press, 1985.

Dulles, Foster Rhea. *Americans Abroad: Two Centuries of European Travel.* Ann Arbor: University of Michigan Press, 1964.

Dwyer, John B. *To Wire the World: Perry M. Collins and the North Pacific Telegraph Expedition.* Westport, Conn.: Praeger, 2001.

Eckes, Alfred E., Jr., and Thomas W. Zeiler. *Globalization and the American Century.* Cambridge: Cambridge University Press, 2003.

Elfers, James E. *The Tour to End All Tours: The Story of Major League Baseball's 1913–1914 World Tour.* Lincoln: University of Nebraska Press, 2003.

Endy, Christopher. "Travel and World Power: Americans in Europe, 1890–1917." *Diplomatic History* 22, no. 4 (Fall 1998): 565–94.

Evans, Christopher H. "Baseball as Civil Religion: The Genesis of an American Creation Story." In *The Faith of 50 Million: Baseball, Religion, and American Culture*, ed. Christopher H. Evans and William R. Herzog II, 13–33. Louisville, Ky.: Westminster John Knox Press, 2002.

Faithfull, Emily. *Three Visits to America.* Edinburgh: D. Douglas, 1884. Available at http://memory.loc.gov/cgi-bin/query/r?ammem/lhbtn:@field(DOCID+@lit(lhbtn05740)).

Farnham, Wallace D. "'The Weakened Spring of Government': A Study in Nineteenth-Century American History." *American Historical Review* 68 (1963): 662–80.

Fatout, Paul. *Mark Twain Speaking.* Iowa City: University of Iowa Press, 1976.

Feifer, Maxine. *Tourism in History: From Imperial Rome to the Present.* New York: Stein and Day, 1985.

Ferguson, Niall. *Empire: How Britain Made the Modern World.* London: Penguin Books, 2004.

Field, James A., Jr. "Transnationalism and the New Tribe." *International Organization* 25 (1971): 353–72.

Fielding, Lawrence W., and Lori K. Miller. "The ABC Trust: A Chapter in the History of Capitalism in the Sporting Goods Industry." *Sport History Review* 29 (1998): 44–58.

Flammarion, Camille. "Of What Use Is the Eiffel Tower?" *Cosmopolitan* 7 (July 1889): 235–43.

Fornay, M. N. "American Locomotives and Cars." *Scribner's Magazine* 4 (August 1888): 193.

Franks, Joel. "The California League of 1886–1893." *Californians* 6 (May–June 1988): 50–56.

———. "Of Heroes and Boors: Early Bay-Area Baseball." *Baseball Research Journal* 16 (1987): 45–47.

Freedman, Stephen. "The Baseball Fad in Chicago, 1865–1870: An Exploration of the Role of Sports in the Nineteenth-Century City." *Journal of Sport History* 5 (1978): 42–64.

Furst, R. Terry. "The Image of Professional Baseball: The Sport Press and the Formation of Ideas about Baseball in Nineteenth-Century America." Ph.D. diss., New School for Social Research, 1986.

Garnham, Neal. "Football and National Identity in Pre–Great War Ireland." *Irish Economic and Social History* 28 (2001): 13–31.

Glazier, Willard. *Peculiarities of American Cities*. Philadelphia: Hubbard Brothers, 1883. Available at http://memory.loc.gov/cgi-bin/query/r?ammem/lhbtn:@ field(DOCID + @lit(lhbtn05993)).

Gordon, Sarah Barringer. "The Mormon Question: Polygamy and Constitutional Conflict in Nineteenth-Century America." *Journal of Supreme Court History* 28 (2003): 14–29.

Gossip, G. H. D. "Cricket in Australia." *Outing* 14 (April 1889): 48.

———. "Cricket in Australia." *Outing* 14 (June 1889): 194.

Green, Ben. *Spinning the Globe: The Rise, Fall, and Return to Greatness of the Harlem Globetrotters*. New York: Amistad, 2005.

Greer, Richard A. "The Royal Tourist—Kalakua's Letters Home from Tokio to London." *Hawaiian Journal of History* 5 (1971): 75–109.

Guterl, Matthew, and Christine Skwiot. "Atlantic and Pacific Crossings: Race, Empire, and 'The Labor Problem' in the Late Nineteenth Century." *Radical History Review* 91 (Winter 2005): 40–61.

Guthrie-Shimizu, Sayuri. "For the Love of the Game: Baseball in Early U.S.–Japanese Encounters and the Rise of a Transnational Sporting Fraternity." *Diplomatic History* 28 (November 2004): 637–62.

Gyory, Andrew. *Closing the Gate: Race, Politics, and the Chinese Exclusion Act*. Chapel Hill: University of North Carolina Press, 1998.

Hall, Joy H. "Images of the French Revolution through Two Centuries." *Consortium on Revolutionary Europe 1750–1850: Selected Papers* (1998): 41–51.

Harney, Gilbert L. *The Lives of Benjamin Harrison and Levi P. Morton*. Providence, R.I.: J. A. & R. A. Reid, 1888.

Harris, Paul. "Cultural Imperialism and American Protestant Missionaries: Collaboration and Dependency in Mid-Nineteenth-Century China." *Pacific Historical Review* 60 (1991): 309–38.

Hartnoll, Phyllis, ed. *The Oxford Companion to the Theatre*. 3rd ed. London: Oxford University Press, 1967.

Harvey, Adrian. "'An Epoch in the Annals of National Sport': Football in Sheffield and the Creation of Modern Soccer and Rugby." *International Journal of the History of Sport* 18 (2001): 53–87.

Hayes, Kevin. "Mark Twain's Earliest London Lecture: Three Unknown Reports." *Studies in American Humor* 3 (1994): 116–19.

Heard, J. "Florence the Beautiful." *Cosmopolitan* 6 (January 1889): 268–70.

Heiss, Mary Ann. "The Evolution of the Imperial Idea and U.S. National Identity." *Diplomatic History* 26 (Fall 2002): 511–41.

Hervé, Lucien, and Barry Bergdoll. *The Eiffel Tower.* New York: Princeton Architectural, 2003.

Hills, Jill. *The Struggle for Control of Global Communication: The Formative Century.* Urbana: University of Illinois Press, 2002.

Hirata, Lucie Cheng. "Free, Indentured, Enslaved: Chinese Prostitutes in Nineteenth-Century America." *Signs* 5 (1979): 3–29.

Hodeir, Catherine. "En route pour le pavillon americain!" [Let's go to the American pavilion!]. *Mouvement Social* 149 (1989): 89–98.

Hoffenberg, Peter. "Colonial Innocents Abroad? Late Nineteenth-Century Australian Visitors to America and the Invention of New Nations." *Australasian Journal of American Studies* 19 (2000): 4–24.

Hoganson, Kristin. "Cosmopolitan Domesticity: Importing the American Dream, 1865–1920." *American Historical Review* 107 (February 2002): 55–83.

———. *Fighting for American Manhood: How Gender Politics Provoked the Spanish-American and Philippine-American Wars.* New Haven, Conn.: Yale University Press. 1998.

Hole, S. Reynolds. *A Little Tour in America.* London: E. Arnold, 1895. Available at http://memory.loc.gov/cgi-bin/query/r?ammem/lhbtn:@field(DOCID+@lit(lhbtn04153)).

Hollenbach, John W. "The Image of the Arab in Nineteenth-Century English and American Literature." *Muslim World* 62 (1972): 195–208.

Holt, Richard. "Contrasting Nationalisms: Sport, Militarism and the Unitary State in Britain and France before 1914." *International Journal of the History of Sport* 12 (1995): 39–54.

———. "Women, Men, and Sport in France, c. 1870–1914: An Introductory Survey." *Journal of Sport History* 18 (1991): 121–34.

Hopkins, A. G., ed. *Globalization in World History.* New York: W. W. Norton, 2002.

———. "The Victorians and Africa: A Reconsideration of the Occupation of Egypt, 1882." *Journal of African History* 27 (1986): 363–91.

Howat, Gerald. *The Great Cricketer.* London: Marylebone Cricket Club, 1998.

Igler, David. "The Industrial Far West: Region and Nation in the Late Nineteenth Century." *Pacific Historical Review* 69 (2000): 159–92.

Ingersoll, Ernest. "The Heart of Colorado." *Cosmopolitan* 5 (September 1888): 423.

Iriye, Akira. "Culture." *Journal of American History* (June 1990): 99–107.

Jacobson, Matthew Frye. *Barbarian Virtues: The United States Encounters Foreign Peoples at Home and Abroad, 1876–1917.* New York: Hill and Wang, 2000.

James, Wilma. "Hawaii's Last King." *Pacific Historian* 24 (1980): 312–15.

Johnes, Martin. "'Poor Man's Cricket': Baseball, Class and Community in South Wales, c. 1880–1950." *International Journal of the History of Sport* 17 (2000): 153–66.

Johnson, Mary. "One Reason for the Inefficiency of Women's Work." *Century* 38 (July 1889): 470–71.

Kaplan, Amy. *Anarchy of Empire in the Making of U.S. Culture.* Cambridge, Mass.: Harvard University Press, 2002.

Karpiel, Frank J., Jr. "Mystic Ties of Brotherhood: Freemasonry, Ritual, and Hawaiian Royalty in the Nineteenth Century." *Pacific Historical Review* 69 (August 2000): 357–97.

Keeling, Drew. "The Transportation Revolution and Transatlantic Migration, 1850–1914." *Research in Economic History* 19 (1999): 39–74.

Kennedy, Charles. "The Captain's Work on an Atlantic Liner." *North American Review* 148 (January 1889): 73–81.

Kimmel, Michael S. "Baseball and the Reconstitution of American Masculinity, 1880–1920." In *Baseball History from Outside the Lines: A Reader*, ed. John E. Dreifort, 47–61. Lincoln: University of Nebraska Press, 2001.

Kincheloe, Pamela J. "Two Visions of Fairyland: Ireland and the Monumental Discourse of the Nineteenth-Century American Tourist," *Irish Studies Review* 7 (1999): 41–51.

Kirsch, George B. "American Cricket: Players and Clubs before the Civil War." *Journal of Sport History* 11 (1984): 28–50.

Knox, Thomas W. *The Republican Party and Its Leaders*. New York: P. F. Collier, 1892.

Koppett, Leonard. *Koppett's Concise History of Major League Baseball*. Philadelphia: Temple University Press, 1998.

Kramer, Paul A. "Empires, Exceptions, and Anglo-Saxons: Race and Rule between the British and United States Empires, 1880–1910." *Journal of American History* 88, no. 4 (2002): 1315–53.

Krenn, Michael L. *Race and U.S. Foreign Policy in the Ages of Territorial and Market Expansion, 1840–1900*. Vol. 2, *Race and U.S. Foreign Policy from the Colonial Period to the Present: A Collection of Essays*. New York: Garland, 1998.

LaFeber, Walter. *The Clash: U.S.–Japanese Relations throughout History*. New York: W. W. Norton, 1997.

———. *The New Empire: An Interpretation of American Expansion, 1860–1898*. Ithaca, N.Y.: Cornell University Press, 1963.

Lambert, Ernest. "Americanized Englishmen." *North American Review* 147 (August 1888): 320.

Lamoreaux, David. "Baseball in the Late Nineteenth Century: The Source of Its Appeal." *Journal of Popular Culture* 11 (1977): 597–613.

Landes, David S. *The Unbound Prometheus: Technological Change and Industrial Development in Western Europe from 1750 to the Present*. 2nd ed. Cambridge: Cambridge University Press, 2003.

Lane, F. C. "The Greatest President the National League Ever Had." *Baseball Magazine* (January 1918): 258–307.

Lautreppe, Le Cocq de. "A Preliminary Walk through the Paris Exposition." *Nation* 48 (March 21, 1889): 241.

Lee, Erika. *At America's Gates: Chinese Immigrants during the Exclusion Era, 1882–1943*. Chapel Hill: University of North Carolina Press, 2003.

Leed, Eric J. *The Mind of the Traveler: From Gilgamesh to Global Tourism*. New York: Basic Books, 1991.

Lemoine, Bertrand. "L'entreprise Eiffel" [The Eiffel business]. *Histoire, Economie et Société* 14 (1995): 273–85.

Levenstein, Harvey. *Seductive Journey: American Tourists in France from Jefferson to the Jazz Age*. Chicago: University of Chicago Press, 1998.

Levine, Peter. *A. G. Spalding and the Rise of Baseball: The Promise of American Sport.* New York: Oxford University Press, 1985.

———. "Business, Missionary Motives behind the 1888–1889 World Tour." *SABR Baseball Research Journal* 13 (1984): 60–63.

Lewis, Robert M. "Cricket and the Beginnings of Organized Baseball in New York City." *International Journal of the History of Sport* 4 (1987): 315–32.

Light, Jonathan Fraser. *The Cultural Encyclopedia of Baseball.* Jefferson, N.C.: McFarland, 1997.

Limerick, Patricia Nelson. *The Legacy of Conquest: The Unbroken Past of the American West.* New York: W. W. Norton, 1988.

Lipset, Seymour Martin. *American Exceptionalism: A Double-Edged Sword.* New York: W. W. Norton, 1996.

Lockley, Timothy. "'The Manly Game': Cricket and Masculinity in Savannah, Georgia, in 1859." *International Journal of the History of Sport* 20 (2003): 77–98.

Love, Eric T. L. *Race over Empire: Racism and U.S. Imperialism, 1865–1900.* Chapel Hill: University of North Carolina Press, 2004.

Lowenfish, Lee. *The Imperfect Diamond: A History of Baseball's Labor Wars,* rev. ed. New York: Da Capo Press, 1991.

Lyberg, Wolf. *Fabulous 100 Years of the IOC: Facts, Figures, and Much Much More.* Lausanne: International Olympic Committee, 1996.

MacCannell, Dean. *The Tourist: A New Theory of the Leisure Class.* New York: Schocken Books, 1976.

MacRaild, Donald. "Parnell and Home Rule." *Modern History Review* 4 (1993): 30–33.

Madsen, Deborah L. *American Exceptionalism.* Jackson: University Press of Mississippi, 1998.

Mandle, W. F. "Cricket and Australian Nationalism in the Nineteenth Century." *Journal of the Royal Australian Historical Society* 59 (1973): 225–42.

———. "Parnell and Sport." *Studia Hibernica* 28 (1994): 103–16.

———. "W. G. Grace as a Victorian Hero." *Historical Studies* 19 (1981): 353–68.

Mangan, J. A. *Athleticism in the Victorian and Edwardian Public School.* London: Cass, 2000.

———. *The Games Ethic and Imperialism.* London: Cass, 1998.

———. "'Muscular, Militaristic and Manly': The British Middle-Class Hero as Moral Messenger." *International Journal of the History of Sport* 13 (1996): 28–47.

Mangan, J. A., and Colm Hickey. "Globalization, the Games Ethic and Imperialism: Further Aspects of the Diffusion of an Ideal." *European Sports History Review* 3 (2001): 105–30.

Marcus, Robert D. *The Grand Old Party: Political Structure in the Gilded Age, 1880–1896.* New York: Oxford University Press, 1971.

Mark, Shelley A., and Jacob Adler. "Claus Spreckels in Hawaii: Impact of a Mainland Interloper on Development of Hawaiian Sugar Industry." *Explorations in Entrepreneurial History* 10 (1958): 22–32.

Marks, Jason. *Around the World in 72 Days.* Pittsburgh, Pa.: Sterlinghouse, 1999.

Mazzi, Frank. "Harbingers of the City: Men and Their Monuments in Nineteenth-Century San Francisco." *Southern California Quarterly* 55 (1973): 141–62.

McClain, Charles J. *In Search of Equality: The Chinese Struggle against Discrimination in Nineteenth-Century America.* Berkeley: University of California Press, 1994.

McCrone, Kathleen E. "Class, Gender, and English Women's Sport, c. 1890–1914." *Journal of Sport History* 18 (Spring 1991): 159–82.

McCullough, David. *Mornings on Horseback.* New York: Simon & Schuster, 1981.

McDevitt, Patrick Francis. "May the Best Man Win: Sport, Masculinity and Nationalism in Great Britain and the Empire, 1884–1933." Ph.D. diss., Rutgers University, 1999.

McMahon, Bill. "Al Spalding." *SABR Baseball Biography Project*, http://bioproj .sabr.org/bioproj.cfm?a = v&v = l&bid = 1274&pid = 13395.

Melville, Tom. "An Aspiration to Cosmopolitanism: Cricket in Nineteenth-Century St. Louis." *Gateway Heritage* 19 (1998): 16–21.

———. "From Ethnic Tradition to Community Institution: Nineteenth-Century Cricket in Small-Town Wisconsin and a Note on the Enigma of a Sporting Discontinuity." *International Journal of the History of Sport* 11 (1994): 281–84.

———. "Our First National Pastime: Cricket in America." *Timeline* 8 (1991): 44–53.

Miller, Donald L. *City of the Century: The Epic of Chicago and the Making of America.* New York: Simon & Schuster, 1996.

Miller, Justice. "The State of Iowa." *Harper's New Monthly Magazine* 74, no. 470 (July 1889): 169–75.

Mitchell, Bruce. "Sporting Traditions: Two Tours and the Beginnings of Baseball in Australia." *Journal of the Australian Society for Sports History* 7 (May 1991): 2–24.

Moon, Ernest. "Some Aspects of Australian Life." *Blackwood's Magazine* 143 (March 1888): 351–65.

Moore, Glenn. "The Great Baseball Tour of 1888–1889: A Tale of Image-Making, Intrigue, and Labour Relations in the Gilded Age." *International Journal of the History of Sport* 11 (December 1994): 431–56.

———. "Ideology on the Sportspage: Newspapers, Baseball, and Ideological Conflict in the Gilded Age." *Journal of Sport History* 23 (Fall 1996): 228–55.

Navailles, Jean-Pierre. "Eiffel's Tower." *History Today* 39 (1989): 38–43.

Ninkovich, Frank. *The United States and Imperialism.* Malden, Mass.: Blackwell, 2001.

Nugent, Walter. "Frontiers and Empires in the Late Nineteenth Century." *Western Historical Quarterly* 20 (1989): 393–408.

Obeidat, Marwan A. "Lured by the Exotic Levant: The Muslim East to the American Traveller of the Nineteenth Century." *Islamic Quarterly* 31 (1987): 167–93.

O'Rell, Max [pseud.]. *A Frenchman in America: Recollections of Men and Things.* New York: Cassell Publishing, 1891. Available at http://memory.loc.gov/cgi-bin/ query/r?ammem/lhbtn:@field(DOCID + @lit(lhbtn01319)).

O'Rourke, Kevin, and Jeffrey G. Williamson. *Globalization and History: The Evolution of a Nineteenth-Century Atlantic Economy.* Cambridge, Mass.: MIT Press, 1999.

Osorio, Jonathan Kay Kamakawiwo. *Dismembering Lahui: A History of the Hawaiian Nation to 1887.* Honolulu: University of Hawaii Press, 2002.

Palmer, Harry Clay. *Athletic Sports in America, England, and Australia.* Philadelphia: Hubbard Brothers, 1889.

Parish, Peter J. "What Made American Nationalism Different?" In *America Compared: American History in International Perspective*, vol. 1, *To 1877*, ed. Carl J. Guarneri. 2nd ed. Boston: Houghton Mifflin, 2005.

Park, Roberta J. "British Sports and Pastimes in San Francisco, 1848–1900." *British Journal of Sports History* 1 (1984): 300–317.

———. "Physiology and Anatomy are Destiny!? Brains, Bodies and Exercise in Nineteenth-Century American Thought." *Journal of Sport History* 18 (Spring 1991): 31–63.

———. "Sport, Gender, and Society in a Transatlantic Victorian Perspective." *British Journal of Sports History* 2 (1985): 5–28.

Parmet, Robert D. "The Presidential Fever of Chauncey De Pew." *New York Historical Society Quarterly* 54 (1970): 268–90.

Parratt, Cartriona M. "Athletic 'Womanhood': Exploring Sources for Female Sport in Victorian and Edwardian England." *Journal of Sport History* 16 (Summer 1989): 140–57.

Perez, Louis A., Jr. "Between Baseball and Bullfighting: The Quest for Nationality in Cuba, 1868–1898." *Journal of American History* 81 (September 1994): 493–517.

Perkins, Bradford. *The Great Rapprochement: England and the United States, 1895–1914*. New York: Atheneum, 1968.

Perry, John Curtis. *Facing West: Americans and the Opening of the Pacific*. Westport, Conn.: Praeger, 1994.

Peterson, Robert. *Only the Ball Was White*. New York: Oxford University Press, 1970.

Phelps, E. J. "Divorce in the United States." *Forum* 8 (December 1889): 350.

Plesur, Milton. *America's Outward Thrust: Approaches to Foreign Affairs, 1865–1890*. Dekalb: Northern Illinois University Press, 1971.

Pomeroy, Earl S. *In Search of the Golden West: The Tourist in Western America*. Reprinted ed. Lincoln: University of Nebraska Press, 1990.

———. *The Pacific Slope: A History of California, Oregon, Washington, Idaho, Utah, and Nevada*. Reprinted ed. Reno: University of Nevada Press, 2003.

Porter, David L., ed. *Biographical Dictionary of American Sports: Baseball*. Rev. and expanded ed. 3 vols. Westport, Conn.: Greenwood Press, 2000.

———. "Cap Anson of Marshalltown: Baseball's First Superstar." *Palimpsest* 61, no. 4 (1980): 98–107.

Porter, Horace. "Railway Passenger Travel." *Scribner's Magazine* 4 (September 1888): 302–11.

Post, Robert M. "Charles Stewart Parnell before Congress." *Quarterly Journal of Speech* 51 (1965): 419–25.

Purdy, Jedediah. "Universal Nation." In *The Imperial Tense: Prospects and Problems of American Empire*, ed. Andrew Bacevich, 102–10. Chicago: Ivan R. Dee, 2003.

Putz, Manfred. "Mark Twain and the Idea of American Superiority at the End of the Nineteenth Century." In *An American Empire: Expansionist Cultures and Policies, 1881–1917*, ed. Serge Ricard, 215–35. Aix-en-Provence, France: Université de Provence, 1990.

Rajapakse, Reginald Lakshman. "Christian Missions, Theosophy, and Trade: A History of American Relations with Ceylon, 1815–1915." Ph.D. diss., University of Pennsylvania, 1974.

Rannella, Mark, and Whitney Walter. "Planned Serendipity: American Travelers and the Transatlantic Voyage in the Nineteenth and Twentieth Centuries." *Journal of Social History* 38 (Winter 2004): 365–83.

Rash, Keith. "The Discovery of Gold at Ballarat." *Victorian Historical Magazine* 25 (1954): 133–43.

Reddin, Paul. *Wild West Shows*. Urbana-Champaign: University of Illinois Press, 1999.

Rideing, William. "The Building of an 'Ocean Greyhound.'" *Scribner's Magazine* 5 (April 1889): 431–42.

Riess, Steven A. "Sport and the Redefinition of American Middle-class Masculinity." *International Journal of the History of Sport* 8 (May 1991): 5–27.

Roberts, Edward. "The City of Denver." *Harper's New Monthly Magazine* 76, no. 456 (May 1888): 946–54.

Robbins, William G. *Colony and Empire: The Capitalist Transformation of the American West*. Lawrence: University Press of Kansas, 1994.

Rosenberg, Emily S. *Spreading the American Dream: American Economic and Cultural Expansion, 1890–1945*. New York: Hill and Wang, 1982.

Rosenberg, Howard W. *Cap Anson 1: When Captaining a Team Meant Something; Leadership in Baseball's Early Years*. Arlington, Va.: Tile Books, 2003.

Roth, Mitchel. *Reading the American West: Primary Source Readings in American History*. New York: Addison Wesley Longman, 1999.

Rothman, Hal K. *Devil's Bargains: Tourism in the Twentieth-Century American West*. Lawrence: University Press of Kansas, 2003.

Royce, Josiah. "Impressions of Australia." *Scribner's Magazine* 9 (1888): 76.

Ruble, Blair A. *Second Metropolis: Pragmatic Pluralism in Gilded Age Chicago, Silver Age Moscow, and Meiji Osaka*. Cambridge: Cambridge University Press, 2001.

Russell, Dave. "Sport and Identity: The Case of Yorkshire County Cricket Club, 1890–1939." *Twentieth Century British History* 7 (1996): 206–30.

Rydell, Robert W. *All the World's a Fair: Visions of Empire at American International Expositions, 1876–1916*. Chicago: University of Chicago Press, 1984.

Rydell, Robert W., and Rob Kroes. *Buffalo Bill in Bologna: The Americanization of the World, 1869–1922*. Chicago: University of Chicago Press, 2005.

Salomone, A. William. "The Nineteenth-Century Discovery of Italy: An Essay in American Cultural History; Prolegomena to a Historiographical Problem." *American Historical Review* 73 (1968): 1359–91.

Salvatore, Victor. "The Man Who Didn't Invent Baseball." *American Heritage* 34 (1983): 65–67.

Schaller, Michael. *The United States and China in the Twentieth Century*. New York: Oxford University Press, 1979.

Schlereth, Thomas J. *Victorian America: Transformations in Everyday Life, 1876–1915*. New York: HarperCollins, 1991.

Schweizer, Niklaus R. "King Kalakaua: An International Perspective." *Hawaiian Journal of History* 25 (1991): 103–20.

Schwendinger, Robert J. "Chinese Sailors: America's Invisible Merchant Marine, 1876–1905." *California History* 57 (1978): 58–69.

Shaffer, Marguerite S. *See America First: Tourism and National Identity, 1880–1940*. Washington, D.C.: Smithsonian Institution Press, 2001.

Shah, Nayan. *Contagious Divide: Epidemics and Race in San Francisco's Chinatown.* Berkeley: University of California Press, 2001.

Sherman, Richard Morey. "American Contacts with Ceylon in the 19th Century: An Introduction to Their Impact." *Journal of the Royal Asiatic Society of Sri Lanka* 35 (1990–1991): 1–8.

Sigaux, Gilbert. *History of Tourism.* Trans. from the French by Joan White. London: Leisure Arts, 1966.

Simmons, Jack. "Railways, Hotels, and Tourism in Great Britain, 1839–1914." *Journal of Contemporary History* 19 (1984): 201–22.

Simons, John. "The 'Englishness' of English Cricket." *Journal of Popular Culture* 29 (1996): 41–50.

Sloan, Edward W. "The Nightingale and the Steamship: Jenny Lind and the Collins Liner *Atlantic.*" *American Neptune* 51, no. 3 (1991): 149–55.

Slotkin, Richard. "Buffalo Bill's 'Wild West' and the Mythologization of the American Empire." In *Cultures of United States Imperialism,* ed. Amy Kaplan and Donald E. Pease, 164–81. Durham, N.C.: Duke University Press, 1993.

Socolofsky, Homer, and Allan B. Spetter. *The Presidency of Benjamin Harrison.* Lawrence: University Press of Kansas, 1987.

Spalding, Albert G. *Baseball: America's National Game.* Lincoln: University of Nebraska Press, 1992.

———. "In the Field Papers: Baseball." *Cosmopolitan* 6 (October 1889): 608–12.

*Spalding's Official Base Ball Guide.* Annual. Chicago: A. G. Spalding & Bros., 1889–1939. Available at http://memory.loc.gov/ammem/spaldinghtml/spaldinghome.html.

Spearman, Frank. "The Great American Desert." *Harper's New Monthly Magazine* 77, no. 458 (July 1888): 232–42.

Spillman, Lyn. "'Neither the Same Nation nor Different Nations': Constitutional Conventions in the United States and Australia." *Comparative Studies in Society and History* 38 (1996): 149–81.

Steinbrink, Jeffrey. "Why the Innocents Went Abroad: Mark Twain and American Tourism in the Late Nineteenth Century." *American Literary Realism* 16 (1983): 278–86.

Stevens, David. *Baseball's Radical for All Seasons: A Biography of John Montgomery Ward.* Lanham, Md.: Scarecrow Press, 1998.

Stout, Neil. "1874 Baseball Tour Not Cricket to British," *Baseball Research Journal* 14 (1985): 83–85.

Stowe, William W. *Going Abroad: European Travel in Nineteenth-Century American Culture.* Princeton, NJ: Princeton University Press, 1994.

Streeby, Shelly. *American Sensations: Class, Empire, and the Production of Popular Culture.* Berkeley: University of California Press, 2002.

Sullivan, Dean A., ed. *Early Innings: A Documentary History of Baseball, 1825–1908.* Lincoln: University of Nebraska Press, 1995.

Tatz, Collin. "Racism and Sport in Australia." *Race & Class* 36 (1995): 43–54.

Thelen, David. "The Nation and Beyond: Transnational Perspectives on United States History." *Journal of American History* 86, no. 3 (1999): 965–75.

Thomas, James. "Wilson Barrett's New School 'Othello.'" *Library Chronicle of the University of Texas at Austin* 22 (1983): 66–87.

Thomas, Phillip Drennon. "The West of Currier and Ives: Nineteenth-Century Lithographs Capture the Frontier Adventure." *American West* 19 (1982): 18–25.

Thorn, John. "Our Game." In *Total Baseball: The Official Encyclopedia of Major League Baseball*, 7th ed., ed. John Thorn, Peter Palmer, and Michael Gershman, 1–10. Kingston, N.Y.: Total Sports Publishing, 2001.

Tissot, Laurent. "How Did the British Conquer Switzerland? Guidebooks, Railways, Travel Agencies, 1850–1914." *Journal of Transport History* 16 (1995): 21–54.

Toghill, P. J. "Dr. W. G. Grace: Cricketer and General Practitioner." *Journal of Medical Biography* 1 (1993): 155–59.

Trocmé, Hélène. "Les Etats-Unis et L'Exposition Universelle de 1889 [The United States and the Universal Exposition of 1889]." *Revue d'Histoire Moderne et Contemporaine* 37 (1990): 283–96.

Trotter, Coutts. "Among the Islands of the South Pacific: Tonga and Samoa." *Littell's Living Age* 5, no. 62 (April–June, 1888): 797.

Turner, Frederick Jackson. *The Frontier in American History*. New York: H. Holt, 1920.

Twain, Mark. *The Innocents Abroad, or The New Pilgrims' Progress*. New York: Bantam Books, 1964.

Twombley, Robert. "Cuds and Snipes: Labor at Chicago's Auditorium Building, 1887–1889." *Journal of American Studies* 31 (1997): 79–101.

Tygiel, Jules. *Past Time: Baseball as History*. New York: Oxford University Press, 2000.

Vambery, Arminius. "Is the Power of England Declining?" *Forum* 6 (November 1888): 221–34.

Van Bottenburg, Maarten. *Global Games*. Urbana: University of Illinois Press, 2001.

Voigt, David Quentin. *American Baseball: From the Gentleman's Sport to the Commissioner System*. Vol. 1. University Park: Pennsylvania State University Press, 1983.

———. "Reflections on Diamonds: American Baseball and American Culture." *Journal of Sport History* 1 (1974): 3–25.

———. "Serfs versus Magnates: A Century of Labor Strife in Major League Baseball." In *The Business of Professional Sports*, ed. Paul D. Staudohar and James A. Mangan, 95–114. Urbana: University of Illinois Press, 1991.

Wallace, Lew. *The Life of Gen. Ben Harrison*. St. Louis: Riverside Publishing, 1888.

Ward, John Montgomery. *Base-Ball: How to Become a Player, with the Origin, History, and Explanation of the Game*. Philadelphia: Athletic Publishing, 1888.

———. "Is the Base-Ball Player Chattel?" *Lippincott's* 40 (August 1887): 310–19.

———. "Our National Game." *Cosmopolitan* 5, no. 6 (October 1888): 443–55.

Warner, Charles Dudley. "Studies of the Great West: III—Chicago." *Harper's New Monthly Magazine* 76, no. 456 (May 1888): 869–79.

———. "Studies of the Great West: IV—Chicago, Second Paper." *Harper's New Monthly Magazine* 77, no. 457 (June 1888): 116–21.

———. "Studies of the Great West: Three Capitals." *Harper's New Monthly Magazine* 77 (July 1888): 259–69.

Warren, Louis S. *Buffalo Bill's America: William Cody and the Wild West Show*. New York: Knopf, 2005.

Warzeski, Jean-Marie. "Mapping the Unknown: Gendered Spaces and the Oriental Other in Travelogues of Egypt by U.S. Women, 1854–1914." *History and Anthropology* 13 (January 2002): 301–17.

West, Elliott. *The Contested Plains: Indians, Goldseekers, and the Rush to Colorado.* Lawrence: University Press of Kansas, 1998.

Wharton, Thomas. "Inter-City and International Cricket in America." *Outing* 18 (June 1889): 172–77.

Whitaker, Hervey W. "Samoa: The Isles of the Navigators." *Century Magazine* 38, no. 1 (May 1889): 17–25.

White, Richard. "Information, Markets, and Corruption: Transcontinental Railroads in the Gilded Age." *Journal of American History* 90 (June 2003): 19–43.

Whitehead, John S. *Completing the Union: Alaska, Hawaii and the Battle for Statehood.* Albuquerque: University of New Mexico Press, 2004.

Wiggins, David K. "Peter Jackson and the Elusive Heavyweight Championship: A Black Athlete's Struggle against the Late Nineteenth-Century Color Line." *Journal of Sport History* 12 (1985): 143–68.

Wilder, Marshall P. "Our English Cousins." *Lippincott's Magazine* 45 (August 1887): 409.

Wilson, A. N. *The Victorians.* London: Hutchinson, 2002.

Wilson, R. L. *Buffalo Bill's Wild West: An American Legend.* London: Chartwell Books, 2004.

Wonham, Henry B. "'I Want a Real Coon': Mark Twain and Late-Nineteenth-Century Caricature." *American Literature* 72 (2000): 117–52.

Wrobel, David M. *The End of American Exceptionalism: Frontier Anxiety from the Old West to the New Deal.* Lawrence: University Press of Kansas, 1993.

Zang, David W. *Fleet Walker's Divided Heart.* Lincoln: University of Nebraska Press, 1995.

# Index

# About the Author

**Thomas Zeiler** is a professor of history and former chair at the University of Colorado, Boulder, who specializes in American foreign relations. He is the author of *Unconditional Defeat: Japan, America, and the End of World War II*; *Free Trade, Free World: The Advent of GATT*; and *Dean Rusk: Defending the American Mission Abroad*.